Civil War Memories

Civil War Memories

Edited by S. T. Joshi

Rutledge Hill Press®
Nashville, Tennessee
A Thomas Nelson Company

Published by Rutledge Hill Press, a Thomas Nelson Company, P.O. Box 141000, Nashville, Tennessee 37214.

Library of Congress Cataloging-in-Publication Data

Civil war memories / edited by S. T. Joshi
 p. cm.
 ISBN 1-55853-809-7 (pbk.)
 1. United States—History—Civil War, 1861–1865—Fiction. 2. American Fiction—19th century. 3. Short stories, American. I. Joshi, S. T., 1958–
PS648.C54 C5345 2000
813'.0108358—dc21   99-087246
                CIP

Printed in the United States of America
1 2 3 4 5 6 7 8 9 — 05 04 03 02 01 00

Contents

Introduction

he American Civil War has probably inspired more miscellaneous commentary—histories, biographies, memoirs, fiction, poetry— than all of America's wars put together." So wrote Daniel Aaron, whose *The Unwritten War* (1973) remains one of the finest studies of the literature that emerged out of the war. And Aaron was of course writing well before the recent resurgence of interest in the Civil War—an interest that has led to widespread coverage of the conflict in books, films, television series, and other media.

And yet, while scholars have charted more than a thousand Civil War novels—from Edmund Kirke's *Among the Pines; or, South in Secession-Time* (1862) to the present day—they have been curiously slow in identifying the equally bountiful number of short stories that have treated all phases of the war, from actual battles to the war's lingering aftermath.

This volume seeks to gather a representative array of short fiction, written either during the war or in the first two or three generations following it. Few of these stories have been reprinted in the context of Civil War literature, and some have not been reprinted at all since their original appearances in magazines, newspapers, or books. Nearly all the tales were written by those who either participated in the war, observed it from near or far, or could profit from first-hand accounts of the war by its survivors. The voices are both Northern and Southern, both male and female, both angry and melancholy, both serious and comic; but they all treat the Civil War as a *watershed* in American history and in the lives of those who experienced it.

The Civil War was a *divisive* war in every sense of the term: it divided the North and the South, and it divided the nineteenth century into two unequal parts, so that what went before seemed curiously irrelevant to those who sought to mend the country's wounds once the conflict was over. No writer whose life-span included the war could avoid coming to terms with it—not even the young Henry James, who sustained his "obscure hurt" as a volunteer fireman in Newport, Rhode Island, nor William Dean Howells, who went abroad during the war to escape his military obligations. Even the elderly Nathaniel Hawthorne, although he would die in 1864 and wrote no actual fiction dealing with the war, managed to write an article about the struggle, while other eminent writers of the time—Ralph Waldo Emerson, Henry Wadsworth Longfellow, Walt Whitman, James Russell Lowell, Herman Melville—chose to express their views of the war in verse.

It was left to other writers to capture fragments of the conflict in short fiction. Ambrose Bierce is preeminent among those who actually served in the war, and his imperishable war memoirs ("Bits of Autobiography") are equalled by his landmark story collection, *Tales of Soldiers and Civilians* (1891). Bierce remarked in a newspaper column that "in my poor little battle-yarns the incidents that come in for special reprobation by the critics as 'improbable' and even 'impossible' are transcripts from memory—things that actually occurred before my eyes." Stephen Crane, the other great literary figure who wrote of the Civil War, could have no such advantage, having been born six years after the war was over; but his remarkable ability to absorb the essence of the conflict merely through reading the standard histories of the war is nowhere more powerfully realized than in *The Red Badge of Courage* (1895). And yet, the shorter pieces included in *The Little Regiment* (1896) feature images no less grounded in his distinctive poetic realism.

Within the compass of a short story, the war must necessarily become a matter of vignettes—narratives of individual battles, individual instances of heroism, or the small triumphs or tragedies that collectively made the war what it was. Lacking the broad panorama of the novel, a short story harps intensely on the minute or the particular—the hapless fate of a deserter in W. C. Morrow's "The Bloodhounds," the fate of some Southern soldiers caught in a feed shed in Stephen Crane's "Three Miraculous Soldiers," the three young women witnessing, and unwillingly participating in, the siege of their New Orleans plantation in Grace E. King's "Bayou L'Ombre." And yet, the necessary limitations of the short story bring into sharper focus the plain fact that the Civil War was a conflict between individuals—sometimes between former friends, sometimes even between father and son.

The complex political, social, and economic ramifications that followed the war were widely treated throughout the later nineteenth century. While some Southerners, like Thomas Nelson Page, fueled their resentment at the destruction of Southern culture by inventing a fantastic antebellum South out of their nostalgic imaginations, others looked toward reconciliation. The New Englander Sarah Orne Jewett and the Marylander Edward Lucas White, writing toward the end of the century, perhaps indulged in a bit of wishful thinking in their accounts of new-found harmony between North and South, but the gesture was in itself significant. The Louisianian Kate Chopin sought a reconciliation of a different kind in "A Wizard from Gettysburg"—one that operated on the intimate level of a single family.

It would be difficult to imagine that a conflict so appalling in its violence as the Civil War could be treated comically, but a few valiant writers nonetheless made the attempt. Mark Twain's tart lampoon "Lucretia Smith's Soldier" may be more in the vein of dark satire than lighthearted humor, but his effort is, after a fashion, surpassed by that of pioneering realist writer John William De Forest, who chose to treat the Ku Klux Klan in a comic vein. In the end, his "An Independent Ku-Klux" is perhaps not very funny, especially since part of the humor is evidently thought to reside in the death of the African-American pursued by a Klansman, but even here we can perhaps see some effort at reconciliation. Humor, irony, and satire are a means of distancing: the reader is compelled to look at the depicted events from a position of superiority over the fools and buffoons inhabiting the tale; and to that extent we are removed from the intensity of the emotions that the war engendered in its participants.

Four decades ago Robert A. Lively, in *Fiction Fights the Civil War* (1957), wrote: ". . . no definitive measure of victory or defeat for Blue or Grey may be deduced from Civil War fiction." What he meant was that Northerners and Southerners alike have produced outstanding literary work in this vein, and it is possible to find excellence of style, manner, and treatment in writers on both sides of the Mason-Dixon Line. Some of the writers included in this volume have perhaps marred their otherwise meritorious tales by the expression of sentiments—particularly racial, social, or political prejudice—that today's readers might find objectionable, but allowance must be made for differing times and differing sensibilities. Later writers—whether it be the Northerner F. Scott Fitzgerald ("The Night Before Chancellorsville") or the Southerner William Faulkner *(The Unvanquished)*, all the way up to Bobbie

Ann Mason's "Shiloh" (1982) and beyond, including the recent Broadway musical *The Civil War*—have continued to find new approaches in dealing with this inexhaustible conflict. But we are perhaps justified in saying that the stories in this volume, dating from 1862 to 1908 and therefore drawing upon first-hand accounts of the conflict, ring true in a way that cannot always be said for their successors.

—S. T. JOSHI

Prologue
THE REVEILLE
1862

BRET HARTE

Francis Brett Harte (1836–1902) was born in Albany, New York, but gained early celebrity in the 1850s as the first important writer of the newly formed state of California. Harte spent much of the Civil War as Secretary of the California Mint, a sinecure that allowed him abundant time for writing. One of his works of this period is the stirring poem "The Reveille," read by Harte at a gathering in San Francisco in 1862 and collected in many editions of his poetry.

Hark! I hear the tramp of thousands,
   And of armèd men the hum;
Lo! a nation's hosts have gathered
   Round the quick alarming drum,—
     Saying, "Come,
     Freemen, come!
Ere your heritage be wasted," said the quick alarming drum.

"Let me of my heart take counsel:
   War is not of life the sum;
Who shall stay and reap the harvest
   When the autumn days shall come?"
     But the drum
     Echoed, "Come!
Death shall reap the braver harvest," said the solemn-
   sounding drum.

"But when won the coming battle,
    What of profit springs therefrom?
What if conquest, subjugation,
    Even greater ills become?"
      But the drum
      Answered, "Come!
You must do the sum to prove it," said the Yankee answer-
    ing drum.

"What if, 'mid the cannons' thunder,
    Whistling shot and bursting bomb,
When my brothers fall around me,
    Should my heart grow cold and numb?"
      But the drum
      Answered, "Come!
Better there in death united, than in life a recreant.—
    Come!"

Thus they answered,—hoping, fearing,
    Some in faith, and doubting some,
Till a trumpet-voice proclaiming
    Said, "My chosen people, come!"
      Then the drum,
      Lo! was dumb,
For the great heart of the nation, throbbing, answered,
    "Lord, we come!"

Part I

Fields of Glory

My Revenge
1864

ANONYMOUS

Perhaps the first volume of short fiction about the Civil War,
Tales of the Picket-Guard was a slim collection, evidently
intended for young adults, published anonymously in Philadelphia
in 1864. It consists of several stories, presented as narratives told by
"picket-guards" (sentries) to while away the tedium of their work.
"My Revenge" is a moving tale of two friends who take opposite
sides in the conflict but are ultimately reconciled.

We met in the beginning of the action, I and my enemy, Richard Withers—he on foot, I mounted. It matters not why I hated him with the fiercest wrath of my nature. "The heart knoweth its own bitterness," and the details, while most painful to me, would be of trifling interest to you. Suffice it that our feud was not a political one. For ten years we were the closest intimates that the same studies, the same tastes, the same arms could make us. I was the elder of the two, and stronger physically; comparatively friendless, as the world takes it, and had no near relatives. Young, solitary, and visionary as we were, it is hard to make you understand what we were to each other. Up to this period of our estrangement, working together, eating together, sleeping together, I can safely say that we had not a grief, not a pleasure, or a vacation, that we did not share with almost boyish single-heartedness. But one single day changed all. We rose in the morning dear friends and lay down at night bitter foes. I was a man of extremes: I either loved or hated with the strength of my heart. The past was forgotten in the present. The ten years of kindness, of congeniality, of almost humanly kindness, were erased as with a sponge. We looked each other in the face with angry, searching eyes—said but a few words (our rage was too deep to be demonstrative), and parted. Then in my solitude I dashed my clenched hand upon the Bible and vowed passionately: "I may wait ten years, Richard Withers! I may wait twenty, thirty, if you will; but, sooner or later, I swear I shall have my revenge!"

And this was the way we met.

I wonder if he thought of that day when he laid his hand upon my bridle-rein and looked up at me with his treacherous blue eyes. I scarcely think he did, or he could not have given me that look. He was beautiful as a girl; indeed, the contrast of his fair, aristocratic face with the regular outline and red, curving lips, to my own rough, dark exterior, might have been partly the secret of my former attraction to him. But the loveliness of an angel, if it had been his, would not have saved him from me then. There was a pistol in his hand, but before he had time to discharge it, I cut at him with my sword, and as the line swept on like a gathering wave, I saw him stagger under the blow, throw up his arms and go down with the press. Bitterly as I hated him, the ghastly face haunted me the long day through.

You all remember how it was at Fredericksburg. How we crossed the river at the wrong point, and under the raking fire of the enemy were so disastrously repulsed.

It was a sad mistake, and fatal to many a brave heart. When night fell I lay upon the field among dead and wounded. I was comparatively helpless. A ball had shivered the cap of my right knee, and my shoulder was laid open with a sabre-cut. The latter bled profusely, but by dint of knotting my handkerchief tightly around it, I managed to stanch it in a measure. For my knee I could do nothing. Consciousness did not forsake me, and the pain was intense; but from the moans and wails of the men about me I judged that others had fared worse than I. Poor fellows! there was many a mother's darling suffering there. Many of my comrades—lads of eighteen or twenty, who had never seen a night from home until they joined the army, spoiled pets of fortune, manly enough at heart, but children in years and constitution, who have been used to have every little ache and scratch compassioned with an almost extravagant sympathy—there crushed and dying, huddled together—some where they had weakly crawled upon their hands and knees—and never a woman's voice to whisper gentle consolation. It was pitchy dark, and a cold, miserable rain was falling upon us, the very heavens weeping over our miseries. Then through the darkness and drizzling rain, through the groans and prayers of the fallen men about me, I heard a familiar voice close to my side:

"Water! water! water! I am dying with thirst—if it be but a swallow— water! For God's sake, give me water!"

I recoiled with dismay. It was the voice of my enemy—the voice of

Richard Withers. They were once very dear to me, those mellow tones; once the pleasantest music I cared to hear. Do you think they so softened me now? You are mistaken; I am candid about it. My blood boiled in my veins when powerless to withdraw from his detested neighborhood. There was water in my canteen. I had filled it before the last ball came. By stretching my hand I could give him a drink, but I did not raise a finger. Vengeance was sweet. I smiled grimly to myself, and said down in my secret heart:

"Not a drop shall cross his lips though he perish. I shall have my revenge."

Do you recoil with horror? Listen how merciful God was to me.

There was a poor little drummer on the other side—a merry, manly boy of twelve or thirteen, the pet and plaything of the regiment. There was something of the German in him; he had been with us from the first, and was reckoned one of the best drummers in the army. But we could never march to the tap of Charlie's drum again. He had got a ball in his lungs, and the exposure and fatigue, together with the wound, had made him light-headed. Poor little child! he crept close to me in the darkness and laid his cheek on my breast. May be he thought it was his own pillow at home; may be he thought it, poor darling, his mother's bosom. God only knows what he thought; but with his hot arm about my neck, and his curly head pressed close to my wicked heart, even then swelling with bitter hatred of my enemy, he began to murmur in his delirium, "Our Father who art in heaven."

I was a rough, bearded man. I had been an orphan for many a long year; but not too many or too long to forget the simple-hearted prayer of my childhood—the dim vision of that mother's face over which the grass had grown for twenty changing summers. Something tender stirred within my hardened heart. It was too dark to see the little face, but the young lips went on brokenly:

"And forgive us our trespasses as we forgive those who trespass against us."

It went through me like a knife—sharper than the sabre-cut, keener than the ball. God was merciful to me, and this young child was the channel of his mercy.

"Forgive our trespasses as we forgive those who trespass against us."

I had never understood the words before. If an angel had spoken it could scarcely have been more of a revelation. For the first time the thought that I might be mortally wounded, that death might be nearer than I dreamed, struck me with awe and horror. The text of a long-forgotten sermon was in my ears: "It is appointed for all men to die, and after death the judgment."

Worse and worse. What measure of mercy could I expect, if the same was meted out that I had meted unto my enemy. The tears welled into my eyes, and trickled my cheeks—the first that I had shed since my boyhood. I felt subdued and strangely moved.

The rain was falling still, but the little head upon my breast was gone. He crept away silently in the darkness. His unconscious mission was fulfilled; he would not return at my call.

Then I lifted myself with great effort. The old bitterness was crushed, but not altogether dead.

"Water! water!" moaned Richard Withers, in his agony.

I dragged myself closer to him.

"God be praised!" I said with a solemn heart. "Dick, old boy—enemy no longer—God be praised! I am willing and able to help you. Drink and be friends."

It had been growing lighter and lighter in the east, and now it was day. Day within and day without. In the first gray glimmer of dawn we looked into each other's ghastly faces for a moment, and then the canteen was at Richard's mouth, and he drank as only the fevered can drink. I watched him with moist eyes, leaning upon my elbow and forgetting the bandaged shoulder. He grasped me with both hands.

Blood-stained and pallid as it was, his face was ingenuous and beautiful as a child's.

"Now let me speak," he said, panting. "You have misjudged me, Rufus. It was all a mistake. I found it out after we parted. I meant to have spoken this morning when I grasped your rein, but—but—"

His generosity spared me the rest.

The wound my hand had inflicted was yet bleeding in his head; but for the blind passion of the blow it must have been mortal. Was vengeance so sweet after all? I felt something warm trickling from my shoulder. The daylight was gone—how dark it was!

"Forgive me, Dick," I murmured, groping about for him with my hands. Then I was blind—then I was cold as ice—then I tumbled down an abyss, and every thing was blank.

"The crisis is past; he will recover," cried a strange voice.

"Thank God! thank God!" cried a familiar one.

I opened my eyes. Where am I? How odd every thing was! Rows of beds stretching down a long, narrow hall, bright with sunshine; and women wearing white caps and peculiar dresses flitting to and fro with noiseless activity, which in my fearful weakness it tired me to watch. My hand lay outside the covers—it was as shadowy as a skeleton's. What had become of my flesh? Was I a child, or a man? A body, or a spirit? I was done with material things altogether, and had been subjected to some refining process, and but now awaked to a new existence. But did they have beds in the other world? I was looking lazily at the opposite one, when some one took my hand. A face was bending over. I looked up with a beating heart. The golden sunshine was on it—on the fair, regular features, and the lips, and the kindly blue eyes.

"Dick!" I gasped, "where have you been all these years?"

"Weeks, you mean," said Richard, with the old smile. "But never mind, now. You are better, dear Rufus—you will live—we shall be happy together again."

It was more a woman's voice than a man's, but Dick had a tender heart.

"Where am I?" I asked, still hazy. "What's the matter with me?"

"Hospital, in the first place," said Richard. "Typhus, in the second. You were taken after that night at Fredericksburg."

It broke upon me at once. I remembered that awful night—I could never forget it again. Weak as a child, I covered my face and burst into tears. Richard was on his knees by my side at once.

"I was a brute to recall it," he whispered remorsefully. "Do not think of it, old boy—you must not excite yourself. It is all forgotten and forgiven."

"Forgive us our trespasses as we forgive those who trespass against us," I prayed from my inmost heart.

"Those words have been in your mouth day and night, ever since you were taken," said my friend.

I lay silent, cogitating.

"Tell me one thing," I asked. "Are we in the North, or South?"

"North. In Philadelphia."

"Then you are a prisoner," I said, mournfully, recalling his principles.

"Not a bit of it."

"What do you mean?"

Richard laughed.

"I have seen the error of my ways. I have taken the oath of allegiance. When you are strong enough we shall fight side by side."

"And the wound in your head?" I asked, with emotion, looking up at his bright, handsome face.

"Don't mention it! It healed up long ago."

"And the little drummer?"

Richard bowed his head upon my hand.

"He was found dead upon the field. Heaven bless him! They said he died praying, with his mother's name upon his lips."

"Revere him as an angel!" I whispered, grasping him by the hand. "But for his dying prayer we had yet been enemies!"

Quite So
1872

THOMAS BAILEY ALDRICH

Thomas Bailey Aldrich (1836–1907) was once a renowned novel-ist and poet, but he has now lapsed into obscurity. Although he spent three years in his youth in New Orleans, Aldrich was emphatically a Northerner, raised in New Hampshire and spending most of his life in New York and Boston, where he was well acquainted with the leading literary figures of his day. Aldrich did not serve in the war, but instead spent the period 1855–64 as an editor and journalist in New York. Aside from several poems, Aldrich wrote three substantial tales about the Civil War: "My Cousin the Colonel" [in Two Bites at a Cherry and Other Tales *(1894)],* "The White Feather" [in A Sea Turn and Other Matters *(1902)], and* "Quite So," *first published in the* Atlantic Monthly *in April 1872 and included in his best-known story collection,* Marjorie Down and Other People *(1873).* "Quite So" *features vivid vignettes of camp life in its account of a shy, reserved soldier from Maine.*

I

Of course that was not his name. Even in the State of Maine, where it is still a custom to maim a child for life by christening him Arioch or Shadrach or Ephraim, nobody would dream of calling a boy "Quite So." It was merely a nickname which we gave him in camp; but it stuck to him with such bur-like tenacity, and is so inseparable from my memory of him, that I do not think I could write definitely of John Bladburn if I were to call him anything but "Quite So."

It was one night shortly after the first battle of Bull Run. The Army of the

9

Potomac, shattered, stunned, and forlorn, was back in its old quarters behind the earthworks. The melancholy line of ambulances bearing our wounded to Washington was not done creeping over Long Bridge; the blue smocks and the gray still lay in windrows on the field of Manassas; and the gloom that weighed down our hearts was like the fog that stretched along the bosom of the Potomac, and enfolded the valley of the Shenandoah. A drizzling rain had set in at twilight, and, growing bolder with the darkness, was beating a dismal tattoo on the tent—the tent of Mess 6, Company A, –th Regiment, N.Y. Volunteers. Our mess, consisting originally of eight men, was reduced to four. Little Billy, as one of the boys grimly remarked, had concluded to remain at Manassas; Corporal Steele we had to leave at Fairfax Court-House, shot through the hip; Hunter and Suydam we had said good-by to that afternoon. "Tell Johnny Reb," says Hunter, lifting up the leather side-piece of the ambulance, "that I'll be back again as soon as I get a new leg." But Suydam said nothing; he only unclosed his eyes languidly and smiled farewell to us.

The four of us who were left alive and unhurt that shameful July day sat gloomily smoking our brier-wood pipes, thinking our thoughts, and listening to the rain pattering against the canvas. That, and the occasional whine of a hungry cur, foraging on the outskirts of the camp for a stray bone, alone broke the silence, save when a vicious drop of rain detached itself meditatively from the ridge-pole of the tent, and fell upon the wick of our tallow candle, making it "cuss," as Ned Strong described it. The candle was in the midst of one of its most profane fits when Blakely, knocking the ashes from his pipe and addressing no one in particular, but giving breath, unconsciously as it were, to the result of his cogitations, observed that "it was considerable of a fizzle."

"The 'on to Richmond' business?"

"Yes."

"I wonder what they'll do about it over yonder," said Curtis, pointing over his right shoulder. By "over yonder" he meant the North in general and Massachusetts especially. Curtis was a Boston boy, and his sense of locality was so strong that, during all his wanderings in Virginia, I do not believe there was a moment, day or night, when he could not have made a bee-line for Faneuil Hall.

"Do about it?" cried Strong. "They'll make about two hundred thousand blue flannel trousers and send them along, each pair with a man in it—all the short men in the long trousers, and all the tall men in the short ones," he added, ruefully contemplating his own leg-gear, which scarcely reached to his ankles.

"That's so," said Blakely. "Just now, when I was tackling the commissary for an extra candle, I saw a crowd of new fellows drawing blankets."

"I say there, drop that!" cried Strong. "All right, sir, didn't know it was you," he added hastily, seeing it was Lieutenant Haines who had thrown back the flap of the tent, and let in a gust of wind and rain that threatened the most serious bronchial consequences to our discontented tallow dip.

"You're to bunk in here," said the lieutenant, speaking to some one outside. The some one stepped in, and Haines vanished in the darkness.

When Strong had succeeded in restoring the candle to consciousness, the light fell upon a tall, shy-looking man of about thirty-five, with long, hay-colored beard and mustache, upon which the rain-drops stood in clusters, like the night-dew on patches of cobweb in a meadow. It was an honest face, with unworldly sort of blue eyes, that looked out from under the broad visor of the infantry cap. With a deferential glance towards us, the new-comer unstrapped his knapsack, spread his blanket over it, and sat down unobtrusively.

"Rather damp night out," remarked Blakely, whose strong hand was supposed to be conversation.

"Quite so," replied the stranger, not curtly, but pleasantly, and with an air as if he had said all there was to be said about it.

"Come from the North recently?" inquired Blakely, after a pause.

"Yes."

"From any place in particular?"

"Maine."

"People considerably stirred up down there?" continued Blakely, determined not to give up.

"Quite so."

Blakely threw a puzzled look over the tent, and seeing Ned Strong on the broad grin, frowned severely. Strong instantly assumed an abstracted air, and began humming softly,

"I wish I was in Dixie."

"The State of Maine," observed Blakely, with a certain defiance of manner not at all necessary in discussing a geographical question, "is a pleasant State."

"In summer," suggested the stranger.

"In summer, I mean," returned Blakely with animation, thinking he had broken the ice. "Cold as blazes in winter, though—isn't it?"

11

The new recruit merely nodded.

Blakely eyed the man homicidally for a moment, and then, smiling one of those smiles of simulated gayety which the novelists inform us are more tragic than tears, turned upon him with withering irony.

"Trust you left the old folks pretty comfortable?"

"Dead."

"The old folks dead!"

"Quite so."

Blakely made a sudden dive for his blanket, tucked it around him with painful precision, and was heard no more.

Just then the bugle sounded "lights out,"—bugle answering bugle in far-off camps. When our not elaborate night-toilets were complete, Strong threw somebody else's old boot at the candle with infallible aim, and darkness took possession of the tent. Ned, who lay on my left, presently reached over to me, and whispered, "I say, our friend 'quite so' is a garrulous old boy! He'll talk himself to death some of these odd times, if he isn't careful. How he *did* run on!"

The next morning, when I opened my eyes, the new member of Mess 6 was sitting on his knapsack, combing his blonde beard with a horn comb. He nodded pleasantly to me, and to each of the boys as they woke up, one by one. Blakely did not appear disposed to renew the animated conversation of the previous night; but while he was gone to make a requisition for what was in pure sarcasm called coffee, Curtis ventured to ask the man his name.

"Bladburn, John," was the reply.

"That's rather an unwieldy name for every-day use," put in Strong. "If it wouldn't hurt your feelings, I'd like to call you Quite So—for short. Don't say no, if you don't like it. Is it agreeable?"

Bladburn gave a little laugh, all to himself, seemingly, and was about to say, "Quite so," when he caught at the words, blushed like a girl, and nodded a sunny assent to Strong. From that day until the end, the sobriquet clung to him.

The disaster at Bull Run was followed, as the reader knows, by a long period of masterly inactivity, so far as the Army of the Potomac was concerned. McDowell, a good soldier, but unlucky, retired to Arlington Heights, and McClellan, who had distinguished himself in Western Virginia, took command of the forces in front of Washington, and bent his energies to reorganizing the demoralized troops. It was a dreary time to the people of the North, who looked fatuously from week to week for "the fall of Richmond;" and it was a dreary time to the denizens of that vast city of tents and forts which stretched in a semicircle before the beleaguered Capitol—so tedious and soul-wearing a time that the hardships of forced marches and the horrors of battle became desirable things to them.

Roll-call morning and evening, guard-duty, dress-parades, an occasional reconnoissance, dominoes, wrestling-matches, and such rude games as could be carried on in camp made up the sum of our lives. The arrival of the mail with letters and papers from home was the event of the day. We noticed that Bladburn neither wrote nor received any letters. When the rest of the boys were scribbling away for dear life, with drum-heads and knapsacks and crackerboxes for writing-desks, he would sit serenely smoking his pipe, but looking out on us through rings of smoke with a face expressive of the tenderest interest.

"Look here, Quite So," Strong would say, "the mail-bag closes in half an hour. Ain't you going to write?"

"I believe not to-day," Bladburn would reply, as if he had written yesterday, or would write to-morrow: but he never wrote.

He had become a great favorite with us, and with all the officers of the regiment. He talked less than any man I ever knew, but there was nothing sinister or sullen in his reticence. It was sunshine,—warmth and brightness, but no voice. Unassuming and modest to the verge of shyness, he impressed every one as a man of singular pluck and nerve.

"Do you know," said Curtis to me one day, "that that fellow Quite So is clear grit, and when we come to close quarters with our Palmetto brethren over yonder, he'll do something devilish?"

"What makes you think so?"

"Well, nothing quite explainable; the exasperating coolness of the man, as much as anything. This morning the boys were teasing Muffin Fan [a small mulatto girl who used to bring muffins into camp three times a week,—at the peril of her life!] and Jemmy Blunt of Company K—you know him—was rather rough on the girl, when Quite So, who had been reading under a tree, shut one finger in his book, walked over to where the boys were skylarking, and with the smile of a juvenile angel on his face lifted Jemmy out of that and set him down gently in front of his own tent. There Blunt sat speechless, staring at Quite So, who was back again under the tree, pegging away at his little Latin grammar."

That Latin grammar! He always had it about him, reading it or turning over its dog's-eared pages at odd intervals and in out-of-the-way places. Half a dozen times a day he would draw it out from the bosom of his blouse, which had taken the shape of the book just over the left breast, look at it as if to assure himself it was all right, and then put the thing back. At night the volume lay beneath his pillow. The first thing in the morning, before he was well awake, his hand would go groping instinctively under his knapsack in search of it.

A devastating curiosity seized upon us boys concerning that Latin grammar, for we had discovered the nature of the book. Strong wanted to steal it one night, but concluded not to. "In the first place," reflected Strong, "I haven't the heart to do it, and in the next place I haven't the moral courage. Quite So would placidly break every bone in my body." And I believe Strong was not far out of the way.

Sometimes I was vexed with myself for allowing this tall, simple-hearted country fellow to puzzle me so much. And yet, was he a simple-hearted country fellow? City bred he certainly was not; but his manner, in spite of his awkwardness, had an indescribable air of refinement. Now and then, too, he dropped a word or a phrase that showed his familiarity with unexpected lines of reading. "The other day," said Curtis, with the slightest elevation of eyebrow, "he had the cheek to correct my Latin for me." In short, Quite So was a daily problem to the members of Mess 6. Whenever he was absent, and Blakely and Curtis and Strong and I got together in the tent, we discussed him, evolving various theories to explain why he never wrote to anybody and why nobody ever wrote to him. Had the man committed some terrible crime, and fled to the army to hide his guilt? Blakely suggested that he must have murdered "the old folks." What did he mean by eternally conning that tattered Latin grammar? And was his name Bladburn, anyhow? Even his imperturbable amiability became suspicious. And then his frightful reticence! If he was the victim of any deep grief or crushing calamity, why didn't he seem unhappy? What business had he to be cheerful?

"It's my opinion," said Strong, "that he's a rival Wandering Jew; the original Jacobs, you know, was a dark fellow."

Blakely inferred from something Bladburn had said, or something he had not said—which was more likely—that he had been a schoolmaster at some period of his life.

"Schoolmaster be hanged!" was Strong's comment. "Can you fancy a schoolmaster going about conjugating baby verbs out of a dratted little spelling-book? No, Quite So has evidently been a—a— Blest if I can imagine *what* he's been!"

Whatever John Bladburn had been, he was a lonely man. Whenever I want a type of perfect human isolation, I shall think of him, as he was in those days, moving remote, self-contained, and alone in the midst of two hundred thousand men.

II

The Indian summer, with its infinite beauty and tenderness, came like a reproach that year to Virginia. The foliage, touched here and there with prismatic tints, drooped motionless in the golden haze. The delicate Virginia creeper was almost minded to put forth its scarlet buds again. No wonder the lovely phantom—this dusky Southern sister of the pale Northern June—lingered not long with us, but, filling the once peaceful glens and valleys with her pathos, stole away rebukefully before the savage enginery of man.

The preparations that had been going on for months in arsenals and foundries at the North were nearly completed. For weeks past the air had been filled with rumors of an advance; but the rumor of to-day refuted the rumor of yesterday, and the Grand Army did not move. Heintzelman's corps was constantly folding its tents, like the Arabs, and as silently stealing away; but somehow it was always in the same place the next morning. One day, at last, orders came down for our brigade to move.

"We're going to Richmond, boys!" shouted Strong, thrusting his head in at the tent; and we all cheered and waved our caps like mad. You see, Big Bethel and Bull Run and Ball's Bluff (the bloody B's, as we used to call them) hadn't taught us any better sense.

Rising abruptly from the plateau, to the left of our encampment, was a tall hill covered with a stunted growth of red-oak, persimmon, and chestnut. The night before we struck tents I climbed up to the crest to take a parting look at a spectacle which custom had not been able to rob of its enchantment. There, at my feet, and extending miles and miles away, lay the camps of the Grand Army, with its camp-fires reflected luridly against the sky. Thousands of lights were twinkling in every direction, some nestling in the valley, some like fire-flies beating their wings and palpitating among the trees, and others stretching in parallel lines and curves, like the street-lamps of a city. Somewhere, far off, a band was playing, at intervals it seemed; and now and then, nearer to, a silvery strain from a bugle shot sharply up through the night, and seemed to lose itself like a rocket among the stars—the patient, untroubled stars. Suddenly a hand was laid upon my arm.

"I'd like to say a word to you," said Bladburn.

With a little start of surprise, I made room for him on the fallen tree where I was seated.

"I mayn't get another chance," he said. "You and the boys have been very kind to me, kinder than I deserve; but sometimes I've fancied that my not saying anything about myself had given you the idea that all was not right in my past. I want to say that I came down to Virginia with a clean record."

"We never really doubted it, Bladburn."

"If I didn't write home," he continued, "it was because I hadn't any home, neither kith nor kin. When I said the old folks were dead, I said it. Am I boring you? If I thought I was"—

"No, Bladburn. I have often wanted you to talk to me about yourself, not from idle curiosity, I trust, but because I liked you that rainy night when you came to camp, and have gone on liking you ever since. This isn't too much to say, when Heaven only knows how soon I may be past saying it or you listening to it."

"That's it," said Bladburn, hurriedly; "that's why I want to talk with you. I've a fancy that I shan't come out of our first battle."

The words gave me a queer start, for I had been trying several days to throw off a similar presentiment concerning him—a foolish presentiment that grew out of a dream.

"In case anything of that kind turns up," he continued, "I'd like you to have my Latin grammar here—you've seen me reading it. You might stick it away in a bookcase, for the sake of old times. It goes against me to think of it falling into rough hands or being kicked about camp and trampled underfoot."

He was drumming softly with his fingers on the volume in the bosom of his blouse.

"I didn't intend to speak of this to a living soul," he went on, motioning me not to answer him; "but something took hold of me to-night and made me follow you up here. Perhaps if I told you all, you would be the more willing to look after the little book in case it goes ill with me. When the war broke out I was teaching school down in Maine, in the same village where my father was schoolmaster before me. The old man when he died left me quite alone. I lived pretty much by myself, having no interests outside of the district school, which seemed in a manner my personal property. Eight years ago last spring a new pupil was brought to the school, a slight slip of a girl, with a sad kind of face and quiet ways. Perhaps it was because she wasn't very strong, and perhaps because she wasn't used over well by those who had charge of her, or perhaps it was because my life was lonely, that my heart warmed to the child. It all seems like a dream now, since that April morning when little Mary stood in front of my desk with her pretty eyes looking down bashfully and her soft hair falling over her face. One day I look up, and six years have gone by—as they go by in dreams—and among the scholars is a tall girl of sixteen, with serious, womanly eyes which I cannot trust myself to look upon. The old life has come to an end. The child has become a woman and can teach the master now. So help me Heaven, I didn't know that I loved her until that day!

"Long after the children had gone home I sat in the school-room with my face resting on my hands. There was her desk, the afternoon shadows falling across it. It never looked empty and cheerless before. I went and stood by the low chair, as I had stood hundreds of times. On the desk was a pile of books, ready to be taken away, and among the rest a small Latin grammar which we had studied together. What little despairs and triumphs and happy hours were associated with it! I took it up curiously, as if it were some gentle dead thing, and turned over the pages, and could hardly see them. Turning the pages, idly so, I came to a leaf on which something was written with ink, in the familiar girlish hand. It was only the words 'Dear John,' through which she had drawn two hasty pencil lines—I wish she hadn't drawn those lines!" added Bladburn, under his breath.

He was silent for a minute or two, looking off towards the camps, where the lights were fading out one by one.

"I had no right to go and love Mary. I was twice her age, an awkward, unsocial man, that would have blighted her youth. I was as wrong as wrong can be. But I never meant to tell her. I locked the grammar in my desk and the secret in my heart for a year. I couldn't bear to meet her in the village, and kept away from every place where she was likely to be. Then she came to me, and sat down at my feet penitently, just as she used to do when she was a child, and asked what she had done to anger me; and then, Heaven forgive me! I told her all, and asked her if she could say with her lips the words she had written, and she nestled in my arms all a-trembling like a bird, and said them over and over again.

"When Mary's family heard of our engagement, there was trouble. They looked higher for Mary than a middle-aged schoolmaster. No blame to them. They forbade me the house, her uncles; but we met in the village and at the neighbors' houses, and I was happy, knowing she loved me. Matters were in this state when the war came on. I had a strong call to look after the old flag, and I hung my head that day when the company raised in our village marched by the school-house to the railroad station; but I couldn't tear myself away. About this time the minister's son, who had been away to college, came to the village. He met Mary here and there, and they became great friends. He was a likely fellow, near her own age, and it was natural they should like one another. Sometimes I winced at seeing him made free of the home from which I was shut out; then I would open the grammar at the leaf where 'Dear John' was written up in the corner, and my trouble was gone. Mary was sorrowful and pale these days, and I think her people were worrying her.

"It was one evening two or three days before we got the news of Bull Run. I had gone down to the burying-ground to trim the spruce hedge set round the old man's lot, and was just stepping into the enclosure, when I heard voices from the opposite side. One was Mary's, and the other I knew to be young Marston's, the minister's son. I didn't mean to listen, but what Mary was saying struck me dumb. *We must never meet again,* she was saying in a wild way. *We must say good-by here, forever,—good-by, good-by!* And I could hear her sobbing. Then, presently, she said, hurriedly, *No, no; my hand, not my lips!* Then it seemed he kissed her hands, and the two parted, one going towards the parsonage, and the other out by the gate near where I stood.

"I don't know how long I stood there, but the night-dews had wet me to the bone when I stole out of the graveyard and across the road to the school-house. I unlocked the door, and took the Latin grammar from the desk and hid it in my bosom. There was not a sound or a light anywhere as I walked out of the village. And now," said Bladburn, rising suddenly from the tree-trunk, "if the little book ever falls in your way, won't you see that it comes to no harm, for my sake, and for the sake of the little woman who was true to me and didn't love me? Wherever she is to-night, God bless her!"

As we descended to camp with our arms resting on each other's shoulder, the watchfires were burning low in the valleys and along the hillsides, and as far as the eye could reach the silent tents lay bleaching in the moonlight.

III

We imagined that the throwing forward of our brigade was the initial movement of a general advance of the army; but that, as the reader will remember, did not take place until the following March. The Confederates had fallen back to Centreville without firing a shot, and the national troops were in possession of Lewinsville, Vienna, and Fairfax Court-House. Our new position was nearly identical with that which we had occupied on the night previous to the battle of Bull Run— on the old turnpike road to Manassas, where the enemy was supposed to be in great force. With a field-glass we could see the Rebel pickets moving in a belt of woodland on our right, and morning and evening we heard the spiteful roll of their snare-drums.

Those pickets soon became a nuisance to us. Hardly a night passed but they fired upon our outposts, so far with no harmful result; but after a while it grew to be a serious matter. The Rebels would crawl out on all-fours from the wood into a field covered with underbrush, and lie there in the dark for hours, waiting for a shot. Then our men took to the rifle-pits— pits ten or twelve feet long by four or five deep, with the loose earth banked up a few inches high on the exposed sides. All the pits bore names, more or less felicitous, by which they were known to their transient ten- ants. One was called "The Pepper-Box," another "Uncle Sam's Well," another "The Reb-Trap," and another, I am constrained to say, was named after a not-to-be-mentioned tropical locality. Though this rude sort of nomenclature predominated, there was no lack of softer titles, such as "Fortress Matilda" and "Castle Mary," and one had, though unintention- ally, a literary flavor to it, "Blair's Grave," which was not popularly consid- ered as reflecting unpleasantly on Nat Blair, who had assisted in making the excavation.

Some of the regiment had discovered a field of late corn in the neigh- borhood, and used to boil a few ears every day, while it lasted, for the boys detailed on the night-picket. The corn-cobs were always scrupulously pre- served and mounted on the parapets of the pits. Whenever a Rebel shot carried away one of these *barbette* guns, there was swearing in that partic- ular trench. Strong, who was very sensitive to this kind of disaster, was complaining bitterly one morning, because he had lost three "pieces" the night before.

"There's Quite So, now," said Strong, "when a Minie-ball comes *ping!* and knocks one of his guns to flinders, he merely smiles, and doesn't at all see the degradation of the thing."

Poor Bladburn! As I watched him day by day going about his duties, in his shy, cheery way, with a smile for every one and not an extra word for anybody, it was hard to believe he was the same man who, that night before we broke camp by the Potomac, had poured out to me the story of his love and sorrow in words that burned in my memory.

While Strong was speaking, Blakely lifted aside the flap of the tent and looked in on us.

"Boys, Quite So was hurt last night," he said, with a white tremor to his lip.

"What!"

"Shot on picket."

"Why, he was in the pit next to mine," cried Strong.

"Badly hurt?"

"Badly hurt."

I knew he was; I need not have asked the question. He never meant to go back to New England!

Bladburn was lying on the stretcher in the hospital-tent. The surgeon had knelt down by him, and was carefully cutting away the bosom of his blouse. The Latin grammar, stained and torn, slipped, and fell to the floor. Bladburn gave me a quick glance. I picked up the book, and as I placed it in his hand, the icy fingers closed softly over mine. He was sinking fast. In a few minutes the surgeon finished his examination. When he rose to his feet there were tears on the weather-beaten cheeks. He was a rough outside, but a tender heart.

"My poor lad," he blurted out, "it's no use. If you've anything to say, say it now, for you've nearly done with this world."

Then Bladburn lifted his eyes slowly to the surgeon, and the old smile flitted over his face as he murmured,

"Quite so."

The Three Hundred
1880

William Chambers Morrow (1854–1923) was a successful but now little-known fiction writer and journalist whose family came from Alabama, where they owned many slaves. Coming to San Francisco shortly after the war, Morrow became acquainted with the leading literary figures in the city (notably Ambrose Bierce), and also became known for his gripping and crisply written tales. Among his novels is Blood-Money (1882), which dealt with the Mussel Slough affair, in which the Southern Pacific Railroad forced settlers off a tract of land they had worked hard to cultivate, leading to a gunfight in 1880 in which some settlers were killed. Morrow, however, published only one short story collection, The Ape, the Idiot and Other People (1897), a distinctive volume of tales of suspense and the supernatural. In several uncollected tales, Morrow wrote vividly of the Civil War. "The Three Hundred," first published in the Argonaut on January 10, 1880, tells of a valiant band of extremely young Southern soldiers.

Three hundred men of remarkable size remained as the bulwark of a cause. Three hundred rifles flashed in the sunlight, and three hundred glistening bayonets pointed with ominous portent to the sky, which was blue. The uniform of the soldiers was gray. They were drawn up for review. There were several peculiarities that distinguished these men from ordinary soldiers in time of war. Their uniforms were bright and new. Three rows of brass buttons ornamented the breast, gold braid in graceful festoon-designs relieved the front, and a stripe of black ran down the outer seam of the trowsers. The caps were surrounded by a black-and-gold band

21

and surmounted by a cockade of white feathers. These facts are worth of note, for the reason that the war was drawing to a close. The soldiers exhibited no signs of fatigue or hardships; their uniforms were not soiled nor ragged, nor slashed by sabres, nor torn by minie-balls.

Let us examine the reasons why this magnificently equipped and excellently drilled battalion was absent from Shiloh, from Seven Pines, from Chickamauga, from Donaldson. Was the Southern army surfeited with men? No. These were of a strange and unusual type. There was not a man who wore a beard. Their faces were rosy and white. Their most striking peculiarity was their size. They were not giants. They were narrow in the shoulders, narrow in the hips, and had legs of disproportionate length. In fact, they appeared to be dwarfs.

Not less remarkable in appearance than the soldiers were those who participated in the review. There was a notable exception in the person of the colonel, who was about forty years of age, of medium stature, straight as an arrow and proud as a king. He had gray eyes that were sharp, quick, intense. His forehead was broad and massive, his hair very gray, his neck powerful and firm. He was every inch a soldier—brave, resolute, daring, calm, prompt. It was upon his companions that the caricaturist could have flung the filthiest ink of bad humor. There were six of these. They were mounted, sat their horses awkwardly and uneasily, were uncouth and ridiculous. One had extremely long legs and large ears; another was so near-sighted that the phalanx appeared to him to be a monstrous pin-cushion, pricked by many needles. Under ordinary circumstances they might have been dignified men; but their surroundings were extraordinary, and they were consequently undignified.

After the review, the colonel asked one of the gentlemen:

"How do you like their appearance?"

"Very much; very much."

"Do you think they will stand?"

"Under your leadership they certainly will, commandant."

The colonel smiled.

"But, commandant," continued the gentleman, "you must remember that it is only at your earnest solicitation that I consented for the little fellows to retain their uniforms and be under fire. I would not have a hair of their heads harmed for all the world."

It was strange that he should speak thus of soldiers!

"I assure you they will be perfectly safe, sir," replied the officer.

"Quite sure?"

"Yes."

"Very well."

"The breastworks will afford ample protection. There will be merely a skirmish. The enemy will not fire upon us; but, on a mock show of resistance, will probably aim high and discharge a round to frighten us. I will return the fire in like manner, and then send up the white flag. I am extremely anxious that the boys should smell burnt powder. It will be a harmless lesson; yet I will lead them to believe I am in earnest. Of course it would be folly to oppose five thousand veterans with three hundred school-boys, twelve or thirteen years old."

They were not soldiers, then, but babes, whom the conscript act had disdained to send to the front. They were cadets; they attended a university, the colonel was the commandant; the horsemen, the Faculty. The boys were under the age of fourteen, the professors, over the age of fifty. They were not bomb-proof, but age-proof.

The commandant mounted his horse, spurred down to the centre of the line, and made the following address:

"Men and soldiers!"

Three hundred young hearts throbbed with pride.

"The enemy is upon us. Sherman is marching to the sea. He leaves in his desolate track chimneys without houses, children without homes, a people without a God!"

He paused. The line trembled.

"You hear his guns. You see the black smoke of burning homes. In less than an hour a brigade of five thousand trained soldiers will sweep down upon you. The South does not despair. She has yet three hundred brave hearts to sacrifice upon the altar of Right."

The line swayed with excitement.

"Your mothers and sisters watch you from afar. Their prayers are with you."

He shook with emotion.

"Richmond has her eyes upon you! If we die, it is the death of the soldier."

He raised his sword:

"If we fall, our dead bodies will be a monument to honor, the inalienable birthright of a Southerner!"

This ingenious and eloquent appeal had a wonderful effect. The colors were unfurled, and the entire line, in the wildest enthusiasm, sent up cheer after cheer. What if the boys were beguiled with a taste of glory? It made them soldiers, men, heroes.

The University was a mile from the town. A fence inclosed the broad campus. Along one side ran the public highway. On the side nearest the town was a large meadow. Not many rods from that side of the inclosure nearest the town was a trench two hundred yards long, protected by an earthwork that rose three feet above the surrounding level. The town was separated from the University by an intervening country, crossed and checked with fences, hedges, and walls of stone, the road cutting a broad passage through the whole. On either side was a row of stately dwellings and magnificent lines of cedar and live-oak, with occasional hedges of arbor-vitæ, Osage orange, or Cherokee rose.

The three hundred were drawn up in line of battle some two hundred yards in advance of the intrenchment. It was the intention of the commandant to fall back after the first fire. He speculated considerably on the nature of the attack. It was uncertain whether the raiders would send out a small detachment, or precipitate the whole column upon the feeble opposition of the boys.

But the commandant had not acted in consonance with his original intentions. He did not place the boys under the protection of the breastwork; they stood upon the open plain.

A cloud of dust was seen in the direction of the town. It was caused by the rapid approach of a company of horsemen. They numbered some seventy men. The heart of the commandant beat rapidly; a crisis was at hand. The advancing cavalrymen reached the meadow and halted. They formed. A command was given; a charge was ordered. The horsemen plied the spur, and bore down, headlong and furious, upon the three hundred.

The commandant saw at a glance their terrible object: they would not shed the blood of the boys, but they would scatter them like chaff, and perhaps trample them in the dust. It was an anxious moment, and the commandant formed a resolution.

"Aim low!" he commanded.

He could not brook the insult.

"Fire!"

There was a terrific crash. When within fifty yards of the young rebels the impetuous charge of the cavalrymen was stopped by a wall of lead. It struck them in the face and blinded them; it crushed their breasts; it shattered their arms. It struck down their horses, some falling to the ground, others, rearing and plunging, fled riderless from the bloody scene. The company was overwhelmed with consternation. A pompous little array of mock soldiers had poured out from three hundred toy rifles an unmerciful hail of death, that scorched the air and tore through the vitals of the veterans.

The soldiers had not fired a gun. They did not retreat—they ran. Death had stalked, unexpected, into their midst. They left a third of their number dead or wounded upon the field. But they were by no means defeated. It was now a point of honor. They rallied and prepared for a second charge.

The feelings that thrilled the breasts of the three hundred at this first taste of victory, the wild energy that sent the hot young blood bounding with redoubled speed through their veins, are things that scoff at portrayal. The faces that were white when the finger pressed the trigger were now glowing with feverish excitement. They stood as firm as a rock, and reloaded their rifles. The commandant praised them.

The cavalrymen advanced and delivered a fire at long range. One little fellow was struck in the breast. He threw up his hands and fell flat upon his face. Those in his immediate vicinity were demoralized, but the commandant galloped to the spot and reassured them. Much as it galled his pride, he saw the advisability of ordering an immediate retreat. He carried a heavy responsibility in the little life that had already gone out. He proceeded to retreat, orderly and slowly, and reserved his fire. He was in despair. Events had taken an altogether unexpected turn. He concluded to surrender. He pulled something white from his pocket, and reached down for a gun from which to wave it.

At that moment his plume fell to the ground, severed by a bullet. He had become a target. In another second a mad ball tore blindly through his heart.

When the commandant fell there was indeed dismay in the ranks. His horse bounded away. The cavalrymen, seeing his fall, again put spur to horse and charged furiously.

But the boys were not without a leader. The senior captain sprang forward, sword in hand, and placed himself in front of the commandant's body. The hat of the latter had fallen; the boy picked it up and placed it upon his own head. It was too large for him. He was a mere child, but his eyes glared dangerously. He raised his sword as the commandant had done, and assumed command. But the line was giving way. It melted. It was lost. Not to be outdone in bravery, the other captains rallied around their commander. Many were flying, but they also returned. The little captain bravely endeavored to form his men, but it was useless. The horsemen were charging them and were quite near. The boy captain shouted at the top of his voice:

"Fire—low!"

Again was the enemy brought to a stand by a short nervous fire, that did little harm. The boys were huddled together like frightened sheep. The commander ordered a retreat to the intrenchment.

He picked up the dead body of his commandant. By a powerful effort he succeeded in placing it across his shoulder. A torrent of warm blood gushed from the ghastly hole in the side and streamed down the boy's breast. It sickened him. The weight of the body was crushing him. He staggered forward a few steps. The odor of the blood invaded his nostrils. He closed his teeth firmly together, and struggled to retain his balance. The body was heavy and unwieldy. The legs swung from side to side and hindered him. He trembled with the exertion. His stomach revolted at the smell of blood. He surged to one side and fell, the body lying across his back. He raised himself upon his hands and knees, and the body rolled upon the ground. He grasped it by the collar, and mustering all his strength, dragged it across the intervening space, and over the embankment.

In the meantime, a cloud of dust far greater than that previously created by the repulsed horsemen was approaching the battle-field from the town. A regiment of eight hundred horse had been dispatched at the moment the firing was heard. It arrived at a most unseasonable time. The Federal company was stung with anger and shame. It had demoralized the enemy, but only temporarily; for he was now safely lodged behind an efficient shelter. The company was compelled to submit to the mortification of a reinforcement. Eight hundred and fifty cavalrymen were now arrayed against three hundred trembling boys.

The solitary figure of a boy stood calmly upon the embankment, in full view of the enemy. He was the leader of the rebel forces. The great mantle of a sorrowful loneliness enveloped him; the sad essence of that oppressing absence of everything but pride pervaded his bearing; he seemed utterly desolate and deserted, but brave, superior, scornful of death. There is not a mother in the world whose heart would not have gone out to that lonely child standing in the shadow of death. She would have clasped him in her arms, and covered his sad, childish face with kisses. His arms were folded. His right hand clasped a sword larger than the one he had previously carried. It was the commandant's. The boy was pale.

He had restored order and confidence. The boys had as yet imbibed no idea of defeat. They were quietly secreted in the trench, rifle in hand, and prepared for another charge.

The storm gathered. A dense blue cloud, charged with a thousand thunderbolts, prepared to burst upon the heads of the three hundred. It advanced, and disgorged a hail of leaden stones. It thundered out destruction, and belched fire and smoke. It rolled onward, hurling death through the air.

The cool commander of the rebels stood upon the embankment unharmed, while the minie-balls rained around him. They threw dirt upon him as they struck the embankment. As the cloud rumbled noisily and thundering over the ground, he seized his opportunity, and shouted at the top of his voice:

"Ready—aim low—fire!"

There was a puff of smoke from the earthwork; a few in the lines of the enemy wavered; but the cloud swept on.

The crisis came. The cloud had become a flood, which poured over the embankment. The boys were scattered to the winds—

All but one. He stood pale and resolute beside the dead body of the commandant. The flood roared and seethed around him; he held the great sword in both hands, to battle with the waves.

A captain approached him and demanded:

"Surrender!"

The boy regarded him scornfully, and grasped the sword more firmly. The captain thought to frighten him by raising his sword as if to strike.

"Surrender!" he repeated.

"Not to you, sir."

The captain was astonished.

"To whom, then?"

"Your colonel."

"My colonel!"

"Yes."

"Why?"

"I demand it."

"For what reason?"

"It is a courtesy due to my rank."

"Who are you?"

"A soldier."

"Your rank?"

"Colonel-commanding."

"And the man lying there?"

The boy gazed down into the upturned face. His breast was seen to heave.

"Who is he?" asked the officer softly.

A tear trembled upon the pale cheek of the boy. Less firmly he answered:

"My father."

Three Miraculous Soldiers
1896

STEPHEN CRANE

Stephen Crane (1871–1900) was of course not even born before the end of the Civil War, yet his ability to portray the war realistically, albeit impressionistically, is remarkable. He achieved his greatest triumph in The Red Badge of Courage *(1895), far and away the finest novel about the war, but in a series of stories included in* The Little Regiment and Other Episodes of the American Civil War *(1896) he achieved similar effects within a more narrow compass. In one story from that collection, "Three Miraculous Soldiers," Crane seriocomically depicts the tribulations of a young Southern girl who seeks to prevent some of her compatriots from being captured by the invading Federals.*

I

The girl was in the front room on the second floor, peering through the blinds. It was the "best room." There was a very new rag carpet on the floor. The edges of it had been dyed with alternate stripes of red and green. Upon the wooden mantel there were two little puffy figures in clay— a shepherd and a shepherdess, probably. A triangle of pink and white wool hung carefully over the edge of this shelf. Upon the bureau there was nothing at all save a spread newspaper, with edges folded to make it into a mat. The quilts and sheets had been removed from the bed and were stacked upon a chair. The pillows and the great feather mattress were muffled and tumbled until they resembled great dumplings. The picture of a man terribly leaden in complexion hung in an oval frame on one white wall and steadily confronted the bureau.

28

From between the slats of the blinds she had a view of the road as it wended across the meadow to the woods, and again where it reappeared crossing the hill, half a mile away. It lay yellow and warm in the summer sunshine. From the long grasses of the meadow came the rhythmic click of the insects. Occasional frogs in the hidden brook made a peculiar chug-chug sound, as if somebody throttled them. The leaves of the wood swung in gentle winds. Through the dark green branches of the pines that grew in the front yard could be seen the mountains, far to the south-east, and inexpressibly blue.

Mary's eyes were fastened upon the little streak of road that appeared on the distant hill. Her face was flushed with excitement, and the hand which stretched in a strained pose on the sill trembled because of the nervous shaking of the wrist. The pines whisked their green needles with a soft hissing sound against the house.

At last the girl turned from the window and went to the head of the stairs. "Well, I just know they're coming, anyhow," she cried argumentatively to the depths.

A voice from below called to her angrily: "They ain't. We've never seen one yet. They never come into this neighbourhood. You just come down here and 'tend to your work insteader watching for soldiers."

"Well, ma, I just know they're coming."

A voice retorted with the shrillness and mechanical violence of occasional housewives. The girl swished her skirts defiantly and returned to the window.

Upon the yellow streak of road that lay across the hillside there now was a handful of black dots—horsemen. A cloud of dust floated away. The girl flew to the head of the stairs and whirled down into the kitchen.

"They're coming! They're coming!"

It was as if she had cried "Fire!" Her mother had been peeling potatoes while seated comfortably at the table. She sprang to her feet. "No—it can't be—how you know it's them—where?" The stubby knife fell from her hand, and two or three curls of potato-skin dropped from her apron to the floor.

The girl turned and dashed upstairs. Her mother followed, gasping for breath, and yet contriving to fill the air with question, reproach, and remonstrance. The girl was already at the window, eagerly pointing. "There! There! See 'em! See 'em!"

Rushing to the window, the mother scanned for an instant the road on the hill. She crouched back with a groan. "It's them, sure as the world! It's them!" She waved her hands in despairing gestures.

The black dots vanished into the wood. The girl at the window was quivering, and her eyes were shining like water when the sun flashes. "Hush! They're in the woods! They'll be here directly." She bent down and intently watched the green archway whence the road emerged. "Hush! I hear 'em coming," she swiftly whispered to her mother, for the elder woman had dropped dolefully upon the mattress and was sobbing. And, indeed, the girl could hear the quick, dull trample of horses. She stepped aside with sudden apprehension, but she bent her head forward in order to still scan the road.

"Here they are!"

There was something very theatrical in the sudden appearance of these men to the eyes of the girl. It was as if a scene had been shifted. The forest suddenly disclosed them—a dozen brown-faced troopers in blue—galloping.

"Oh, look!" breathed the girl. Her mouth was puckered into an expression of strange fascination, as if she had expected to see the troopers change into demons and gloat at her. She was at last looking upon those curious beings who rode down from the North—those men of legend and colossal tale—they who were possessed of such marvellous hallucinations.

The little troop rode in silence. At its head was a youthful fellow with some dim yellow stripes upon his arm. In his right hand he held his carbine, slanting upward, with the stock resting upon his knee. He was absorbed in a scrutiny of the country before him.

At the heels of the sergeant the rest of the squad rode in thin column, with creak of leather and tinkle of steel and tin. The girl scanned the faces of the horsemen, seeming astonished vaguely to find them of the type she knew.

The lad at the head of the troop comprehended the house and its environments in two glances. He did not check the long, swinging stride of his horse. The troopers glanced for a moment like casual tourists, and then returned to their study of the region in front. The heavy thudding of the hoofs became a small noise. The dust, hanging in sheets, slowly sank.

The sobs of the woman on the bed took form in words which, while strong in their note of calamity, yet expressed a querulous mental reaching for some near thing to blame. "And it'll be lucky fer us if we ain't both butchered in our sleep—plundering and running off horses—old Santo's gone—you see if he ain't—plundering—"

"But, ma," said the girl, perplexed and terrified in the same moment, "they've gone."

"Oh, but they'll come back!" cried the mother, without pausing her wail. "They'll come back—trust them for that—running off horses. O

John, John! why did you, why did you?" She suddenly lifted herself and sat rigid, staring at her daughter. "Mary," she said in a tragic whisper, "the kitchen door isn't locked!" Already she was bended forward to listen, her mouth agape, her eyes fixed upon her daughter.

"Mother," faltered the girl.

Her mother again whispered, "The kitchen door isn't locked."

Motionless and mute, they stared into each other's eyes.

At last the girl quavered, "We better—we better go and lock it." The mother nodded. Hanging arm in arm, they stole across the floor toward the head of the stairs. A board of the floor creaked. They halted and exchanged a look of dumb agony.

At last they reached the head of the stairs. From the kitchen came the bass humming of the kettle and frequent sputterings and cracklings from the fire. These sounds were sinister. The mother and the girl stood incapable of movement. "There's somebody down there!" whispered the elder woman.

Finally, the girl made a gesture of resolution. She twisted her arm from her mother's hands and went two steps downward. She addressed the kitchen: "Who's there?" Her tone was intended to be dauntless. It rang so dramatically in the silence that a sudden new panic seized them, as if the suspected presence in the kitchen had cried out to them. But the girl ventured again: "Is there anybody there?" No reply was made save by the kettle and the fire.

With a stealthy tread the girl continued her journey. As she neared the last step the fire crackled explosively, and the girl screamed. But the mystic presence had not swept around the corner to grab her, so she dropped to a seat on the step and laughed. "It was—was only the—the fire," she said, stammering hysterically.

Then she arose with sudden fortitude and cried: "Why, there isn't anybody there! I know there isn't." She marched down into the kitchen. In her face was dread, as if she half expected to confront something, but the room was empty. She cried joyously: "There's nobody here! Come on down, ma." She ran to the kitchen door and locked it.

The mother came down to the kitchen. "Oh, dear, what a fright I've had! It's given me the sick headache. I know it has."

"Oh, ma," said the girl.

"I know it has—I know it. Oh, if your father was only here! He'd settle those Yankees mighty quick—he'd settle 'em! Two poor helpless women—"

"Why, ma, what makes you act so? The Yankees haven't—"

"Oh, they'll be back—they'll be back. Two poor helpless women! Your father and your uncle Asa and Bill off gallivanting around and fighting when they ought to be protecting their home! That's the kind of men they are. Didn't I say to your father just before he left—?"

"Ma," said the girl, coming suddenly from the window, "the barn door is open. I wonder if they took old Santo."

"Oh, of course they have—of course— Mary, I don't see what we are going to do—I don't see what we are going to do."

The girl said, "Ma, I'm going to see if they took old Santo."

"Mary," cried the mother, "don't you dare!"

"But think of poor old Sant, ma."

"Never you mind old Santo. We're lucky to be safe ourselves, I tell you. Never mind old Santo. Don't you dare to go out there, Mary—Mary!"

The girl had unlocked the door and stepped out upon the porch. The mother cried in despair, "Mary!"

"Why, there isn't anybody out here," the girl called in response. She stood for a moment with a curious smile upon her face, as of gleeful satisfaction at her daring.

The breeze was waving the boughs of the apple trees. A rooster with an air importantly courteous was conducting three hens upon a foraging tour. On the hillside at the rear of the grey old barn the red leaves of a creeper flamed amid the summer foliage. High in the sky clouds rolled toward the north. The girl swung impulsively from the little stoop and ran toward the barn.

The great door was open, and the carved peg which usually performed the office of a catch lay on the ground. The girl could not see into the barn because of the heavy shadows. She paused in a listening attitude and heard a horse munching placidly. She gave a cry of delight and sprang across the threshold. Then she suddenly shrank back and gasped. She had confronted three men in grey seated upon the floor with their legs stretched out and their backs against Santo's manger. Their dust-covered countenances were expanded in grins.

II

As Mary sprang backward and screamed, one of the calm men in grey, still grinning, announced, "I knowed you'd holler." Sitting there comfortably, the three surveyed her with amusement.

Mary caught her breath, throwing her hand up to her throat. "Oh!" she said, "you—you frightened me!"

"We're sorry, lady, but couldn't help it no way," cheerfully responded another. "I knowed you'd holler when I seen you coming yere, but I raikoned we couldn't help it no way. We hain't a-troubling this yere barn, I don't guess. We been doing some mighty tall sleeping yere. We done woke when them Yanks loped past."

"Where did you come from? Did—did you escape from the—the Yankees?" The girl still stammered and trembled.

The three soldiers laughed. "No, m'm. No, m'm. They never cotch us. We was in a muss down the road yere about two mile. And Bill yere, they gi'n it to him in the arm, kehplunk. And they pasted me thar, too. Curious. And Sim yere, he didn't get nothing, but they chased us all quite a little piece, and we done lose track of our boys."

"Was it—was it those who passed here just now? Did they chase you?"

The men in grey laughed again. "What—them? No, indeedee! There was a mighty big swarm of Yanks and a mighty big swarm of our boys, too. What—that little passel? No, m'm."

She became calm enough to scan them more attentively. They were much begrimed and very dusty. Their grey clothes were tattered. Splashed mud had dried upon them in reddish spots. It appeared, too, that the men had not shaved in many days. In the hats there was a singular diversity. One soldier wore the little blue cap of the Northern infantry, with corps emblem and regimental number; one wore a great slouch hat with a wide hole in the crown; and the other wore no hat at all. The left sleeve of one man and the right sleeve of another had been slit, and the arms were neatly bandaged with clean cloths. "These hain't no more than two little cuts," explained one. "We stopped up yere to Mis' Leavitt's—she said her name was—and she bind them for us. Bill yere, he had the thirst come on him. And the fever too. We—"

"Did you ever see my father in the army?" asked Mary. "John Hinckson—his name is."

The three soldiers grinned again, but they replied kindly: "No, m'm. No, m'm, we hain't never. What is he—in the cavalry?"

"No," said the girl. "He and my uncle Asa and my cousin—his name is Bill Parker—they are all with Longstreet—they call him."

"Oh," said the soldiers. "Longstreet? Oh, they're a good smart ways from yere. 'Way off up nawtheast. There hain't nothing but cavalry down yere. They're in the infantry, probably."

"We haven't heard anything from them for days and days," said Mary.

"Oh, they're all right in the infantry," said one man, to be consoling. "The infantry don't do much fighting. They go bellering out in a big swarm and only a few of 'em get hurt. But if they was in the cavalry—the cavalry—"

Mary interrupted him without intention. "Are you hungry?" she asked.

The soldiers looked at each other, struck by some sudden and singular shame. They hung their heads. "No, m'm," replied one at last.

Santo, in his stall, was tranquilly chewing and chewing. Sometimes he looked benevolently over at them. He was an old horse, and there was something about his eyes and his forelock which created the impression that he wore spectacles. Mary went and patted his nose. "Well, if you are hungry, I can get you something," she told the men. "Or you might come to the house."

"We wouldn't dast go to the house," said one. "That passel of Yanks was only a scouting crowd, most like. Just an advance. More coming, likely."

"Well, I can bring you something," cried the girl eagerly. "Won't you let me bring you something?"

"Well," said a soldier with embarrassment, "we hain't had much. If you could bring us a little snack-like—just a snack—we'd—"

Without waiting for him to cease, the girl turned toward the door. But before she had reached it she stopped abruptly. "Listen!" she whispered. Her form was bent forward, her head turned and lowered, her hand extended toward the men in a command for silence.

They could faintly hear the thudding of many hoofs, the clank of arms, and frequent calling voices.

"By cracky, it's the Yanks!" The soldiers scrambled to their feet and came toward the door. "I knowed that first crowd was only an advance."

The girl and the three men peered from the shadows of the barn. The view of the road was intersected by tree trunks and a little henhouse. However, they could see many horsemen streaming down the road. The horsemen were in blue. "Oh, hide—hide—hide!" cried the girl, with a sob in her voice.

"Wait a minute," whispered a grey soldier excitedly. "Maybe they're going along by. No, by thunder, they hain't! They're halting. Scoot, boys!"

They made a noiseless dash into the dark end of the barn. The girl, standing by the door, heard them break forth an instant later in clamorous whispers. "Where'll we hide? Where'll we hide? There hain't a place to hide!" The girl turned and glanced wildly about the barn. It seemed true. The stock of hay had grown low under Santo's endless munching, and from occasional levyings by passing troopers in grey. The poles of the mow were barely covered, save in one corner where there was a little bunch.

The girl espied the great feed-box. She ran to it and lifted the lid. "Here! here!" she called. "Get in here."

They had been tearing noiselessly around the rear part of the barn. At her low call they came and plunged at the box. They did not all get in at the same moment without a good deal of a tangle. The wounded men gasped and muttered, but they at last were flopped down on the layer of feed which covered the bottom. Swiftly and softly the girl lowered the lid, and then turned like a flash toward the door.

No one appeared there, so she went close to survey the situation. The troopers had dismounted and stood in silence by their horses. A grey-bearded man, whose red cheeks and nose shone vividly above the whiskers, was strolling about with two or three others. They wore double-breasted coats, and faded yellow sashes were wound under their black leather sword-belts. The grey-bearded soldier was apparently giving orders, pointing here and there.

Mary tiptoed to the feed-box. "They've all got off their horses," she said to it. A finger projected from a knot-hole near the top and said to her very plainly, "Come closer." She obeyed, and then a muffled voice could be heard: "Scoot for the house, lady, and if we don't see you again, why, much obliged for what you done."

"Good-bye," she said to the feed-box.

She made two attempts to walk dauntlessly from the barn, but each time she faltered and failed just before she reached the point where she could have been seen by the blue-coated troopers. At last, however, she made a sort of rush forward and went out into the bright sunshine.

The group of men in double-breasted coats wheeled in her direction at the instant. The grey-bearded officer forgot to lower his arm, which had been stretched forth in giving an order.

She felt that her feet were touching the ground in a most unnatural manner. Her bearing, she believed, was suddenly grown awkward and ungainly. Upon her face she thought that this sentence was plainly written: "There are three men hidden in the feed-box."

The grey-bearded soldier came toward her. She stopped; she seemed about to run away. But the soldier doffed his little blue cap and looked amiable. "You live here, I presume?" he said.

"Yes," she answered.

"Well, we are obliged to camp here for the night, and as we've got two wounded men with us I don't suppose you'd mind if we put them in the barn."

"In—in the barn?"

He became aware that she was agitated. He smiled assuringly. "You needn't be frightened. We won't hurt anything around here. You'll all be safe enough."

The girl balanced on one foot and swung the other to and fro in the grass. She was looking down at it. "But—but I don't think ma would like it if—if you took the barn."

The old officer laughed. "Wouldn't she?" said he. "That's so. Maybe she wouldn't." He reflected for a time and then decided cheerfully: "Well, we will have to go ask her, anyhow. Where is she? In the house?"

"Yes," replied the girl, "she's in the house. She—she'll be scared to death when she sees you!"

"Well, you go and ask her then," said the soldier, always wearing a benign smile. "You go ask her and then come and tell me."

When the girl pushed open the door and entered the kitchen, she found it empty. "Ma!" she called softly. There was no answer. The kettle still was humming its low song. The knife and the curl of potato-skin lay on the floor.

She went to her mother's room and entered timidly. The new, lonely aspect of the house shook her nerves. Upon the bed was a confusion of coverings. "Ma!" called the girl, quaking in fear that her mother was not there to reply. But there was a sudden turmoil of the quilts, and her mother's head was thrust forth. "Mary!" she cried, in what seemed to be a supreme astonishment, "I thought—I thought—"

"Oh, ma," blurted the girl, "there's over a thousand Yankees in the yard, and I've hidden three of our men in the feed-box!"

The elder woman, however, upon the appearance of her daughter had begun to thresh hysterically about on the bed and wail.

"Ma!" the girl exclaimed, "and now they want to use the barn—and our men in the feed-box! What shall I do, ma? What shall I do?"

Her mother did not seem to hear, so absorbed was she in her grievous flounderings and tears. "Ma!" appealed the girl. "Ma!"

For a moment Mary stood silently debating, her lips apart, her eyes fixed. Then she went to the kitchen window and peeked.

The old officer and the others were staring up the road. She went to another window in order to get a proper view of the road, and saw that they were gazing at a small body of horsemen approaching at a trot and raising much dust. Presently she recognized them as the squad that had passed the house earlier, for the young man with the dim yellow chevron still rode at their head. An unarmed horseman in grey was receiving their close attention.

As they came very near to the house she darted to the first window again. The grey-bearded officer was smiling a fine broad smile of satisfaction. "So you got him?" he called out. The young sergeant sprang from his horse, and his brown hand moved in a salute. The girl could not hear his reply. She saw the unarmed horseman in grey stroking a very black moustache and looking about him coolly and with an interested air. He appeared so indifferent that she did not understand he was a prisoner until she heard the greybeard call out: "Well, put him in the barn. He'll be safe there, I guess." A party of troopers moved with the prisoner toward the barn.

The girl made a sudden gesture of horror, remembering the three men in the feed-box.

III

The busy troopers in blue scurried about the long lines of stamping horses. Men crooked their backs and perspired in order to rub with cloths or bunches of grass these slim equine legs upon whose splendid machinery they depended so greatly. The lips of the horses were still wet and frothy from the steel bars which had wrenched at their mouths all day. Over their backs and about their noses sped the talk of the men.

"Moind where yer plug is steppin', Finerty! Keep 'im aff me!"

"An ould elephant! He shtrides like a schoolhouse."

"Bill's little mar'—she was plum beat when she come in with Crawford's crowd."

"Crawford's the hardest-ridin' cavalryman in the army. An' he don't use up a horse, neither—much. They stay fresh when the others are most a-droppin'."

"Finerty, will yeh moind that cow a' yours?"

Amid a bustle of gossip and banter, the horses retained their air of solemn rumination, twisting their lower jaws from side to side and sometimes rubbing noses dreamfully.

Over in front of the barn three troopers sat talking comfortably. Their carbines were leaned against the wall. At their side and outlined in the black of the open door stood a sentry, his weapon resting in the hollow of his arm. Four horses, saddled and accoutred, were conferring with their heads close together. The four bridle-reins were flung over a post.

Upon the calm green of the land, typical in every way of peace, the hues of war brought thither by the troops shone strangely. Mary, gazing curiously, did not feel that she was contemplating a familiar scene. It was no longer the home acres. The new blue, steel, and faded yellow thoroughly dominated the old green and brown. She could hear the voices of the men, and it seemed from their tone that they had camped there for years. Everything with them was usual. They had taken possession of the landscape in such a way that even the old marks appeared strange and formidable to the girl.

Mary had intended to go and tell the commander in blue that her mother did not wish his men to use the barn at all, but she paused when she heard him speak to the sergeant. She thought she perceived then that it mattered little to him what her mother wished, and that an objection by her or by anybody would be futile. She saw the soldiers conduct the prisoner in grey into the barn, and for a long time she watched the three chatting guards and the pondering sentry. Upon her mind in desolate weight was the recollection of the three men in the feed-box.

It seemed to her that in a case of this description it was her duty to be a heroine. In all the stories she had read when at boarding-school in Pennsylvania, the girl characters, confronted with such difficulties, invariably did hairbreadth things. True, they were usually bent upon rescuing and recovering their lovers, and neither the calm man in grey nor any of the three in the feed-box was lover of hers; but then, a real heroine would not pause over this minor question. Plainly a heroine would take measures to rescue the four men. If she did not at least make the attempt, she would be false to those carefully constructed ideals which were the accumulation of years of dreaming.

But the situation puzzled her. There was the barn with only one door, and with four armed troopers in front of this door, one of them with his back to the rest of the world, engaged, no doubt, in a steadfast contemplation of the calm man and, incidentally, of the feed-box. She knew, too, that even if she should open the kitchen door, three heads and perhaps four would turn casually in her direction. Their ears were real ears.

Heroines, she knew, conducted these matters with infinite precision and dispatch. They severed the hero's bonds, cried a dramatic sentence, and stood between him and his enemies until he had run far enough away. She saw well, however, that even should she achieve all things up to the point where she might take glorious stand between the escaping and the pursuers, those grim troopers in blue would not pause. They would run around her, make a circuit. One by one she saw the gorgeous contrivances and expedients of fiction fall before the plain, homely difficulties of this situation. They were of no service. Sadly, ruefully, she thought of the calm man and of the contents of the feed-box.

The sum of her invention was that she could sally forth to the commander of the blue cavalry and, confessing to him that there were three of her friends and his enemies secreted in the feed-box, pray him to let them depart unmolested. But she was beginning to believe the old greybeard to be a bear. It was hardly probable that he would give this plan his support. It was more probable that he and some of his men would at once descend upon the feed-box and confiscate her three friends. The difficulty with her idea was that she could not learn its value without trying it, and then in case of failure it would be too late for remedies and other plans. She reflected that war made men very unreasonable.

All that she could do was to stand at the window and mournfully regard the barn. She admitted this to herself with a sense of deep humiliation. She was not, then, made of that fine stuff, that mental satin, which enabled some other beings to be of such mighty service to the distressed. She was defeated by a barn with one door, by four men with eight eyes and eight ears—trivialities that would not impede the real heroine.

The vivid white light of broad day began slowly to fade. Tones of grey came upon the fields, and the shadows were of lead. In this more sombre atmosphere the fires built by the troops down in the far end of the orchard grew more brilliant, becoming spots of crimson colour in the dark grove.

The girl heard a fretting voice from her mother's room. "Mary!" She hastily obeyed the call. She perceived that she had quite forgotten her mother's existence in this time of excitement.

The elder woman still lay upon the bed. Her face was flushed, and perspiration stood amid new wrinkles upon her forehead. Weaving wild glances from side to side, she began to whimper. "Oh, I'm just sick—I'm just sick! Have those men gone yet? Have they gone?"

The girl smoothed a pillow carefully for her mother's head. "No, ma. They're here yet. But they haven't hurt anything—it doesn't seem. Will I get you something to eat?"

Her mother gestured her away with the impatience of the ill. "No—no—just don't bother me. My head is splitting, and you know very well that nothing can be done for me when I get one of these spells. It's trouble—that's what makes them. When are those men going? Look here, don't you go 'way. You stick close to the house now."

"I'll stay right here," said the girl. She sat in the gloom and listened to her mother's incessant moaning. When she attempted to move, her mother cried out at her. When she desired to ask if she might try to alleviate the pain, she was interrupted shortly. Somehow her sitting in passive silence within hearing of this illness seemed to contribute to her mother's relief. She assumed a posture of submission. Sometimes her mother projected questions concerning the local condition, and although she laboured to be graphic and at the same time soothing, unalarming, her form of reply was always displeasing to the sick woman, and brought forth ejaculations of angry impatience.

Eventually the woman slept in the manner of one worn from terrible labour. The girl went slowly and softly to the kitchen. When she looked from the window, she saw the four soldiers still at the barn door. In the west, the sky was yellow. Some tree trunks intersecting it appeared black as streaks of ink. Soldiers hovered in blue clouds about the bright splendour of the fires in the orchard. There were glimmers of steel.

The girl sat in the new gloom of the kitchen and watched. The soldiers lit a lantern and hung it in the barn. Its rays made the form of the sentry seem gigantic. Horses whinnied from the orchard. There was a low hum of human voices. Sometimes small detachments of troopers rode past the front of the house. The girl heard the abrupt calls of sentries. She fetched some food and ate it from her hand, standing by the window. She was so afraid that something would occur that she barely left her post for an instant.

A picture of the interior of the barn hung vividly in her mind. She recalled the knot-holes in the boards at the rear, but she admitted that the prisoners could not escape through them. She remembered some inadequacies of the roof, but these also counted for nothing. When confronting the problem, she felt her ambitions, her ideals, tumbling headlong like cottages of straw.

Once she felt that she had decided to reconnoitre at any rate. It was night; the lantern at the barn and the camp-fires made everything without their circle into masses of heavy mystic blackness. She took two steps toward the door. But there she paused. Innumerable possibilities of danger had assailed her mind. She returned to the window and stood wavering. At last, she went swiftly to the door, opened it, and slid noiselessly into the darkness.

For a moment she regarded the shadows. Down in the orchard the camp-fires of the troops appeared precisely like a great painting, all in reds upon a black cloth. The voices of the troopers still hummed. The girl started slowly off in the opposite direction. Her eyes were fixed in a stare; she studied the darkness in front for a moment, before she ventured upon a forward step. Unconsciously, her throat was arranged for a sudden shrill scream. High in the tree branches she could hear the voice of the wind, a melody of the night, low and sad, the plaint of an endless, incommunicable sorrow. Her own distress, the plight of the men in grey—these near matters as well as all she had known or imagined of grief—everything was expressed in this soft mourning of the wind in the trees. At first she felt like weeping. This sound told her of human impotency and doom. Then later the trees and the wind breathed strength to her, sang of sacrifice, of dauntless effort, of hard carven faces that did not blanch when Duty came at midnight or at noon.

She turned often to scan the shadowy figures that moved from time to time in the light at the barn door. Once she trod upon a stick, and it flopped, crackling in the intolerable manner of all sticks. At this noise, however, the guards at the barn made no sign. Finally, she was where she could see the knot-holes in the rear of the structure gleaming like pieces of metal from the effect of the light within. Scarcely breathing in her excitement, she glided close and applied an eye to a knot-hole. She had barely achieved one glance at the interior before she sprang back shuddering.

For the unconscious and cheerful sentry at the door was swearing away in flaming sentences, heaping one gorgeous oath upon another, making a conflagration of his description of his troop-horse.

"Why," he was declaring to the calm prisoner in grey, "you ain't got a horse in your hull damned army that can run forty rod with that there little mar'!"

As in the outer darkness Mary cautiously returned to the knot-hole, the three guards in front suddenly called in low tones: "S-s-s-h!" "Quit, Pete; here comes the lieutenant." The sentry had apparently been about to resume his declamation, but at these warnings he suddenly posed in a soldierly manner.

A tall and lean officer with a smooth face entered the barn. The sentry saluted primly. The officer flashed a comprehensive glance about him. "Everything all right?"

"All right, sir."

This officer had eyes like the points of stilettos. The lines from his nose to the corners of his mouth were deep and gave him a slightly disagreeable aspect, but somewhere in his face there was a quality of singular thoughtfulness, as of the absorbed student dealing in generalities, which was utterly in opposition to the rapacious keenness of the eyes, which saw everything.

Suddenly he lifted a long finger and pointed. "What's that?"

"That? That's a feed-box, I suppose."

"What's in it?"

"I don't know. I—"

"You ought to know," said the officer sharply. He walked over to the feed-box and flung up the lid. With a sweeping gesture he reached down and scooped a handful of feed. "You ought to know what's in everything when you have prisoners in your care," he added, scowling.

During the time of this incident, the girl had nearly swooned. Her hands searched weakly over the boards for something to which to cling. With the pallor of the dying she had watched the downward sweep of the officer's arm, which after all had only brought forth a handful of feed. The result was a stupefaction of her mind. She was astonished out of her senses at this spectacle of three large men metamorphosed into a handful of feed.

IV

It is perhaps a singular thing that this absence of the three men from the feed-box at the time of the sharp lieutenant's investigation should terrify the girl more than it should joy her. That for which she had prayed had come to pass. Apparently the escape of these men in the face of every improbability had been granted her, but her dominating emotion was fright. The feed-box was a mystic and terrible machine, like some dark magician's trap. She felt it almost possible that she should see the three weird men floating spectrally away through the air. She glanced with swift apprehension behind her, and, when the dazzle from the lantern's light had left her eyes, saw only the dim hillside stretched in solemn silence.

The interior of the barn possessed for her another fascination because it was now uncanny. It contained that extraordinary feed-box. When she peeped again at the knot-hole, the calm grey prisoner was seated upon the feed-box, thumping it with his dangling, careless heels as if it were in no wise his conception of a remarkable feed-box. The sentry also stood facing it. His carbine he held in the hollow of his arm. His legs were spread apart, and he mused. From with out came the low mumble of the three other troopers. The sharp lieutenant had vanished.

The trembling yellow light of the lantern caused the figures of the men to cast monstrous wavering shadows. There were spaces of gloom which shrouded ordinary things in impressive garb. The roof presented an inscrutable blackness, save where small rifts in the shingles glowed phosphorescently. Frequently old Santo put down a thunderous hoof. The heels of the prisoner made a sound like the booming of a wild kind of drum. When the men moved their heads, their eyes shone with ghoulish whiteness, and their complexions were always waxen and unreal. And there was that profoundly strange feed-box, imperturbable with its burden of fantastic mystery.

Suddenly from down near her feet the girl heard a crunching sound, a sort of nibbling, as if some silent and very discreet terrier was at work upon the turf. She faltered back; here was, no doubt, another grotesque detail of this most unnatural episode. She did not run, because physically she was in the power of these events. Her feet chained her to the ground in submission to this march of terror after terror. As she stared at the spot from which this sound seemed to come, there floated through her mind a vague, sweet vision—a vision of her safe little room, in which at this hour she usually was sleeping.

The scratching continued faintly and with frequent pauses, as if the terrier was then listening. When the girl first removed her eyes from the knot-hole the scene appeared of one velvet blackness; then gradually objects loomed with a dim lustre. She could see now where the tops of the trees joined the sky, and the form of the barn was before her, dyed in heavy purple. She was ever about to shriek, but no sound came from her constricted throat. She gazed at the ground with the expression of countenance of one who watches the sinister-moving grass where a serpent approaches.

Dimly she saw a piece of sod wrenched free and drawn under the great foundation beam of the barn. Once she imagined that she saw human hands, not outlined at all, but sufficient in colour, form, or movement to make subtle suggestion.

Then suddenly a thought that illuminated the entire situation flashed in her mind like a light. The three men, late of the feed-box, were beneath the floor of the barn and were now scraping their way under this beam. She did not consider for a moment how they could come there. They were marvellous creatures. The supernatural was to be expected of them. She no longer trembled, for she was possessed upon this instant of the most unchangeable species of conviction. The evidence before her amounted to no evidence at all, but nevertheless her opinion grew in an instant from an irresponsible acorn to a rooted and immovable tree. It was as if she was on a jury.

She stooped down hastily and scanned the ground. There she indeed saw a pair of hands hauling at the dirt where the sod had been displaced. Softly, in a whisper like a breath, she said, "Hey!"

The dim hands were drawn hastily under the barn. The girl reflected for a moment. Then she stooped and whispered: "Hey! It's me!"

After a time there was a resumption of the digging. The ghostly hands began once more their cautious mining. She waited. In hollow reverberations from the interior of the barn came the frequent sounds of old Santo's lazy movements. The sentry conversed with the prisoner.

At last the girl saw a head thrust slowly from under the beam. She perceived the face of one of the miraculous soldiers from the feed-box. A pair of eyes glintered and wavered, then finally settled upon her, a pale statue of a girl. The eyes became lit with a kind of humorous greeting. An arm gestured at her.

Stooping, she breathed, "All right." The man drew himself silently back under the beam. A moment later the pair of hands resumed their cautious task. Ultimately the head and arms of the man were thrust strangely from the earth. He was lying on his back. The girl thought of the dirt in his hair. Wriggling slowly and pushing at the beam above him, he forced his way out of the curious little passage. He twisted his body and raised himself upon his hands. He grinned at the girl and drew his feet carefully from under the beam. When he at last stood erect beside her, he at once began mechanically to brush the dirt from his clothes with his hands. In the barn the sentry and his prisoner were evidently engaged in an argument.

The girl and the first miraculous soldier signalled warily. It seemed that they feared that their arms would make noises in passing through the air. Their lips moved, conveying dim meanings.

In this sign-language the girl described the situation in the barn. With guarded motions, she told him of the importance of absolute stillness. He nodded, and then in the same manner he told her of his two companions under the barn floor. He informed her again of their wounded state, and wagged his head to express his despair. He contorted his face, to tell how sore were their arms; and jabbed the air mournfully, to express their remote geographical position.

This signalling was interrupted by the sound of a body being dragged or dragging itself with slow, swishing sound under the barn. The sound was too loud for safety. They rushed to the hole and began to semaphore until a shaggy head appeared with rolling eyes and quick grin.

With frantic downward motions of their arms they suppressed this grin and with it the swishing noise. In dramatic pantomime they informed this head of the terrible consequences of so much noise. The head nodded, and painfully, but with extreme care, the second man pushed and pulled himself from the hole.

In a faint whisper the first man said, "Where's Sim?"

The second man made low reply: "He's right here." He motioned reassuringly toward the hole.

When the third head appeared, a soft smile of glee came upon each face, and the mute group exchanged expressive glances.

When they all stood together, free from this tragic barn, they breathed a long sigh that was contemporaneous with another smile and another exchange of glances.

One of the men tiptoed to a knot-hole and peered into the barn. The sentry was at that moment speaking. "Yes, we know 'em all. There isn't a house in this region that we don't know who is in it most of the time. We collar 'em once in a while—like we did you. Now, that house out yonder, we—"

The man suddenly left the knot-hole and returned to the others. Upon his face, dimly discerned, there was an indication that he had made an astonishing discovery. The others questioned him with their eyes, but he simply waved an arm to express his inability to speak at that spot. He led them back toward the hill, prowling carefully. At a safe distance from the barn he halted, and as they grouped eagerly about him, he exploded in an intense undertone: "Why, that—that's Cap'n Sawyer they got in yonder."

"Cap'n Sawyer!" incredulously whispered the other men.

But the girl had something to ask. "How did you get out of that feed-box?"

He smiled. "Well, when you put us in there, we was just in a minute when we allowed it wasn't a mighty safe place, and we allowed we'd get out. And we did. We skedaddled round and round until it 'peared like we was going to get cotched, and then we flung ourselves down in the cow-stalls where it's low-like—just dirt floor—and then we just naturally went a-whooping under the barn floor when the Yanks come. And we didn't know Cap'n Sawyer by his voice nohow. We heard 'im discoursing, and we allowed it was a mighty pert man, but we didn't know that it was him. No, m'm."

These three men, so recently from a situation of peril, seemed suddenly to have dropped all thought of it. They stood with sad faces looking at the barn. They seemed to be making no plans at all to reach a place of more complete safety. They were halted and stupefied by some unknown calamity.

"How do you raikon they cotch him, Sim?" one whispered mournfully.

"I don't know," replied another in the same tone.

Another with a low snarl expressed in two words his opinion of the methods of Fate: "Oh, hell!"

The three men started then as if simultaneously stung, and gazed at the young girl who stood silently near them. The man who had sworn began to make agitated apology: "Pardon, miss! 'Pon my soul, I clean forgot you was by. 'Deed, and I wouldn't swear like that if I had knowed. 'Deed, I wouldn't."

The girl did not seem to hear him. She was staring at the barn. Suddenly she turned and whispered, "Who is he?"

"He's Cap'n Sawyer, m'm," they told her sorrowfully. "He's our own cap'n. He's been in command of us yere since a long time. He's got folks about yere. Raikon they cotch him while he was a-visiting."

She was still for a time, and then, awed, she said: "Will they—will they hang him?"

"No, m'm. Oh, no, m'm. Don't raikon no such thing. No, m'm."

The group became absorbed in a contemplation of the barn. For a time no one moved or spoke. At last the girl was aroused by slight sounds, and, turning, she perceived that the three men who had so recently escaped from the barn were now advancing toward it.

V

The girl, waiting in the darkness, expected to hear the sudden crash and uproar of a fight as soon as the three creeping men should reach the barn. She reflected in an agony upon the swift disaster that would befall any enterprise so desperate. She had an impulse to beg them to come away. The grass rustled in silken movements as she sped toward the barn.

When she arrived, however, she gazed about her bewildered. The men were gone. She searched with her eyes, trying to detect some moving thing, but she could see nothing.

Left alone again, she began to be afraid of the night. The great stretches of darkness could hide crawling dangers. From sheer desire to see a human, she was obliged to peep again at the knot-hole. The sentry had apparently wearied of talking. Instead, he was reflecting. The prisoner still sat on the feed-box, moodily staring at the floor. The girl felt in one way that she was looking at a ghastly group in wax. She started when the old horse put down an echoing hoof. She wished the men would speak; their silence reinforced the strange aspect. They might have been two dead men.

The girl felt impelled to look at the corner of the interior where were the cow-stalls. There was no light there save the appearance of peculiar grey haze which marked the track of the dimming rays of the lantern. All else was sombre shadow. At last she saw something move there. It might have been as small as a rat, or it might have been a part of something as large as a man. At any rate, it proclaimed that something in that spot was alive. At one time she saw it plainly, and at other times it vanished, because her fixture of gaze caused her occasionally to greatly tangle and blur those peculiar shadows and faint lights. At last, however, she perceived a human head. It was monstrously dishevelled and wild. It moved slowly forward until its glance could fall upon the prisoner and then upon the sentry. The wandering rays caused the eyes to glitter like silver. The girl's heart pounded so that she put her hand over it.

The sentry and the prisoner remained immovably waxen, and over in the gloom the head thrust from the floor watched them with its silver eyes.

Finally, the prisoner slipped from the feed-box and, raising his arms, yawned at great length. "Oh, well," he remarked, "you boys will get a good licking if you fool around here much longer. That's some satisfaction, any-how, even if you did bag me. You'll get a good walloping." He reflected for a moment, and decided: "I'm sort of willing to be captured if you fellows only get a damned good licking for being so smart."

The sentry looked up and smiled a superior smile. "Licking, hey? Nixey!" He winked exasperatingly at the prisoner. "You fellows are not fast enough, my boy. Why didn't you lick us at—? and at—? and at—?" He named some of the great battles.

To this the captive officer blurted in angry astonishment: "Why, we did!"

The sentry winked again in profound irony. "Yes—I know you did. Of course. You whipped us, didn't you? Fine kind of whipping that was! Why, we—"

He suddenly ceased, smitten mute by a sound that broke the stillness of the night. It was the sharp crack of a distant shot that made wild echoes among the hills. It was instantly followed by the hoarse cry of a human voice, a far-away yell of warning, singing of surprise, peril, fear of death. A moment later there was a distant fierce spattering of shots. The sentry and the prisoner stood facing each other, their lips apart, listening.

The orchard at that instant awoke to sudden tumult. There were the thud and scramble and scamper of feet, the mellow, swift clash of arms, men's voices in question, oath, command, hurried and unhurried, resolute and frantic. A horse sped along the road at a raging gallop. A loud voice shouted, "What is it, Ferguson?" Another voice yelled something incoherent. There was a sharp, discordant chorus of command. An uproarious volley suddenly rang from the orchard. The prisoner in grey moved from his intent, listening attitude. Instantly the eyes of the sentry blazed, and he said with a new and terrible sternness: "Stand where you are!"

The prisoner trembled in his excitement. Expressions of delight and triumph bubbled to his lips. "A surprise, by Gawd! Now—now, you'll see!"

The sentry stolidly swung his carbine to his shoulder. He sighted carefully along the barrel until it pointed at the prisoner's head, about at his nose. "Well, I've got you, anyhow. Remember that! Don't move!"

The prisoner could not keep his arms from nervously gesturing. "I won't; but—"

"And shut your mouth!"

The three comrades of the sentry flung themselves into view. "Pete—devil of a row!—can you—"

"I've got him," said the sentry calmly and without moving. It was as if the barrel of the carbine rested on piers of stone. The three comrades turned and plunged into the darkness.

In the orchard it seemed as if two gigantic animals were engaged in a mad, floundering encounter, snarling, howling in a whirling chaos of noise and motion. In the barn the prisoner and his guard faced each other in silence.

As for the girl at the knot-hole, the sky had fallen at the beginning of this clamour. She would not have been astonished to see the stars swinging from their abodes, and the vegetation, the barn, all blow away. It was the end of everything, the grand universal murder. When two of the three miraculous soldiers who formed the original feed-box corps emerged in detail from the hole under the beam and slid away into the darkness, she did no more than glance at them.

Suddenly she recollected the head with silver eyes. She started forward and again applied her eyes to the knot-hole. Even with the din resounding from the orchard, from up the road and down the road, from the heavens and from the deep earth, the central fascination was this mystic head. There, to her, was the dark god of the tragedy.

The prisoner in grey at this moment burst into a laugh that was no more than a hysterical gurgle. "Well, you can't hold that gun out for ever! Pretty soon you'll have to lower it."

The sentry's voice sounded slightly muffled, for his cheek was pressed against the weapon. "I won't be tired for some time yet."

The girl saw the head slowly rise, the eyes fixed upon the sentry's face. A tall, black figure slunk across the cow-stalls and vanished in back of old Santo's quarters. She knew what was to come to pass. She knew this grim thing was upon a terrible mission, and that it would reappear again at the head of the little passage between Santo's stall and the wall, almost at the sentry's elbow; and yet when she saw a faint indication as of a form crouching there, a scream from an utterly new alarm almost escaped her.

The sentry's arms, after all, were not of granite. He moved restively. At last he spoke in his even, unchanging tone: "Well, I guess you'll have to climb into that feed-box. Step back and lift the lid."

"Why, you don't mean—"

"Step back!"

The girl felt a cry of warning arising to her lips as she gazed at this sentry. She noted every detail of his facial expression. She saw, moreover, his mass of brown hair bunching disgracefully about his ears, his clear eyes lit now with a hard, cold light, his forehead puckered in a mighty scowl, the ring upon the third finger of the left hand. "Oh, they won't kill him! Surely they won't kill him!" The noise of the fight in the orchard was the loud music, the thunder and lightning, the rioting of the tempest which people love during the critical scene of a tragedy.

When the prisoner moved back in reluctant obedience, he faced for an instant the entrance of the little passage, and what he saw there must have been written swiftly, graphically in his eyes. And the sentry read it and knew then that he was upon the threshold of his death. In a fraction of time, certain information went from the grim thing in the passage to the prisoner, and from the prisoner to the sentry. But at that instant the black formidable figure arose, towered, and made its leap. A new shadow flashed across the floor when the blow was struck.

As for the girl at the knot-hole, when she returned to sense she found herself standing with clenched hands and screaming with her might.

As if her reason had again departed from her, she ran around the barn, in at the door, and flung herself sobbing beside the body of the soldier in blue.

The uproar of the fight became at last coherent, inasmuch as one party was giving shouts of supreme exultation. The firing no longer sounded in crashes; it was now expressed in spiteful crackles, the last words of the combat, spoken with feminine vindictiveness.

Presently there was a thud of flying feet. A grimy, panting, red-faced mob of troopers in blue plunged into the barn, became instantly frozen to attitudes of amazement and rage, and then roared in one great chorus: "He's gone!"

The girl who knelt beside the body upon the floor turned toward them her lamenting eyes and cried: "He's not dead, is he? He can't be dead?"

They thronged forward. The sharp lieutenant who had been so particular about the feed-box knelt by the side of the girl and laid his head against the chest of the prostrate soldier. "Why, no," he said, rising and looking at the man. "He's all right. Some of you boys throw some water on him."

"Are you sure?" demanded the girl, feverishly.

"Of course! He'll be better after a while."

"Oh," said she softly, and then looked down at the sentry. She started to arise, and the lieutenant reached down and hoisted rather awkwardly at her arm.

"Don't you worry about him. He's all right."

She turned her face with its curving lips and shining eyes once more toward the unconscious soldier upon the floor. The troopers made a lane to the door, the lieutenant bowed, the girl vanished.

"Queer," said a young officer. "Girl very clearly worst kind of rebel, and yet she falls to weeping and wailing like mad over one of her enemies. Be around in the morning with all sorts of doctoring—you see if she ain't. Queer."

The sharp lieutenant shrugged his shoulders. After reflection he shrugged his shoulders again. He said: "War changes many things; but it doesn't change everything, thank God!"

Three and One Are One
1908

AMBROSE BIERCE

Aside from Stephen Crane, Ambrose Bierce (1842–1914?) is the best-known literary figure of the nineteenth century to write Civil War fiction, and he is perhaps the best writer who actually served in the war. Joining an Indiana regiment at the outbreak of the war, Bierce saw action in several of the bloodiest and most important battles of the war—Shiloh, Chickamauga, Stones River, and Missionary Ridge. He wrote of his war experiences in several essays gathered together as "Bits of Autobiography" [in the first volume of his Collected Works *(1909)]. After the war he went to San Francisco, where he served as a journalist on several papers, most notably William Randolph Hearst's San Francisco* Examiner *(1887–1906). The bulk of the Civil War tales published in the landmark collection* Tales of Soldiers and Civilians *(1891) first appeared in the* Examiner. *In later years Bierce wrote for Hearst's* Cosmopolitan, *and it is there that the brief but gripping Civil War ghost story, "Three and One Are One," appeared, in the October 1908 issue.*

*I*n the year 1861 Barr Lassiter, a young man of twenty-two, lived with his parents and an elder sister near Carthage, Tennessee. The family were in somewhat humble circumstances, subsisting by cultivation of a small and not very fertile plantation. Owning no slaves, they were not rated among "the best people" of their neighborhood; but they were honest persons of good education, fairly well mannered and as respectable as any family could be if uncredentialed by personal dominion over the sons and daughters of Ham. The elder Lassiter had that severity of manner that so frequently affirms an uncompromising devotion to duty, and conceals a warm and affectionate disposition. He was of the iron of which martyrs are made, but in the heart of the matrix had lurked a nobler metal, fusible at a milder heat, yet never coloring nor softening the hard exterior. By both heredity and environment something of the man's inflexible character had touched the other members of the family; the Lassiter home, though not devoid of domestic affection, was a veritable citadel of duty, and duty—ah, duty is as cruel as death!

When the war came on it found in the family, as in so many others in that State, a divided sentiment; the young man was loyal to the Union, the others savagely hostile. This unhappy division begot an insupportable domestic bitterness, and when the offending son and brother left home with the avowed purpose of joining the Federal army not a hand was laid in his, not a word of farewell was spoken, not a good wish followed him out into the world whither he went to meet with such spirit as he might whatever fate awaited him.

Making his way to Nashville, already occupied by the Army of General Buell, he enlisted in the first organization that he found, a Kentucky regiment of cavalry, and in due time passed through all the stages of military evolution from raw recruit to experienced trooper. A right good trooper he was, too, although in his oral narrative from which this tale is made there was no mention of that; the fact was learned from his surviving comrades. For Barr Lassiter has answered "Here" to the sergeant whose name is Death.

Two years after he had joined it his regiment passed through the region whence he had come. The country thereabout had suffered severely from the ravages of war, having been occupied alternately (and simultaneously) by the belligerent forces, and a sanguinary struggle had occurred in the immediate vicinity of the Lassiter homestead. But of this the young trooper was not aware.

Finding himself in camp near his home, he felt a natural longing to see his parents and sister, hoping that in them, as in him, the unnatural animosities of the period had been softened by time and separation. Obtaining a leave of absence, he set foot in the late summer afternoon, and soon after the rising of the full moon was walking up the gravel path leading to the dwelling in which he had been born.

Soldiers in war age rapidly, and in youth two years are a long time. Barr Lassiter felt himself an old man, and had almost expected to find the place a ruin and a desolation. Nothing, apparently, was changed. At the sight of each dear and familiar object he was profoundly affected. His heart beat audibly, his emotion nearly suffocated him; an ache was in his throat.

Unconsciously he quickened his pace until he almost ran, his long shadow making grotesque efforts to keep its place beside him.

The house was unlighted, the door open. As he approached and paused to recover control of himself his father came out and stood bare-headed in the moonlight.

"Father!" cried the young man, springing forward with outstretched hand—"Father!"

The elder man looked him sternly in the face, stood a moment motionless and without a word withdrew into the house. Bitterly disappointed, humiliated, inexpressibly hurt and altogether unnerved, the soldier dropped upon a rustic seat in deep dejection, supporting his head upon his trembling hand. But he would not have it so: he was too good a soldier to accept repulse as defeat. He rose and entered the house, passing directly to the "sitting-room."

It was dimly lighted by an uncurtained east window. On a low stool by the hearthside, the only article of furniture in the place, sat his mother, staring into a fireplace strewn with blackened embers and cold ashes. He spoke to her—tenderly, interrogatively, and with hesitation, but she neither answered, nor moved, nor seemed in any way surprised.

True, there had been time for her husband to apprise her of their guilty son's return. He moved nearer and was about to lay his hand upon her arm, when his sister entered from an adjoining room, looked him full in the face, passed him without a sign of recognition and left the room by a door that was partly behind him. He had turned his head to watch her, but when she was gone his eyes again sought his mother. She too had left the place.

Barr Lassiter strode to the door by which he had entered. The moonlight on the lawn was tremulous, as if the sward were a rippling sea. The trees and their black shadows shook as in a breeze. Blended with its borders, the gravel walk seemed unsteady and insecure to step on. This young soldier knew the optical illusions produced by tears. He felt them on his cheek, and saw them sparkle on the breast of his trooper's jacket. He left the house and made his way back to camp.

The next day, with no very definite intention, with no dominant feeling that he could rightly have named, he again sought the spot. Within a half-mile of it he met Bushrod Albro, a former playfellow and schoolmate, who greeted him warmly.

"I am going to visit my home," said the soldier.

The other looked at him rather sharply, but said nothing.

"I know," continued Lassiter, "that my folks have not changed, but—"

"There have been changes," Albro interrupted—"everything changes. I'll go with you if you don't mind. We can talk as we go."

But Albro did not talk.

Instead of a house they found only fire-blackened foundations of stone, enclosing an area of compact ashes pitted by rains.

Lassiter's astonishment was extreme.

"I could not find the right way to tell you," said Albro. "In the fight a year ago your house was burned by a Federal shell."

"And my family—where are they?"

"In Heaven, I hope. All were killed by the shell."

Part II

Heroes and Heroines

John Lamar
1862

REBECCA HARDING DAVIS

Rebecca Harding Davis (1831–1910) was a well-known nineteenth-century writer whose life and work are now being redis-covered. Her mother had eloped with an Englishman, Richard Harding, and moved to Alabama; Rebecca grew up there and in Virginia. In 1861 she published in the Atlantic Monthly *a grim account entitled "Life in the Iron-Mills," and from then on she published widely in the leading magazines of the day. While the Civil War was in progress, she married L. Clarke Davis and settled in Philadelphia; in 1864 she gave birth to Richard Harding Davis, who would later become a widely popular novelist. "John Lamar," published in the* Atlantic Monthly *of April 1862, is believed by some scholars to be the first work of fiction about the Civil War. Davis went on to write several other tales using the war as a backdrop, including "David Gaunt" (*Atlantic Monthly, *September–October 1862) and "Paul Blecker" (*Atlantic Monthly, *May–July 1863), as well as the novel* Waiting for the Verdict *(1867), which focused on the aftermath of the war and the attempts to reconcile tensions between the North and the South, especially in regard to racial equal-ity. "John Lamar" tells of the curious bond between Lamar, a cap-tured Southern soldier, and his African-American slave, Ben.*

The guard-house was, in fact, nothing but a shed in the middle of a stubblefield. It had been built for a cider-press last summer; but since Captain Dorr had gone into the army, his regiment had camped over half his plantation, and the shed was boarded up, with heavy wickets at either end, to hold whatever prisoners might fall into their hands from

Floyd's forces. It was a strong point for the Federal troops, his farm,—a sort of wedge in the Rebel Cheat counties of Western Virginia. Only one prisoner was in the guard-house now. The sentry, a raw boat-hand from Illinois, gaped incessantly at him through the bars, not sure if the "Secesh" were limbed and headed like other men; but the November fog was so thick that he could discern nothing but a short, squat man, in brown clothes and white hat, heavily striding to and fro. A negro was crouching outside, his knees cuddled in his arms to keep warm: a field-hand, you could be sure from the face, a grisly patch of flabby black, with a dull eluding word of something, you could not tell what, in the points of eyes,— treachery or gloom. The prisoner stopped, cursing him about something: the only answer was a lazy rub of the heels.

"Got any 'baccy, Mars' John?" he whined, in the middle of the hottest oath.

The man stopped abruptly, turning his pockets inside out.

"That's all, Ben," he said, kindly enough. "Now begone, you black devil!"

"Dem's um, Mars'! Goin' 'mediate,"—catching the tobacco, and lolling down full length as his master turned off again.

Dave Hall, the sentry, stared reflectively, and sat down.

"Ben? Who air you next?"—nursing his musket across his knees, baby-fashion.

Ben measured him with one eye, polished the quid in his greasy hand, and looked at it.

"Pris'ner o' war," he mumbled, finally,—contemptuously; for Dave's trousers were in rags like his own, and his chilblained toes stuck through the shoe-tops. Cheap white trash, clearly.

"Yer master's some at swearin'. Heow many, neow, hes he like you, down to Georgy?"

The boatman's bony face was gathering a woful pity. He had enlisted to free the Uncle Toms, and carry God's vengeance to the Legrees. Here they were, a pair of them.

Ben squinted another critical survey of the "miss'able Linkinite."

"How many wells hev *yer* poisoned since yer set out?" he muttered.

The sentry stopped.

"How many 'longin' to de Lamars? 'Bout as many as der's dam' Yankees in Richmond 'baccy-houses!"

Something in Dave's shrewd, whitish eye warned him off.

"Ki yi! yer white nigger, yer!" he chuckled, shuffling down the stubble.

Dave clicked his musket,—then, choking down an oath into a grim

Methodist psalm, resumed his walk, looking askance at the coarse-moulded face of the prisoner peering through the bars, and the diamond studs in his shirt,—bought with human blood, doubtless. The man was the black curse of slavery itself in the flesh, in his thought somehow, and he hated him accordingly. Our men of the Northwest have enough brawny Covenanter muscle in their religion to make them good haters for opinion's sake.

Lamar, the prisoner, watched him with a lazy drollery in his sluggish black eyes. It died out into sternness, as he looked beyond the sentry. He had seen this Cheat country before; this very plantation was his grandfather's a year ago, when he had come up from Georgia here, and loitered out the summer months with his Virginia cousins, hunting. That was a pleasant summer! Something in the remembrance of it flashed into his eyes, dewy, genial; the man's leather-covered face reddened like a child's. Only a year ago,—and now— The plantation was Charley Dorr's now, who had married Ruth. This very shed he and Dorr had planned last spring, and now Charley held him a prisoner in it. The very thought of Charley Dorr warmed his heart. Why, he could thank God there were such men. True grit, every inch of his little body! There, last summer, how he had avoided Ruth until the day when he (Lamar) was going away!—then he told him he meant to try and win her. "She cared most for you always," Lamar had said, bitterly; "why have you waited so long?" "You loved her first, John, you know." That was like a man! He remembered that even that day, when his pain was breathless and sharp, the words made him know that Dorr was fit to be her husband.

Dorr was his friend. The word meant much to John Lamar. He thought less meanly of himself, when he remembered it. Charley's prisoner! An odd chance! Better that than to have met in battle. He thrust back the thought, the sweat oozing out on his face,—something within him muttering, "For Liberty! I would have killed him, so help me God!"

He had brought despatches to General Lee, that he might see Charley, and the old place, and—Ruth again; there was a gnawing hunger in his heart to see them. Fool! what was he to them? The man's face grew slowly pale, as that of a savage or an animal does, when the wound is deep and inward.

The November day was dead, sunless: since morning the sky had had only enough life in it to sweat out a few muddy drops, that froze as they fell: the cold numbed his mouth as he breathed it. This stubbly slope was where he and his grandfather had headed the deer: it was covered with hundreds of dirty, yellow tents now. Around there were hills like uncouth monsters, swathed in ice, holding up the soggy sky; shivering pine-forests;

unmeaning, dreary flats; and the Cheat, coiled about the frozen sinews of the hills, limp and cold, like a cord tying a dead man's jaws. Whatever outlook of joy or worship this region had borne on its face in time gone, it turned to him to-day nothing but stagnation, a great death. He wondered idly, looking at it, (for the old Huguenot brain of the man was full of morbid fancies,) if it were winter alone that had deadened color and pulse out of these full-blooded hills, or if they could know the colder horror crossing their threshold, and forgot to praise God as it came.

Over that farthest ridge the house had stood. The guard (he had been taken by a band of Snake-hunters, back in the hills) had brought him past it. It was a heap of charred rafters. "Burned in the night," they said, "when the old Colonel was alone." They were very willing to show him this, as it was done by his own party, the Secession "Bush-whackers"; took him to the wood-pile to show him where his grandfather had been murdered, (there was a red mark,) and buried, his old hands above the ground. "Colonel said 't was a job fur us to pay up; so we went to the village an' hed a scrimmage,"—pointing to gaps in the hedges where the dead Bush-whackers yet lay unburied. He looked at them, and at the besotted faces about him, coolly. Snake-hunters and Bush-whackers, he knew, both armies used in Virginia as tools for rapine and murder: the sooner the Devil called home his own, the better. And yet, it was not God's fault, surely, that there were such tools in the North, any more than that in the South Ben was—Ben. Something was rotten in freer States than Denmark, he thought.

One of the men went into the hedge, and brought out a child's golden ringlet as a trophy. Lamar glanced in, and saw the small face in its woollen hood, dimpled yet, though dead for days. He remembered it. Jessy Birt, the ferryman's little girl. She used to come up to the house every day for milk. He wondered for which flag *she* died. Ruth was teaching her to write. *Ruth!* Some old pain hurt him just then, nearer than even the blood of the old man or the girl crying to God from the ground. The sergeant mistook the look. "They'll be buried," he said, gruffly. "Ye brought it on yerselves." And so led him to the Federal camp.

The afternoon grew colder, as he stood looking out of the guard-house. Snow began to whiten through the gray. He thrust out his arm through the wicket, his face kindling with childish pleasure, as he looked closer at the fairy stars and crowns on his shaggy sleeve. If Floy were here! She never had seen snow. When the flakes had melted off, he took a case out of his pocket to look at Floy. His sister,—a little girl who had no mother, nor father, nor lover, but Lamar. The man among his brother officers in Richmond was coarse, arrogant, of dogged courage, keen palate at the table, as keen eye on the turf. Sickly little Floy, down at home, knew the way to something below all this: just as they of the Rommany blood see below the muddy boulders of the streets the enchanted land of Boabdil bare beneath. Lamar polished the ivory painting with his breath, remembering that he had drunk nothing for days. A child's face, of about twelve, delicate,—a breath of fever or cold would shatter such weak beauty; big, dark eyes, (her mother was pure Castilian,) out of which her little life looked irresolute into the world, uncertain what to do there. The painter, with an unapt fancy, had clustered about the Southern face the Southern emblem, buds of the magnolia, unstained, as yet, as pearl. It angered Lamar, remembering how the creamy whiteness of the full-blown flower exhaled passion of which the crimsonest rose knew nothing,—a content, ecstasy, in animal life. Would Floy— Well, God help them both! they needed help. Three hundred souls was a heavy weight for those thin little hands to hold sway over,—to lead to hell or heaven. Up North they could have worked for her, and gained only her money. So Lamar reasoned, like a Georgian: scribbling a letter to "My Baby" on the wrapper of a newspaper,—drawing the shapes of the snowflakes,—telling her he had reached their grandfather's plantation, but "have not seen our Cousin Ruth yet, of whom you may remember I have told you, Floy. When you grow up, I should like you to be just such a woman; so remember, my darling, if I"— He scratched the last words out: why should he hint to her that he could die? Holding his life loose in his hand, though, had brought things closer to him lately,—God and death, this war, the meaning of it all. But he would keep his brawny body between these terrible realities and Floy, yet awhile. "I want you," he wrote, "to leave the plantation, and go with your old maumer to the village. It will be safer there." He was sure the letter would reach her. He had a plan to escape to-night, and he could put it into a post inside the lines. Ben was to get a small hand-saw that would open the wicket; the guards were not hard to elude. Glancing up, he saw the negro stretched by a camp-fire, listening to the gaunt boatman, who was off duty. Preaching Abolitionism, doubtless: he could hear Ben's derisive shouts of laughter. "And so, good bye, Baby Florence!" he scrawled. "I wish I could send you some of this snow, to show you what the floor of heaven is like."

While the snow fell faster without, he stopped writing, and began idly drawing a map of Georgia on the tan-bark with a stick. Here the Federal troops could effect a landing: he knew the defences at that point. If they did? He thought of these Snake-hunters who had found in the war a peculiar road for themselves downward with no gallows to stumble over, fancied he saw them skulking through the fields at Cedar Creek, closing around the house, and behind them a mass of black faces and bloody bayonets. Floy alone, and he here,—like a rat in a trap! "God keep my little girl!" he wrote, unsteadily. "God bless you, Floy!" he gasped for breath, as if he had been writing with his heart's blood. Folding up the paper, he hid it inside his shirt and began his dogged walk, calculating the chances of escape. Once out of this shed, he could baffle a blood-hound, he knew the hills so well.

His head bent down, he did not see a man who stood looking at him over the wicket. Captain Dorr. A puny little man, with thin yellow hair, and womanish face: but not the less the hero of his men,—they having found out, somehow, that muscle was not the solidest thing to travel on in war-times. Our regiments of "roughs" were not altogether crowned with laurel at Manassas! So the men built more on the old Greatheart soul in the man's blue eyes: one of those souls born and bred pure, sent to teach, that can find breath only in the free North. His hearty "Hillo!" startled Lamar.

"How are you, old fellow?" he said, unlocking the gate and coming in.

Lamar threw off his wretched thoughts, glad to do it. What need to bor-row trouble? He liked a laugh,—had a lazy, jolly humor of his own. Dorr had finished drill, and come up, as he did every day, to freshen himself with an hour's talk to this warm, blundering fellow. In this dismal war-work, (though his whole soul was in that, too,) it was like putting your hands to a big blaze. Dorr had no near relations; Lamar—they had played marbles together—stood to him where a younger brother might have stood. Yet, as they talked, he could not help his keen eye seeing him just as he was.

Poor John! he thought: the same uncouth-looking effort of humanity that he had been at Yale. No wonder the Northern boys jeered him, with his slothways, his mouthed English, torpid eyes, and brain shut up in that worst of mud-moulds,—belief in caste. Even now, going up and down the tan-bark, his step was dead, sodden, like that of a man in whose life God had not yet wakened the full live soul. It was wakening, though, Dorr thought. Some pain or passion was bringing the man in him out of the flesh, vigilant, alert, aspirant. A different man from Dorr.

In fact, Lamar was just beginning to think for himself, and of course his thoughts were defiant, intolerant. He did not comprehend how his com-panion could give his heresies such quiet welcome, and pronounce sentence of death on them so coolly. Because Dorr had gone farther up the mountain, had he the right to make him follow in the same steps? The right,—that was it. By brute force, too? Human freedom, eh? Consequently, their talks were stormy enough. To-day, however, they were on trivial matters.

"I've brought the General's order for your release at last, John. It confines you to this district, however."

Lamar shook his head.

"No parole for me! My stake outside is too heavy for me to remain a prisoner on anything but compulsion. I mean to escape, if I can. Floy has nobody but me, you know, Charley."

There was a moment's silence.

"I wish," said Dorr, half to himself, "the child was with her cousin Ruth. If she could make her a woman like herself!"

"You are kind," Lamar forced out, thinking of what might have been a year ago.

Dorr had forgotten. He had just kissed little Ruth at the door-step, coming away: thinking, as he walked up to camp, how her clear thought, narrow as it was, was making his own higher, more just; wondering if the tears on her face last night, when she got up from her knees after prayer, might not help as much in the great cause of truth as the life he was ready to give. He was so used to his little wife now, that he could look to no hour of his past life, nor of the future coming ages of event and work, where she was not present,—very flesh of his flesh, heart of his heart. A gulf lay between them and the rest of the world. It was hardly probable he could see her as a woman towards whom another man looked across the gulf, dumb, hopeless, defrauded of his right.

"She sent you some flowers, by the way, John,—the last in the yard,—and bade me be sure and bring you down with me. Your own colors, you see?—to put you in mind of home,"—pointing to the crimson asters flaked with snow.

The man smiled faintly: the smell of the flowers choked him: he laid them aside. God knows he was trying to wring out this bitter old thought: he could not look in Dorr's frank eyes while it was there. He must escape to-night: he never would come near them again, in this world, or beyond death,—never! He thought of that like a man going to drag through eternity with half his soul gone. Very well: there was man enough left in him to work honestly and bravely, and to thank God for that good pure love he yet had. He turned to Dorr with flushed face, and began talking of Floy in hearty earnest,—glancing at Ben coming up the hill, thinking that escape depended on him.

"I ordered your man up," said Captain Dorr. "Some canting Abolitionist had him open-mouthed down there."

The negro came in, and stood in the corner, listening while they talked. A gigantic fellow, with a gladiator's muscles. Stronger than that Yankee captain, he thought,—than either of them: better breathed,—drawing the air into his brawny chest. "A man and a brother." Did the fool think he didn't know that before? He had a contempt for Dave and his like. Lamar would have told you Dave's words were true, but despised the man as a crude, unlicked bigot. Ben did the same, with no words for the idea. The negro instinct in him recognized gentle blood by any of its signs,—the transparent animal life, the reticent eye, the mastered voice: he had better men than Lamar at home to learn it from. It is a trait of serfdom, the keen eye to measure the inherent rights of a man to be master. A negro or a Catholic Irishman does not need "Sartor Resartus" to help him to see through any clothes. Ben leaned, half-asleep, against the wall, some old thoughts creeping out of their hiding-places through the torpor, like rats to the sunshine: the boatman's slang had been hot and true enough to rouse them in his brain.

"So, Ben," said his master, as he passed once, "your friend has been persuading you to exchange the cotton-fields at Cedar Creek for New-York alleys, eh?"

"Ki!" laughed Ben, "white darkey. Mind ole dad, Mars' John, as took off in der swamp? Um asked dat Linkinite ef him saw dad up Norf. Guess him's free now. Ki! ole dad!"

"The swamp was the place for him," said Lamar. "I remember."

"Dunno," said the negro, surlily: "him's dad, af'er all: tink him's free now,"—and mumbled down into a monotonous drone about

"Oh yo, bredern, is yer gwine ober Jordern?"

Half-asleep, they thought,—but with dull questionings at work in his brain, some queer notions about freedom, of that unknown North, mostly mixed with his remembrance of his father, a vicious old negro, that in Pennsylvania would have worked out his salvation in the under cell of the penitentiary, but in Georgia, whipped into heroism, had betaken himself into the swamp, and never returned. Tradition among the Lamar slaves said he had got off to Ohio, of which they had as clear an idea as most of us have of heaven. At any rate, old Kite became a mystery, to be mentioned with awe at fish-bakes and barbecues. He was this uncouth wretch's father,—do you understand? The flabby-faced boy, flogged in the cotton-field for whining after his dad, or hiding away part of his flitch and molasses for months in hopes the old man would come back, was rather a comical object, you would have thought. Very different his, from the feeling with which you left your mother's grave,—though as yet we have not invented names for the emotions of those people. We'll grant that it hurt Ben a little, however. Even the young polypus, when it is torn from the old one, bleeds a drop or two, they say. As he grew up, the great North glimmered through his thought, a sort of big field,—a paradise of no work, no flogging, and white bread every day, where the old man sat and ate his fill.

The second point in Ben's history was that he fell in love. Just as you did,—with the difference, of course: though the hot sun, or the perpetual foot upon his breast, does not make our black Prometheus less fierce in his agony of hope or jealousy than you, I am afraid. It was Nan, a pale mulatto house-servant, that the field-hand took into his dull, lonesome heart to make life of, with true-love defiance of caste. I think Nan liked him very truly. She was lame and sickly, and if Ben was black and a picker, and stayed in the quarters, he was strong, like a master to her in some ways: the only thing she could call hers in the world was the love the clumsy boy gave her. White women feel in that way sometimes, and it makes them very tender to men not their equals. However, old Mrs. Lamar, before she died, gave her house-servants their free papers, and Nan was among them. So she set off, with all the finery little Floy could give her: went up into that great, dim North. She never came again.

The North swallowed up all Ben knew or felt outside of his hot, hated work, his dread of a lashing on Saturday night. All the pleasure left him was 'possum and hominy for Sunday's dinner. It did not content him. The spasmodic religion of the field-negro does not teach endurance. So it came, that the slow tide of discontent ebbing in everybody's heart towards some unreached sea set in his ignorant brooding towards that vague country which the only two who cared for him had found. If he forgot it through the dogged, sultry days, he remembered it when the overseer scourged the dull tiger-look into his eyes, or when, husking corn with the others at night, the smothered negro-soul, into which their masters dared not look, broke out in their wild, melancholy songs. Aimless, unappealing, yet no prayer goes up to God more keen in its pathos. You find, perhaps, in Beethoven's seventh symphony the secrets of your heart made manifest, and suddenly think of a Somewhere to come, where your hope waits for you with late fulfilment. Do not laugh at Ben, then, if he dully told in his song the story of all he had lost, or gave to his heaven a local habitation and a name.

From the place where he stood now, as his master and Dorr walked up and down, he could see the purplish haze beyond which the sentry had told him lay the North. The North! Just beyond the ridge. There was a pain in his head, looking at it; his nerves grew cold and rigid, as yours do when something wrings your heart sharply: for there are nerves in these black carcasses, thicker, more quickly stung to madness than yours. Yet if any savage longing, smouldering for years, was heating to madness now in his brain, there was no sign of it in his face. Vapid, with sordid content, the huge jaws munching tobacco slowly, only now and then the beady eye shot a sharp glance after Dorr. The sentry had told him the Northern army had come to set the slaves free; he watched the Federal officer keenly.

"What ails you, Ben?" said his master. "Thinking over your friend's sermon?"

Ben's stolid laugh was ready.

"Done forgot dat, Mars'. Wouldn't go, nohow. Since Mars' sold dat cussed Joe, gorry good times 't home. Dam' Abolitioner say we ums all goin' Norf,"—with a stealthy glance at Dorr.

"That's more than your philanthropy bargains for, Charley," laughed Lamar.

The men stopped; the negro skulked nearer, his whole senses sharpened into hearing. Dorr's clear face was clouded.

"This slave question must be kept out of the war. It puts a false face on it."

"I thought one face was what it needed," said Lamar. "You have too many slogans. Strong government, tariff, Sumter, a bit of bunting, eleven dollars a month. It ought to be a vital truth that would give soul and *vim* to a body with the differing members of your army. You, with your ideal theory, and Billy Wilson with his 'Blood and Baltimore!' Try human freedom. That's high and sharp and broad."

Ben drew a step closer.

"You are shrewd, Lamar. I am to go below all constitutions or expediency or existing rights, and tell Ben here that he is free? When once the Government accepts that doctrine, you, as a Rebel, must be let alone."

The slave was hid back in the shade.

"Dorr," said Lamar, "you know I'm a groping, ignorant fellow, but it seems to me that prating of constitutions and existing rights is surface talk; there is a broad common-sense underneath, by whose laws the world is governed, which your statesmen don't touch often. You in the North, in your dream of what shall be, shut your eyes to what is. You want a republic where every man's voice shall be heard in the council, and the majority shall rule. Granting that the free population are educated to a fitness for this,—(God forbid I should grant it with the Snake-hunters before my eyes!)—look here!"

He turned round, and drew the slave out into the light: he crouched down, gaping vacantly at them.

"There is Ben. What, in God's name, will you do with him? Keep him a slave, and chatter about self-government? Pah! The country is paying in blood for the lie, to-day. Educate him for freedom, by putting a musket in his hands? We have this mass of heathendom drifted on our shores by your will as well as mine. Try to bring them to a level with the whites by a wrench, and you'll waken out of your dream to a sharp reality. Your Northern philosophy ought to be old enough to teach you that spasms in the body-politic shake off no atom of disease,—that reform, to be enduring, must be patient, gradual, inflexible as the Great Reformer. 'The mills of God,' the old proverb says, 'grind surely.' But, Dorr, they grind exceeding slow!"

Dorr watched Lamar with an amused smile. It pleased him to see his brain waking up, eager, vehement. As for Ben, crouching there, if they talked of him like a clod, heedless that his face deepened in stupor, that his eyes had caught a strange, gloomy treachery,—we all do the same, you know.

"What is your remedy, Lamar? You have no belief in the right of Secession, I know," said Dorr.

"It's a bad instrument for a good end. Let the white Georgian come out of his sloth, and the black will rise with him. Jefferson Davis may not intend it, but God does. When we have our Lowell, our New York, when we are a self-sustaining people instead of lazy land-princes, Ben here will have climbed the second of the great steps of Humanity. Do you laugh at us?" said Lamar, with a quiet self-reliance. "Charley, it needs only work and ambition to cut the brute away from my face, and it will leave traits very like your own. Ben's father was a Guinea fetich-worshipper; when we stand where New England does, Ben's son will be ready for his freedom."

"And while you theorize," laughed Dorr, "I hold you a prisoner, John, and Ben knows it is his right to be free. He will not wait for the grinding of the mill, I fancy."

Lamar did not smile. It was womanish in the man, when the life of great nations hung in doubt before them, to go back so constantly to little Floy sitting in the lap of her old black maumer. But he did it,—with the quick thought that to-night he must escape, that death lay in delay.

While Dorr talked, Lamar glanced significantly at Ben. The negro was not slow to understand,—with a broad grin, touching his pocket, from which projected the dull end of a hand-saw. I wonder what sudden pain made the negro rise just then, and come close to his master, touching him with a strange affection and remorse in his tired face, as though he had done him some deadly wrong.

"What is it, old fellow?" said Lamar, in his boyish way. "Homesick, eh? There's a little girl in Georgia that will be glad to see you and your master, and take precious good care of us when she gets us safe again. That's true, Ben!" laying his hand kindly on the man's shoulder, while his eyes went wandering off to the hills lying South.

"Yes, Mars'," said Ben, in a low voice, suddenly bringing a blacking-brush, and beginning to polish his master's shoes,—thinking, while he did it, of how often Mars' John had interfered with the overseers to save him from a flogging,—(Lamar, in his lazy way, was kind to his slaves,)—thinking of little Mist' Floy with an odd tenderness and awe, as a gorilla might of a white dove: trying to think thus,—the simple, kindly nature of the negro struggling madly with something beneath, new and horrible. He understood enough of the talk of the white men to know that there was no help for him,—none. Always a slave. Neither you nor I can ever know what those words meant to him. The pale purple mist where the North lay was never to be passed. His dull eyes turned to it constantly,—with a strange look, such as the lost women might have turned to the door, when Jesus shut it: they forever outside. There was a way to help himself? The stubby black finders holding the brush grew cold and clammy,—noting withal, the poor wretch in his slavish way, that his master's clothes were finer than the Northern captain's, his hands whiter, and proud that it was so,—holding Lamar's foot daintily, trying to see himself in the shoe, smoothing down the trousers with a boorish, affectionate touch,—with the same fierce whisper in his ear, Would the shoes ever be cleaned again? would the foot move to-morrow?

It grew late. Lamar's supper was brought up from Captain Dorr's, and placed on the bench. He poured out a goblet of water.

"Come, Charley, let's drink. To Liberty! It is a war-cry for Satan or Michael."

They drank, laughing, while Ben stood watching. Dorr turned to go, but Lamar called him back,—stood resting his hand on his shoulder: he never thought to see him again, you know.

"Look at Ruth, yonder," said Dorr, his face lighting. "She is coming to meet us. She thought you would be with me."

Lamar looked gravely down at the low field-house and the figure at the gate. He thought he could see the small face and earnest eyes, though it was far off, and night was closing.

"She is waiting for you, Charley. Go down. Good night, old chum!"

If it cost any effort to say it, Dorr saw nothing of it.

"Good night, Lamar! I'll see you in the morning."

He lingered. His old comrade looked strangely alone and desolate.

"John!"

"What is it, Dorr?"

"If I could tell the Colonel you would take the oath? For Floy's sake."

The man's rough face reddened.

"You should know me better. Good bye."

"Well, well, you are mad. Have you no message for Ruth?"

There was a moment's silence.

"Tell her I say, God bless her!"

Dorr stopped and looked keenly in his face,—then, coming back, shook hands again, in a different way from before, speaking in a lower voice,—

"God help us all, John! Good night!"—and went slowly down the hill.

It was nearly night, and bitter cold. Lamar stood where the snow drifted in on him, looking out through the horizonless gray.

"Come out o' dem cold, Mars' John," whined Ben, pulling at his coat.

As the night gathered, the negro was haunted with a terrified wish to be kind to his master. Something told him that the time was short. Here and there through the far night some tent-fire glowed in a cone of ruddy haze, through which the thick-falling snow shivered like flakes of light. Lamar watched only the square block of shadow where Dorr's house stood. The door opened at last, and a broad, cheerful gleam shot out red darts across the white waste without; then he saw two figures go in together. They paused a moment; he put his head against the bars, straining his eyes, and saw that the woman turned, shading her eyes with her hand, and looked up to the side of the mountain where the guard-house lay,—with a kindly look, perhaps, for the prisoner out in the cold. A kind look: that was all. The door shut on them. Forever: so, good night, Ruth!

He stood there for an hour or two, leaning his head against the muddy planks, smoking. Perhaps, in his coarse fashion, he took the trouble of his manhood back to the same God he used to pray to long ago. When he turned at last, and spoke, it was with a quiet, strong voice, like one who would fight through life in a manly way. There was a grating sound at the back of the shed: it was Ben, sawing through the wicket, the guard having lounged off to supper. Lamar watched him, noticing that the negro was unusually silent. The plank splintered, and hung loose.

"Done gone, Mars' John, now,"—leaving it, and beginning to replenish the fire.

"That's right, Ben. We'll start in the morning. That sentry at two o'clock sleeps regularly."

Ben chuckled, heaping up the sticks.

"Go on down to the camp, as usual. At two, Ben, remember! We will be free to-night, old boy!"

The black face looked up from the clogging smoke with a curious stare.

"Ki! we'll be free to-night, Mars'!"—gulping his breath.

Soon after, the sentry unlocked the gate, and he shambled off out into the night. Lamar, left alone, went closer to the fire, and worked busily at some papers he drew from his pocket: maps and schedules. He intended to write until two o'clock; but the blaze dying down, he wrapped his blanket about him, and lay down on the heaped straw, going on sleepily, in his brain, with his calculations.

The negro, in the shadow of the shed, watched him. A vague fear beset him,—of the vast, white cold,—the glowering mountains,—of himself; he clung to the familiar face, like a man drifting out into an unknown sea, clutching some relic of the shore. When Lamar fell asleep, he wandered uncertainly towards the tents. The world had grown new, strange; was he Ben, picking cotton in the swamp-edge?—plunging his fingers with a shudder in the icy drifts. Down in the glowing torpor of the Santilla flats, where the Lamar plantations lay, Ben had slept off as maddening hunger for life and freedom as this of to-day; but here, with the winter air stinging every nerve to life, with the perpetual mystery of the mountains terrifying his bestial nature down, the strength of the man stood up: groping, blind, malignant, it may be; but whose fault was that? He was half-frozen: the physical pain sharpened the keen doubt conquering his thought. He sat down in the crusted snow, looking vacantly about him, a man, at last,—but wakening, like a new-born soul, into a world of unutterable solitude. Wakened dully, slowly; sitting there far into the night, pondering stupidly on his old life; crushing down and out the old parasite affection for his master, the old fears, the old weight threatening to press out his thin life; the muddy blood heating, firing with the same heroic dream that bade Tell and Garibaldi lift up their hands to God, and cry aloud that they were men and free: the same,—God-given, burning in the imbruted veins of a Guinea slave. To what end? May God be merciful to America while she answers the question! He sat, rubbing his cracked, bleeding feet, glancing stealthily at the southern hills. Beyond them lay all that was past; in an hour he would follow Lamar back to—what? He lifted his hands up to the sky, in his silly way sobbing hot tears. "Gor-a'mighty, Mars' Lord, I'se tired," was all the prayer he made. The pale purple mist was gone from the

North; the ridge behind which love, freedom waited, struck black across the sky, a wall of iron. He looked at it drearily. Utterly alone: he had always been alone. He got up at last, with a sigh.

"It's a big world,"—with a bitter chuckle,—"but der's no room in it fur poor Ben."

He dragged himself through the snow to a light in a tent where a voice in a wild drone, like that he had heard at negro camp-meetings, attracted him. He did not go in: stood at the tent-door, listening. Two or three of the guard stood around, leaning on their muskets; in the vivid fire-light rose the gaunt figure of the Illinois boatman, swaying to and fro as he preached. For the men were honest, God-fearing souls, members of the same church, and Dave, in all integrity of purpose, read aloud to them,— the cry of Jeremiah against the foul splendors of the doomed city,—waving, as he spoke, his bony arm to the South. The shrill voice was that of a man wrestling with his Maker. The negro's fired brain caught the terrible meaning of the words,—found speech in it: the wide, dark night, the solemn silence of the men, were only fitting audience.

The man caught sight of the slave, and, laying down his book, began one of those strange exhortations in the manner of his sect. Slow at first, full of unutterable pity. There was room for pity. Pointing to the human brute crouching there, made once in the image of God,—the saddest wreck of His green footstool: to the great stealthy body, the revengeful jaws, the foreboding eyes. Soul, brains,—a man, wifeless, homeless, nationless, hawked, flung from trader to trader for a handful of dirty shinplasters. "Lord God of hosts," cried the man, lifting up his trembling hands, "lay not this sin to our charge!" There was a scar on Ben's back where the lash had buried itself: it stung now in the cold. He pulled his clothes tighter, that they should not see it; the scar and the words burned into his heart: the childish nature of the man was gone; the vague darkness in it took a shape and name. The boatman had been praying for him; the low words seemed to shake the night:—

"Hear the prayer of Thy servant, and his supplications! Is not this what Thou hast chosen: to loose the bands, to undo the heavy burdens, and let the oppressed go free? O Lord, hear! O Lord, hearken and do! Defer not for Thine own sake, O my God!"

"What shall I do?" said the slave, standing up.

The boatman paced slowly to and fro, his voice chording in its dull monotone with the smothered savage muttering in the negro's brain.

"The day of the Lord cometh; it is nigh at hand. Who can abide it?

What saith the prophet Jeremiah? 'Take up a burden against the South. Cry aloud, spare not. Woe unto Babylon, for the day of her vengeance is come, the day of her visitation! Call together the archers against Babylon; camp against it round about; let none thereof escape. Recompense her: as she hath done unto my people, be it done unto her. A sword is upon Babylon: it shall break in pieces the shepherd and his flock, the man and the woman, the young man and the maid. I will render unto her the evil she hath done in my sight, saith the Lord.'"

It was the voice of God: the scar burned fiercer; the slave came forward boldly,—

"Mars'er, what shall I do?"

"Give the poor devil a musket," said one of the men. "Let him come with us, and strike a blow for freedom."

He took a knife from his belt, and threw it to him, then sauntered off to his tent.

"A blow for freedom?" mumbled Ben, taking it up.

"Let us sing to the praise of God," said the boatman, "the sixty-eighth psalm," lining it out while they sang,—the scattered men joining, partly to keep themselves awake. In old times David's harp charmed away the demon from a human heart. It roused one now, never to be laid again. A dull, droning chant, telling how the God of Vengeance rode upon the wind, swift to loose the fetters of the chained, to make desert the rebellious land; with a chorus, or refrain, in which Ben's wild, melancholy cry sounded like the wail of an avenging spirit:—

"That in the blood of enemies
Thy foot imbrued may be:
And of thy dogs dipped in the same
The tongues thou mayest see."

The meaning of that was plain; he sang it lower and more steadily each time, his body swaying in cadence, the glitter in his eye more steely.

Lamar, asleep in his prison, was wakened by the far-off plaintive song: he roused himself, leaning on one elbow, listening with a half-smile. It was Naomi they sang, he thought,—an old-fashioned Methodist air that Floy had caught from the negroes, and used to sing to him sometimes. Every night, down at home, she would come to his parlor-door to say goodnight: he thought he could see the little figure now in its white nightgown, and hear the bare feet pattering on the matting. When he was alone, she would come in, and sit on his lap awhile, and kneel down before she went away, her head on his knee, to say her prayers, as she called it. Only God knew how many times he had remained alone after hearing those prayers, saved from nights of drunken debauch. He thought he felt Floy's pure little hand on his forehead now, as if she were saying her usual "Good night, Bud." He lay down to sleep again, with a genial smile on his face, listening to the hymn.

"It's the same God," he said,—"Floy's and theirs."

Outside, as he slept, a dark figure watched him. The song of the men ceased. Midnight, white and silent, covered the earth. He could hear only the slow breathing of the sleeper. Ben's black face grew ashy pale, but he did not tremble, as he crept, cat-like, up to the wicket, his blubber lips apart, the white teeth clenched.

"It's for Freedom, Mar's Lord!" he gasped, looking up to the sky, as if he expected an answer. "Gor-a'mighty, it's for Freedom!" And went in.

A belated bird swooped through the cold moonlight into the valley, and vanished in the far mountain-cliffs with a low, fearing cry, as though it had passed through Hades.

They had broken down the wicket: he saw them lay the heavy body on the lumber outside, the black figures hurrying over the snow. He laughed low, savagely, watching them. Free now! The best of them despised him; the years past of cruelty and oppression turned back, fused in a slow, deadly current of revenge and hate, against the race that had trodden him down. He felt the iron muscles of his fingers, looked close at the glittering knife he held, chuckling at the strange smell it bore. Would the Illinois boatman blame him, if it maddened him? And if Ben took the fancy to put it to his throat, what right has he to complain? Has not he also been a dweller in Babylon? He hesitated a moment in the cleft of the hill, choosing his way, exultantly. He did not watch the North now; the quiet old dream of content was gone; his thick blood throbbed and surged with passions of which you and I know nothing: he had a lost life to avenge. His native air, torrid, heavy with latent impurity, drew him back: a fitter breath than this cold snow for the animal in his body, the demon in his soul, to triumph and wallow in. He panted, thinking of the saffron hues of the Santilla flats, of the white, stately dwellings, the men that went in and out from them, quiet, dominant,—feeling the edge of his knife. It was his turn to be master now! He ploughed his way doggedly through the snow,— panting, as he went,—a hotter glow in his gloomy eyes. It was his turn for

pleasure now: he would have his fill! Their wine and their gardens and—
He did not need to choose a wife from his own color now. He stopped,
thinking of little Floy, with her curls and great listening eyes, watching at
the door for her brother. He had watched her climb up into his arms and
kiss his cheek. She never would do that again! He laughed aloud, shrilly. By
God! she should keep the kiss for other lips! Why should he not say it?

Up on the hill the night-air throbbed colder and holier. The guards stood
about in the snow, silent, troubled. This was not like a death in battle: it put
them in mind of home, somehow. All that the dying man said was,
"Water," now and then. He had been sleeping, when struck, and never had
thoroughly wakened from his dream. Captain Poole, of the Snake-hunters,
had wrapped him in his own blanket, finding nothing more could be done.
He went off to have the Colonel summoned now, muttering that it was "a
damned shame." They put snow to Lamar's lips constantly, being hot and
parched; a woman, Dorr's wife, was crouching on the ground beside him,
chafing his hands, keeping down her sobs for fear they would disturb him.
He opened his eyes at last, and knew Dorr, who held his head.

"Unfasten my coat, Charley. What makes it so close here?"

Dorr could not speak.

"Shall I lift you up, Captain Lamar?" asked Dave Hall, who stood leaning on his rifle.

He spoke in a subdued tone, Babylon being far off for the moment.
Lamar dozed again before he could answer.

"Don't try to move him,—it is too late," said Dorr, sharply.

The moonlight steeped mountain and sky in a fresh whiteness. Lamar's
face, paling every moment, hardening, looked in it like some solemn work
of an untaught sculptor. There was a breathless silence. Ruth, kneeling
beside him, felt his hand grow slowly colder than snow. He moaned, his
voice going fast,—

"At two, Ben, old fellow! We'll be free to-night!"

Dave, stooping to wrap the blanket, felt his hand wet: he wiped it with
a shudder.

"As he hath done unto My people, be it done unto him!" he muttered,
but the words did not comfort him.

Lamar moved, half-smiling.

"That's right Floy. What is it she says? 'Now I lay me down'— I forget.
Good night. Kiss me, Floy."

He waited,—looked up uneasily. Dorr looked at his wife: she stooped,
and kissed his lips. Charley smoothed back the hair from the damp face

with as tender a touch as a woman's. Was he dead? The white moonlight was not more still than the calm face.

Suddenly the night-air was shattered by a wild, revengeful laugh from the hill. The departing soul rushed back, at the sound, to life, full consciousness. Lamar started from their hold,—sat up.

"It was Ben," he said, slowly.

In that dying flash of comprehension, it may be, the wrongs of the white man and the black stood clearer to his eyes than ours: the two lives trampled down. The stern face of the boatman bent over him: he was trying to stanch the flowing blood. Lamar looked at him: Hall saw no bitterness in the look,—a quiet, sad question rather, before which his soul lay bare. He felt the cold hand touch his shoulder, saw the pale lips move.

"Was this well done?" they said.

Before Lamar's eyes the rounded arch of gray receded, faded into dark; the negro's fierce laugh filled his ear: some woful thought at the sound wrung his soul, as it halted at the gate. It caught at the simple faith his mother taught him.

"Yea," he said aloud, "though I walk through the valley of the shadow of death, I will fear no evil: for Thou art with me."

Dorr gently drew down the uplifted hand. He was dead.

"It was a manly soul," said the Northern captain, his voice choking, as he straightened the limp hair.

"He trusted in God? A strange delusion!" muttered the boatman.

Yet he did not like that they should leave him alone with Lamar, as they did, going down for help. He paced to and fro, his rifle on his shoulder, arming his heart with strength to accomplish the vengeance of the Lord against Babylon. Yet he could not forget the murdered man sitting there in the calm moonlight, the dead face turned towards the North,—the dead face, whereon little Floy's tears should never fall. The grave, unmoving eyes seemed to the boatman to turn to him with the same awful question. "Was this well done?" they said. He thought in eternity they would rise before him, sad, unanswered. The earth, he fancied, lay whiter, colder,—the heaven farther off; the war, which had become a daily business, stood suddenly before him in all its terrible meaning. God, he thought, had met in judgment with His people. Yet he uttered no cry of vengeance against the doomed city. With the dead face before him, he bent his eyes to the ground, humble, uncertain,—speaking out of the ignorance of his own weak, human soul.

"The day of the Lord is nigh," he said; "it is at hand; and who can abide it?"

My Contraband
1869

LOUISA MAY ALCOTT

Louisa May Alcott (1832–1888) was born in Germantown, Pennsylvania, but her family soon moved to Concord, Massachusetts, where she and her father—the well-known educator and philosopher Amos Bronson Alcott—became closely acquainted with Emerson, Thoreau, and other leading literary figures. In late 1862 Alcott boldly entered the war as an army nurse, but after only six weeks of service she contracted typhoid fever and had to be brought home. Nevertheless, her experiences led to the writing of Hospital Sketches *(1863), a series of letters about being a war nurse. Although Alcott later gained great fame with* Little Women *(1868), she has in recent years come to be known as the anonymous author of numerous "thrillers" published in the popular magazines of the day. She also wrote a few stories about the Civil War, including "My Contraband," a moving tale of racial tension and reconcillation, which was first published in* Hospital Sketches and Camp and Fireside Stories *(1869).*

octor Franck came in as I sat sewing up the rents in an old shirt, that Tom might go tidily to his grave. New shirts were needed for living, and there was no wife or mother to "dress him handsome when he went to meet the Lord," as one woman said, describing the fine funeral she had pinched herself to give her son.

"Miss Dane, I'm in a quandary," began the Doctor, with that expression of countenance which says as plainly as words, "I want to ask a favor, but I wish you'd save me the trouble."

"Can I help you out of it?"

"Faith! I don't like to propose it, but you certainly can, if you please."

"Then name it, I beg."

"You see a Reb has just been brought in crazy with typhoid; a bad case every way; a drunken, rascally little captain somebody took the trouble to capture, but whom nobody wants to take the trouble to cure. The wards are full, the ladies worked to death, and willing to be for our own boys, but rather slow to risk their lives for a Reb. Now, you've had the fever, you like queer patients, your mate will see to your ward for a while, and I will find you a good attendant. The fellow won't last long, I fancy; but he can't die without some sort of care, you know. I've put him in the fourth story of the west wing, away from the rest. It is airy, quiet, and comfortable there. I'm on that ward, and will do my best for you in every way. Now, then, will you go?"

"Of course I will, out of perversity, if not common charity; for some of these people think that because I'm an abolitionist I am also a heathen, and I should rather like to show them that, though I cannot quite love my enemies, I am willing to take care of them."

"Very good; I thought you'd go; and speaking of abolition reminds me that you can have a contraband for servant, if you like. It is that fine mulatto fellow who was found burying his rebel master after the fight, and, being badly cut over the head, our boys brought him along. Will you have him?"

"By all means,—for I'll stand to my guns on that point, as on the other; these black boys are far more faithful and handy than some of the white scamps given me to serve, instead of being served by. But is this man well enough?"

"Yes, for that sort of work, and I think you'll like him. He must have been a handsome fellow before he got his face slashed; not much darker than myself; his master's son, I dare say, and the white blood makes him rather high and haughty about some things. He was in a bad way when he came in, but vowed he'd die in the street rather than turn in with the black fellows below; so I put him up in the west wing, to be out of the way, and he's seen to the captain all the morning. When can you go up?"

"As soon as Tom is laid out, Skinner moved, Haywood washed, Marble dressed, Charley rubbed, Downs taken up, Upham laid down, and the whole forty fed."

We both laughed, though the Doctor was on his way to the dead-house and I held a shroud on my lap. But in a hospital one learns that cheerfulness is one's salvation; for, in an atmosphere of suffering and death, heaviness of heart would soon paralyze usefulness of hand, if the blessed gift of smiles had been denied us.

In an hour I took possession of my new charge, finding a dissipated-looking boy of nineteen or twenty raving in the solitary little room, with no one near him but the contraband in the room adjoining. Feeling decidedly more interest in the black man than in the white, yet remembering the Doctor's hint of his being "high and haughty," I glanced furtively at him as I scattered chloride of lime about the room to purify the air, and settled matters to suit myself. I had seen many contrabands, but never one so attractive as this. All colored men are called "boys," even if their heads are white; this boy was five-and-twenty at least, strong-limbed and manly, and had the look of one who never had been cowed by abuse or worn with oppressive labor. He sat on his bed doing nothing; no book, no pipe, no pen or paper anywhere appeared, yet anything less indolent or listless than his attitude and expression I never saw. Erect he sat, with a hand on either knee, and eyes fixed on the bare wall opposite, so rapt in some absorbing thought as to be unconscious of my presence, though the door stood wide open and my movements were by no means noiseless. His face was half averted, but I instantly approved the Doctor's taste, for the profile which I saw possessed all the attributes of comeliness belonging to his mixed race. He was more quadroon than mulatto, with Saxon features, Spanish complexion darkened by exposure, color in lips and cheek, waving hair, and an eye full of the passionate melancholy which in such men always seems to utter a mute protest against the broken law that doomed them at their birth. What could he be thinking of? The sick boy cursed and raved, I rustled to and fro, steps passed the door, bells rang, and the steady rumble of army-wagons came up from the street, still he never stirred. I had seen colored people in what they call "the black sulks," when, for days, they neither smiled nor spoke, and scarcely ate. But this was something more than that; for the man was not dully brooding over some small grievance; he seemed to see an all-absorbing fact or fancy recorded on the wall, which was a blank to me. I wondered if it were some deep wrong or sorrow, kept alive by memory and impotent regret; if he mourned for the dead master to whom he had been faithful to the end; or if the liberty now his were robbed of half its sweetness by the knowledge that some one near and dear to him still languished in the hell from which he had escaped. My heart quite warmed to him at that idea; I wanted to know and comfort him; and, following the impulse of the moment, I went in and touched him on the shoulder.

In an instant the man vanished and the slave appeared. Freedom was too new a boon to have wrought its blessed changes yet; and as he started up, with his hand at his temple, and an obsequious "Yes, Missis," any romance that had gathered round him fled away, leaving the saddest of all sad facts in living guise before me. Not only did the manhood seem to die out of him, but the comeliness that first attracted me; for, as he turned, I saw the ghastly wound that had laid open cheek and forehead. Being partly healed, it was no longer bandaged, but held together with strips of that transparent plaster which I never see without a shiver, and swift recollections of the scenes with which it is associated in my mind. Part of his black hair had been shorn away, and one eye was nearly closed; pain so distorted, and the cruel sabre-cut so marred that portion of his face, that, when I saw it, I felt as if a fine medal had been suddenly reversed, showing me a far more striking type of human suffering and wrong than Michael Angelo's bronze prisoner. By one of those inexplicable processes that often teach us how little we understand ourselves, my purpose was suddenly changed; and, though I went in to offer comfort as a friend, I merely gave an order as a mistress.

"Will you open these windows? this man needs more air."

He obeyed at once, and, as he slowly urged up the unruly sash, the handsome profile was again turned toward me, and again I was possessed by my first impression so strongly that I involuntarily said,—

"Thank you."

Perhaps it was fancy, but I thought that in the look of mingled surprise and something like reproach which he gave me, there was also a trace of grateful pleasure. But he said, in that tone of spiritless humility these poor souls learn so soon,—

"I isn't a white man, Missis, I'se a contraband."

"Yes, I know it; but a contraband is a free man, and I heartily congratulate you."

He liked that; his face shone, he squared his shoulders, lifted his head, and looked me full in the eye with a brisk,—

"Thank ye, Missis; anything more to do fer yer?"

"Doctor Franck thought you would help me with this man, as there are many patients and few nurses or attendants. Have you had the fever?"

"No, Missis."

"They should have thought of that when they put him here; wounds and fevers should not be together. I'll try to get you moved."

He laughed a sudden laugh: if he had been a white man, I should have called it scornful; as he was a few shades darker than myself, I suppose it must be considered an insolent, or at least an unmannerly one.

"It don't matter, Missis. I'd rather be up here with the fever than down with those niggers; and there isn't no other place fer me."

Poor fellow! that was true. No ward in all the hospital would take him in to lie side by side with the most miserable white wreck there. Like the bat in Æsop's fable, he belonged to neither race; and the pride of one and the helplessness of the other, kept him hovering alone in the twilight a great sin has brought to overshadow the whole land.

"You shall stay, then; for I would far rather have you than my lazy Jack. But are you well and strong enough?"

"I guess I'll do, Missis."

He spoke with a passive sort of acquiescence,—as if it did not much matter if he were not able, and no one would particularly rejoice if he were.

"Yes, I think you will. By what name shall I call you?"

"Bob, Missis."

Every woman has her pet whim; one of mine was to teach the men self-respect by treating them respectfully. Tom, Dick, and Harry would pass, when lads rejoiced in those familiar abbreviations; but to address men often old enough to be my father in that style did not suit my old-fashioned ideas of propriety. This "Bob" would never do; I should have found it as easy to call the chaplain "Gus" as my tragical-looking contraband by a title so strongly associated with the tail of a kite.

"What is your other name?" I asked. "I like to call my attendants by their last names rather than by their first."

"I'se got no other, Missis; we has our masters' names, or do without. Mine's dead, and I won't have anything of his 'bout me."

"Well, I'll call you Robert, then, and you may fill this pitcher for me, if you will be so kind."

He went; but, through all the tame obedience years of servitude had taught him, I could see that the proud spirit his father gave him was not yet subdued, for the look and gesture, with which he repudiated his master's name were a more effective declaration of independence than any Fourth-of-July orator could have prepared.

We spent a curious week together. Robert seldom left his room, except upon my errands; and I was a prisoner all day, often all night, by the bedside of the rebel. The fever burned itself rapidly away, for there seemed little vitality to feed it in the feeble frame of this old young man, whose life had been none of the most righteous, judging from the revelations made by his unconscious lips; since more than once Robert authoritatively silenced him, when my gentler hushings were of no avail, and blasphemous wanderings or ribald camp-songs made my cheeks burn and Robert's face assume an aspect of disgust. The captain was the gentleman in the world's eye, but the contraband was the gentleman in mine;—I was a fanatic, and that accounts for such depravity of taste, I hope. I never asked Robert of himself, feeling that somewhere there was a spot still too sore to bear the lightest touch; but, from his language, manner, and intelligence, I inferred that his color had procured for him the few advantages within the reach of a quick-witted, kindly-treated slave. Silent, grave, and thoughtful, but most serviceable, was my contraband; glad of the books I brought him, faithful in the performance of the duties I assigned to him, grateful for the friendliness I could not but feel and show toward him. Often I longed to ask what purpose was so visibly altering his aspect with such daily deepening gloom. But I never dared, and no one else had either time or desire to pry into the past of this specimen of one branch of the chivalrous "F.F.Vs."

On the seventh night, Dr. Franck suggested that it would be well for some one, besides the general watchman of the ward, to be with the captain, as it might be his last. Although the greater part of the two preceding nights had been spent there, of course I offered to remain,—for there is a strange fascination in these scenes, which renders one careless of fatigue and unconscious of fear until the crisis is past.

"Give him water as long as he can drink, and if he drops into a natural sleep, it may save him. I'll look in at midnight, when some change will probably take place. Nothing but sleep or a miracle will keep him now. Good-night."

Away went the Doctor; and, devouring a whole mouthful of grapes, I lowered the lamp, wet the captain's head, and sat down on a hard stool to begin my watch. The captain lay with his hot, haggard face turned toward me, filling the air with his poisonous breath, and feebly muttering, with lips and tongue so parched that the sanest speech would have been difficult to understand. Robert was stretched on his bed in the inner room, the door of which stood ajar, that a fresh draught from his open window might carry the fever-fumes away through mine. I could just see a long, dark figure, with the lighter outline of a face, and, having little else to do just then, I fell to thinking of this curious contraband, who evidently prized his freedom highly, yet seemed in no haste to enjoy it. Dr. Franck had offered to send him on to safer quarters, but he had said, "No, thank yer, sir, not yet," and then had gone away to fall into one of those black moods of his, which began to disturb me, because I had no power to lighten them. As I sat listening to the clocks from the steeples all about us, I amused myself with planning Robert's future, as I often did my own, and had dealt out to him a generous hand of trumps wherewith to play this game of life which hitherto had gone so cruelly against him, when a harsh choked voice called,—

"Lucy!"

It was the captain, and some new terror seemed to have gifted him with momentary strength.

"Yes, here's Lucy," I answered, hoping that by following the fancy I might quiet him,—for his face was damp with the clammy moisture, and his frame shaken with the nervous tremor that so often precedes death. His dull eye fixed upon me, dilating with a bewildered look of incredulity and wrath, till he broke out fiercely,—

'That's a lie! she's dead,—and so's Bob, damn him!"

Finding speech a failure, I began to sing the quiet tune that had often soothed delirium like this; but hardly had the line,—

"See gentle patience smile on pain,"

passed my lips, when he clutched me by the wrist, whispering like one in mortal fear,—

"Hush! she used to sing that way to Bob, but she never would to me. I swore I'd whip the devil out of her, and I did; but you know before she cut her throat she said she'd haunt me, and there she is!"

He pointed behind me with an aspect of such pale dismay, that I involuntarily glanced over my shoulder and started as if I had seen a veritable ghost; for, peering from the gloom of that inner room, I saw a shadowy face, with dark hair all about it, and a glimpse of scarlet at the throat. An instant showed me that it was only Robert leaning from his bed's foot, wrapped in a gray army-blanket, with his red shirt just visible above it, and his long hair disordered by sleep. But what a strange expression was on his face! The unmarred side was toward me, fixed and motionless as when I first observed it,—less absorbed now, but more intent. His eye glittered, his lips were apart like one who listened with every sense, and his whole aspect reminded me of a hound to which some wind had brought the scent of unsuspected prey.

"Do you know him, Robert? Does he mean you?"

"Laws, no, Missis; they all own half-a-dozen Bobs: but hearin' my name woke me; that's all."

He spoke quite naturally, and lay down again, while I returned to my charge, thinking that this paroxysm was probably his last. But by another hour I perceived a hopeful change; for the tremor had subsided, the cold dew was gone, his breathing was more regular, and Sleep, the healer, had descended to save or take him gently away. Doctor Franck looked in at midnight, bade me keep all cool and quiet, and not fail to administer a certain draught as soon as the captain woke. Very much relieved, I laid my head on my arms, uncomfortably folded on the little table, and fancied I was about to perform one of the feats which practice renders possible,— "sleeping with one eye open," as we say: a half-and-half doze, for all senses sleep but that of hearing; the faintest murmur, sigh, or motion will break it, and give one back one's wits much brightened by the brief permission to "stand at ease." On this night the experiment was a failure, for previous vigils, confinement, and much care had rendered naps a dangerous indulgence. Having roused half-a-dozen times in an hour to find all quiet, I dropped my heavy head on my arms, and, drowsily resolving to look up again in fifteen minutes, fell fast asleep.

The striking of a deep-voiced clock awoke me with a start. "That is one," thought I; but, to my dismay, two more strokes followed, and in remorseful haste I sprang up to see what harm my long oblivion had done. A strong hand put me back into my seat, and held me there. It was Robert. The instant my eye met his my heart began to beat, and all along my nerves tingled that electric flash which foretells a danger that we cannot see. He was very pale, his mouth grim, and both eyes full of sombre fire; for even the wounded one was open now, all the more sinister for the deep scar above and below. But his touch was steady, his voice quiet, as he said,—

"Sit still, Missis; I won't hurt yer, nor scare yer, ef I can help it, but yer waked too soon."

"Let me go, Robert,—the captain is stirring,—I must give him something."

"No, Missis, yer can't stir an inch. Look here!"

Holding me with one hand, with the other he took up the glass in which I had left the draught, and showed me it was empty.

"Has he taken it?" I asked, more and more bewildered.

"I flung it out o' winder, Missis; he'll have to do without."

"But why, Robert? why did you do it?"

"'Kase I hate him!"

Impossible to doubt the truth of that; his whole face showed it, as he spoke through his set teeth, and launched a fiery glance at the unconscious captain. I could only hold my breath and stare blankly at him, wondering what mad act was coming next. I suppose I shook and turned white, as women have a foolish habit of doing when sudden danger daunts them;

for Robert released my arm, sat down upon the bedside just in front of me, and said, with the ominous quietude that made me cold to see and hear,—

"Don't yer be frightened, Missis; don't try to run away, fer the door's locked and the key in my pocket; don't yer cry out, fer yer'd have to scream a long while, with my hand on yer mouth, 'efore yer was heard. Be still, an' I'll tell yer what I'm gwine to do."

"Lord help us! he has taken the fever in some sudden, violent way, and is out of his head. I must humor him till some one comes"; in pursuance of which swift determination, I tried to say, quite composedly,—

"I will be still and hear you; but open the window. Why did you shut it?"

"I'm sorry I can't do it, Missis; but yer'd jump out, or call, if I did, an' I'm not ready yet. I shut it to make yer sleep, an' heat would do it quicker'n anything else I could do."

The captain moved, and feebly muttered "Water!" Instinctively I rose to give it to him, but the heavy hand came down upon my shoulder, and in the same decided tone Robert said,—

"The water went with the physic; let him call."

"Do let me go to him! he'll die without care!"

"I mean he shall;—don't yer meddle, if yer please, Missis."

In spite of his quiet tone and respectful manner, I saw murder in his eyes, and turned faint with fear; yet the fear excited me, and, hardly knowing what I did, I seized the hands that had seized me, crying,—

"No, no; you shall not kill him! It is base to hurt a helpless man. Why do you hate him? He is not your master."

"He's my brother."

I felt that answer from head to foot, and seemed to fathom what was coming, with a prescience vague, but unmistakable. One appeal was left to me, and I made it.

"Robert, tell me what it means? Do not commit a crime and make me accessory to it. There is a better way of righting wrong than by violence;— let me help you find it."

My voice trembled as I spoke, and I heard the frightened flutter of my heart; so did he, and if any little act of mine had ever won affection or respect from him, the memory of it served me then. He looked down, and seemed to put some question to himself; whatever it was, the answer was in my favor, for when his eyes rose again, they were gloomy, but not desperate.

"I *will* tell yer, Missis; but mind, this makes no difference; the boy is mine. I'll give the Lord a chance to take him fust: if He don't, I shall."

"Oh, no! remember he is your brother."

An unwise speech; I felt it as it passed my lips, for a black frown gathered on Robert's face, and his strong hands closed with an ugly sort of grip. But he did not touch the poor soul gasping there behind him, and seemed content to let the slow suffocation of that stifling room end his frail life.

"I'm not like to forget dat, Missis, when I've been thinkin' of it all this week. I knew him when they fetched him in, an' would 'a' done it long 'fore this, but I wanted to ask where Lucy was; he knows,—he told tonight,—an' now he's done for."

"Who is Lucy?" I asked hurriedly, intent on keeping his mind busy with any thought but murder.

With one of the swift transitions of a mixed temperament like this, at my question Robert's deep eyes filled, the clenched hands were spread before his face, and all I heard were the broken words,—

"My wife,—he took her—"

In that instant every thought of fear was swallowed up in burning indignation for the wrong, and a perfect passion of pity for the desperate man so tempted to avenge an injury for which there seemed no redress but this. He was no longer slave or contraband, no drop of black blood marred him in my sight, but an infinite compassion yearned to save, to help, to comfort him. Words seemed so powerless I offered none, only put my hand on his poor head, wounded, homeless, bowed down with grief for which I had no cure, and softly smoothed the long, neglected hair, pitifully wondering the while where was the wife who must have loved this tenderhearted man so well.

The captain moaned again, and faintly whispered, "Air!" but I never stirred. God forgive me! just then I hated him as only a woman thinking of a sister woman's wrong could hate. Robert looked up; his eyes were dry again, his mouth grim. I saw that, said, "Tell me more," and he did; for sympathy is a gift the poorest may give, the proudest stoop to receive.

"Yer see, Missis, his father,—I might say ours, ef I warn't ashamed of both of 'em,—his father died two years ago, an' left us all to Marster Ned,—that's him here, eighteen then. He always hated me, I looked so like old Marster: he don't,—only the light skin an' hair. Old Marster was kind to all of us, me 'specially, an' bought Lucy off the next plantation down there in South Carolina, when he found I liked her. I married her, all I could; it warn't much, but we was true to one another till Marster Ned come home a year after an' made hell fer both of us. He sent my old mother to be used up in his rice-swamp in Georgy; he found me with my pretty Lucy, an' though young Miss cried, an' I prayed to him on my knees, an' Lucy run away, he wouldn't have no mercy; he brought her back, an'—took her."

"Oh, what did you do?" I cried, hot with helpless pain and passion.

How the man's outraged heart sent the blood flaming up into his face and deepened the tones of his impetuous voice, as he stretched his arm across the bed, saying, with a terribly expressive gesture,—

"I half murdered him, an' to-night I'll finish."

"Yes, yes—but go on now; what came next?"

He gave me a look that showed no white man could have felt a deeper degradation in remembering and confessing these last acts of brotherly oppression.

"They whipped me till I couldn't stand, an' then they sold me further South. Yer thought I was a white man once,—look here!"

With a sudden wrench he tore the shirt from neck to waist, and on his strong, brown shoulders showed me furrows deeply ploughed, wounds which, though healed, were ghastlier to me than any in that house. I could not speak to him, and, with the pathetic dignity a great grief lends the humblest sufferer, he ended his brief tragedy by simply saying,—

"That's all, Missis. I'se never seen her since, an' now I never shall in this world,—maybe not in t'other."

"But, Robert, why think her dead? The captain was wandering when he said those sad things; perhaps he will retract them when he is sane. Don't despair; don't give up yet."

"No, Missis, I 'spect he's right; she was too proud to bear that long. It's like her to kill herself. I told her to, if there was no other way; an' she always minded me, Lucy did. My poor girl! Oh, it warn't right! No, by God, it warn't!"

As the memory of this bitter wrong, this double bereavement, burned in his sore heart, the devil that lurks in every strong man's blood leaped up; he put his hand upon his brother's throat, and, watching the white face before him, muttered low between his teeth,—

"I'm lettin' him go too easy; there's no pain in this; we a'n't even yet. I wish he knew me. Marster Ned! it's Bob; where's Lucy?"

From the captain's lips there came a long faint sigh, and nothing but a flutter of the eyelids showed that he still lived. A strange stillness filled the room as the elder brother held the younger's life suspended in his hand, while wavering between a dim hope and a deadly hate. In the whirl of thoughts that went on in my brain, only one was clear enough to act upon.

I must prevent murder, if I could,—but how? What could I do up there alone, locked in with a dying man and a lunatic?—for any mind yielded utterly to any unrighteous impulse is mad while the impulse rules it. Strength I had not, nor much courage, neither time nor will for stratagem, and chance only could bring me help before it was too late. But one weapon I possessed,—a tongue,—often a woman's best defence; and sympathy, stronger than fear, gave me power to use it. What I said Heaven only knows, but surely Heaven helped me; words burned on my lips, tears streamed from my eyes, and some good angel prompted me to use the one name that had power to arrest my hearer's hand and touch his heart. For at that moment I heartily believed that Lucy lived, and this earnest faith roused in him a like belief.

He listened with the lowering look of one in whom brute instinct was sovereign for the time,—a look that makes the noblest countenance base. He was but a man,—a poor, untaught, outcast, outraged man. Life had few joys for him; the world offered him no honors, no success, no home, no love. What future would this crime mar? and why should he deny himself that sweet, yet bitter morsel called revenge? How many white men, with all New England's freedom, culture, Christianity, would not have felt as he felt then? Should I have reproached him for a human anguish, a human longing for redress, all now left him from the ruin of his few poor hopes? Who had taught him that self-control, self-sacrifice, are attributes that make men masters of the earth, and lift them nearer heaven? Should I have urged the beauty of forgiveness, the duty of devout submission? He had no religion, for he was no saintly "Uncle Tom," and Slavery's black shadow seemed to darken all the world to him, and shut out God. Should I have warned him of penalties, of judgments, and the potency of law? What did he know of justice, or the mercy that should temper that stern virtue, when every law, human and divine, had been broken on his hearthstone? Should I have tried to touch him by appeals to filial duty, to brotherly love? How had his appeals been answered? What memories had father and brother stored up in his heart to plead for either now? No,—all these influences, these associations, would have proved worse than useless, had I been calm enough to try them. I was not; but instinct, subtler than reason, showed me the one safe clue by which to lead this troubled soul from the labyrinth in which it groped and nearly fell. When I paused, breathless, Robert turned to me, asking, as if human assurances could strengthen his faith in Divine Omnipotence,—

"Do you believe, if I let Marster Ned live, the Lord will give me back my Lucy?"

"As surely as there is a Lord, you will find her here or in the beautiful hereafter, where there is no black or white, no master and no slave."

He took his hand from his brother's throat, lifted his eyes from my face to the wintry sky beyond, as if searching for that blessed country, happier even than the happy North. Alas, it was the darkest hour before the dawn!—there was no star above, no light below but the pale glimmer of the lamp that showed the brother who had made him desolate. Like a blind man who believes there is a sun, yet cannot see it, he shook his head, let his arms drop nervelessly upon his knees, and sat there dumbly asking that question which many a soul whose faith is firmer fixed than his has asked in hours less dark than this,—"Where is God?" I saw the tide had turned, and strenuously tried to keep this rudderless life-boat from slipping back into the whirlpool wherein it had been so nearly lost.

"I have listened to you, Robert; now hear me, and heed what I say, because my heart is full of pity for you, full of hope for your future, and a desire to help you now. I want you to go away from here, from the temptation of this place, and the sad thoughts that haunt it. You have conquered yourself once, and I honor you for it, because, the harder the battle, the more glorious the victory; but it is safer to put a greater distance between you and this man. I will write you letters, give you money, and send you to good old Massachusetts to begin your new life a freeman,—yes, and a happy man; for when the captain is himself again, I will learn where Lucy is, and move heaven and earth to find and give her back to you. Will you do this, Robert?"

Slowly, very slowly, the answer came; for the purpose of a week, perhaps a year, was hard to relinquish in an hour.

"Yes, Missis, I will."

"Good! Now you are the man I thought you, and I'll work for you with all my heart. You need sleep, my poor fellow; go, and try to forget. The captain is alive, and as yet you are spared that sin. No, don't look there; I'll care for him. Come, Robert, for Lucy's sake."

Thank Heaven for the immortality of love! for when all other means of salvation failed, a spark of this vital fire softened the man's iron will, until a woman's hand could bend it. He let me take from him the key, let me draw him gently away, and lead him to the solitude which now was the most healing balm I could bestow. Once in his little room, he fell down on his bed and lay there, as if spent with the sharpest conflict of his life. I slipped the bolt across his door, and unlocked my own, flung up the window, steadied myself with a breath of air, then rushed to Doctor Franck.

He came; and till dawn we worked together, saving one brother's life, and taking earnest thought how best to secure the other's liberty. When the sun came up as blithely as if it shone only upon happy homes, the Doctor went to Robert. For an hour I heard the murmur of their voices; once I caught the sound of heavy sobs, and for a time a reverent hush, as if in the silence that good man were ministering to soul as well as body. When he departed he took Robert with him, pausing to tell me he should get him off as soon as possible, but not before we met again.

Nothing more was seen of them all day; another surgeon came to see the captain, and another attendant came to fill the empty place. I tried to rest, but could not, with the thought of poor Lucy tugging at my heart, and was soon back at my post again, anxiously hoping that my contraband had not been too hastily spirited away. Just as night fell there came a tap, and, opening, I saw Robert literally "clothed, and in his right mind." The Doctor had replaced the ragged suit with tidy garments, and no trace of the tempestuous night remained but deeper lines upon the forehead, and the docile look of a repentant child. He did not cross the threshold, did not offer me his hand,—only took off his cap, saying, with a traitorous falter in his voice,—

"God bless yer, Missis! I'm gwine."

I put out both my hands, and held his fast.

"Good-by, Robert! Keep up good heart, and when I come home to Massachusetts we'll meet in a happier place than this. Are you quite ready, quite comfortable for your journey?"

"Yes, Missis, yes; the Doctor's fixed everything! I'se gwine with a friend of his; my papers are all right, an' I'm as happy as I can be till I find"—

He stopped there; then went on, with a glance into the room,—

"I'm glad I didn't do it, an' I thank yer, Missis, fer hinderin' me—thank yer hearty; but I'm afraid I hate him jest the same."

Of course he did; and so did I; for these faulty hearts of ours cannot turn perfect in a night, but need frost and fire, wind and rain, to ripen and make them ready for the great harvest-home. Wishing to divert his mind, I put my poor mite into his hand, and, remembering the magic of a certain little book, I gave him mine, on whose dark cover whitely shone the Virgin Mother and the Child, the grand history of whose life the book contained. The money went into Robert's pocket with a grateful murmur, the book into his bosom, with a long look and a tremulous—

"I never saw *my* baby, Missis."

I broke down then; and though my eyes were too dim to see, I felt the touch of lips upon my hands, heard the sound of departing feet, and knew my contraband was gone.

When one feels an intense dislike, the less one says about the subject of it the better; therefore I shall merely record that the captain lived,—in time was exchanged; and that, whoever the other party was, I am convinced the Government got the best of the bargain. But long before this occurred, I had fulfilled my promise to Robert; for as soon as my patient recovered strength of memory enough to make his answer trustworthy, I asked without any circumlocution,—

"Captain Fairfax, where is Lucy?"

And too feeble to be angry, surprised, or insincere, he straightway answered,—

"Dead, Miss Dane."

"And she killed herself when you sold Bob?"

"How the devil did you know that?" he muttered, with an expression half-remorseful, half-amazed; but I was satisfied, and said no more.

Of course this went to Robert, waiting far away there in a lonely home,—waiting, working, hoping for his Lucy. It almost broke my heart to do it; but delay was weak, deceit was wicked; so I sent the heavy tidings, and very soon the answer came,—only three lines; but I felt that the sustaining power of the man's life was gone.

"I tort I'd never see her any more; I'm glad to know she's out of trouble. I thank yer, Missis; an' if they let us, I'll fight fer yer till I'm killed, which I hope will be 'fore long."

Six months later he had his wish, and kept his word.

Every one knows the story of the attack on Fort Wagner; but we should not tire yet of recalling how our Fifty-Fourth, spent with three sleepless nights, a day's fast, and a march under the July sun, stormed the fort as night fell, facing death in many shapes, following their brave leaders through a fiery rain of shot and shell, fighting valiantly for "God and Governor Andrew,"—how the regiment that went into action seven hundred strong, came out having had nearly half its number captured, killed, or wounded, leaving their young commander to be buried, like a chief of earlier times, with his body-guard around him, faithful to the death. Surely, the insult turns to honor, and the wide grave needs no monument but the heroism that consecrates it in our sight; surely, the hearts that held him nearest, see through their tears a noble victory in the seeming sad defeat; and surely, God's benediction was bestowed, when this loyal soul answered, as Death called the roll, "Lord, here am I, with the brothers Thou hast given me!"

The future must show how well that fight was fought; for though Fort Wagner once defied us, public prejudice is down; and through the cannon-smoke of that black night, the manhood of the colored race shines before many eyes that would not see, rings in many ears that would not hear, wins many hearts that would not hitherto believe.

When the news came that we were needed, there was none so glad as I to leave teaching contrabands, the new work I had taken up, and go to nurse "our boys," as my dusky flock so proudly called the wounded of the Fifty-Fourth. Feeling more satisfaction, as I assumed my big apron and turned up my cuffs, than if dressing for the President's levee, I fell to work in Hospital No. 10 at Beaufort. The scene was most familiar, and yet strange; for only dark faces looked up at me from the pallets so thickly laid along the floor, and I missed the sharp accent of my Yankee boys in the slower, softer voices calling cheerily to one another, or answering my questions with a stout, "We'll never give it up, Missis, till the last Reb's dead," or, "If our people's free, we can afford to die."

Passing from bed to bed, intent on making one pair of hands do the work of three, at least, I gradually washed, fed, and bandaged my way down the long line of sable heroes, and coming to the very last, found that he was my contraband. So old, so worn, so deathly weak and wan, I never should have known him but for the deep scar on his cheek. That side lay uppermost, and caught my eye at once; but even then I doubted, such an awful change had come upon him, when, turning to the ticket just above his head, I saw the name, "Robert Dane." That both assured and touched me, for, remembering that he had no name, I knew that he had taken mine. I longed for him to speak to me, to tell how he had fared since I lost sight of him, and let me perform some little service for him in return for many he had done for me; but he seemed asleep; and as I stood re-living that strange night again, a bright lad, who lay next him softly waving an old fan across both beds, looked up and said,—

"I guess you know him, Missis?"

"You are right. Do you?"

"As much as any one was able to, Missis."

"Why do you say 'was,' as if the man were dead and gone?"

"I s'pose because I know he'll have to go. He's got a bad jab in the breast, an' is bleedin' inside, the Doctor says. He don't suffer any, only gets weaker 'n' weaker every minute. I've been fannin' him this long while, an' he's talked a little; but he don't know me now, so he's most gone, I guess."

There was so much sorrow and affection in the boy's face, that I remembered something, and asked, with redoubled interest,—

"Are you the one that brought him off? I was told about a boy who nearly lost his life in saving that of his mate."

I dare say the young fellow blushed, as any modest lad might have done; I could not see it, but I heard the chuckle of satisfaction that escaped him, as he glanced from his shattered arm and bandaged side to the pale figure opposite.

"Lord, Missis, that's nothin'; we boys always stan' by one another, an' I warn't goin' to leave him to be tormented any more by them cussed Rebs. He's been a slave once, though he don't look half so much like it as me, an' I was born in Boston."

He did not; for the speaker was as black as the ace of spades,—being a sturdy specimen, the knave of clubs would perhaps be a fitter representative,—but the dark freeman looked at the white slave with the pitiful, yet puzzled expression I have so often seen on the faces of our wisest men, when this tangled question of Slavery presented itself, asking to be cut or patiently undone.

"Tell me what you know of this man; for, even if he were awake, he is too weak to talk."

"I never saw him till I joined the regiment, an' no one 'peared to have got much out of him. He was a shut-up sort of feller, an' didn't seem to care for anything but gettin' at the Rebs. Some say he was the fust man of us that enlisted; I know he fretted till we were off, an' when we pitched into Old Wagner, he fought like the devil."

"Were you with him when he was wounded? How was it?"

"Yes, Missis. There was somethin' queer about it; for he 'peared to know the chap that killed him, an' the chap knew him. I don't dare to ask, but I rather guess one owned the other some time; for, when they clinched, the chap sung out, 'Bob!' an' Dane, 'Marster Ned!'—then they went at it."

I sat down suddenly, for the old anger and compassion struggled in my heart, and I both longed and feared to hear what was to follow.

"You see, when the Colonel,—Lord keep an' send him back to us!—it a'n't certain yet, you know, Missis, though it's two days ago we lost him,— well, when the Colonel shouted, 'Rush on, boys, rush on!' Dane tore away as if he was goin' to take the fort alone; I was next him, an' kept close as we went through the ditch an' up the wall. Hi! warn't that a rusher!" and the boy flung up his well arm with a whoop, as if the mere memory of that stirring moment came over him in a gust of irrepressible excitement.

"Were you afraid?" I said, asking the question women often put, and receiving the answer they seldom fail to get.

"No, Missis!"—emphasis on the "Missis"—"I never thought of anything but the damn' Rebs, that scalp, slash, an' cut our ears off, when they git us. I was bound to let daylight into one of 'em at least, an' I did. Hope he liked it!"

"It is evident that you did. Now go on about Robert, for I should be at work."

"He was one of the fust up; I was just behind, an' though the whole thing happened in a minute, I remember how it was, for all I was yellin' an' knockin' round like mad. Just where we were, some sort of an officer was wavin' his sword an' cheerin' on his men; Dane saw him by a big flash that come by; he flung away his gun, give a leap, an' went at that feller as if he was Jeff, Beauregard, an' Lee, all in one. I scrabbled after as quick as I could, but was only up in time to see him git the sword straight through him an' drop into the ditch. You needn't ask what I did next, Missis, for I don't quite know myself; all I'm clear about is, that I managed somehow to pitch that Reb into the fort as dead as Moses, git hold of Dane, an' bring him off. Poor old feller! we said we went in to live or die; he said he went in to die, an' he's done it."

I had been intently watching the excited speaker; but as he regretfully added those last words I turned again, and Robert's eyes met mine,—those melancholy eyes, so full of an intelligence that proved he had heard, remembered, and reflected with that preternatural power which often out-lives all other faculties. He knew me, yet gave no greeting; was glad to see a woman's face, yet had no smile wherewith to welcome it; felt that he was dying, yet uttered no farewell. He was too far across the river to return or linger now; departing thought, strength, breath, were spent in one grateful look, one murmur of submission to the last pang he could ever feel. His lips moved, and, bending to them, a whisper chilled my cheek, as it shaped the broken words,—

"I'd 'a' done it,—but it's better so,—I'm satisfied."

Ah! well he might be,—for, as he turned his face from the shadow of the life that was, the sunshine of the life to be touched it with a beautiful content, and in the drawing of a breath my contraband found wife and home, eternal liberty and God.

The Bloodhounds
1879

W. C. MORROW

W. C. Morrow's Southern upbringing did not prevent him from writing the following grim tale, "The Bloodhounds" (first published in the Argonaut *on December 13, 1879), which extends sympathy to a Southern deserter ruthlessly hunted down by dogs.*

In 1864 the horrors of war spread over the South like a pall of death. Not only did they stalk among the soldiers to strip the rags from their backs; to starve them or to feed them on rotten meat; to place them in the deadly path of the Minié or the murderous grape; to mow them down with foul disease and loathsome suffering, but they sent conscription, to feed mothers on despair and children on stones, and hunger to take up its abode at the fireside of the poor. The facilities of the transitory and feeble government for supplying means of sustenance to poor families were inadequate in remote and sparsely settled communities; and now that the husband, on whom had depended the livelihood of his family, had been armed with a musket and ordered to the front, there was no lack of anguish and the distressing cry of children for bread. The despairing mother wrote to her husband on paper that was blotted with tears, and from every word there stared at him the suffering faces of his children and the imploring look that no parent can withstand. So the stanch soldier, who could unflinchingly storm a rampart or face a cannon, and who looked upon death as his companion and honor as his future shroud, employed his affections as his grave-digger, and sneaked away in the darkness like a thief. Desertion and death were synonymous terms, and the man sacrificed his life to feed his children. Depletion of the ranks by desertion assumed such alarming proportions that the War Department stretched forth its relentless arm and

93

stained its sword with the blood of its own men. It was not a question of bread for children, but of men for the vanguard. Desertion was, in point of numbers, equivalent to death on the battlefield, so far as it affected the strength of the line; in point of discipline it was a thousand times worse. A man's life was worth nothing unless it served to check the career of a rifle-ball directed at the vitals of the government. To such a desperate strait had the war policy of the Confederate Government been reduced that, in order to discourage a defection that was becoming epidemic, a patrol was employed, which, with the assistance of hounds in rare instances, hunted the deserters down and hanged them in chains, or shot them blindfolded, with their faces to the wall.

One day a deserter named Martin was at work in a cornfield attached to his humble dwelling. Four or five pale, ragged, emaciated children were amusing themselves in the yard, and a homely, care-worn woman was bending over a washtub, while her infant, with hollowed eyes and wasted limbs, was playing in the dirt at her side. The man had been at home unmolested for two months, and had come to experience a faint sense of security. When darkness came on he shouldered his hoe and trudged to the house, taking in his arms a few pine knots which were to furnish light for the evening. The family sat down to a supper of corn-bread, which they washed down with a disgusting drink, too familiar in those days to nearly all classes, and especially to those on whom the finger of war pressed most heavily. It was made from corn, roasted until it was black; it was called "coffee," and was drunk without sugar.

"Well, Mary," said the husband, "the corn will be in roasting-ear in two weeks, and we will have something fit to eat."

"Yes," said the woman.

"And then, you know, the birds will begin to flock in, and I can trap a few of them and get meat."

"Yes."

"I think we're going to get along first rate. I don't believe the war will last three months longer. You know one reason for so much desertion is that a great many soldiers have no idea now that we can ever whip the North, and they think that if they desert the Confederacy will go under before the patrol can catch them. I'm thinking that I am almost out of danger."

"I hope so, William; but there's no telling."

"All right, Mary; but they can't take me alive."

This declaration was made with such a calm and quiet determination that the poor woman looked anxiously at the hard lines about his eyes and mouth. She knew that he meant it, and that the loaded revolver he always carried would never hesitate a moment.

In striking contrast to the woman, the man was of powerful build. His hardships in the army had toughened his muscles and strengthened his large bones and supple joints. In a simple measure of strength he would have been a match for two ordinary men. His shoulders were broad and erect, and his arms and legs large and full of power.

They sat silently watching the blazing knots in the broad fire-place, the woman wearily engaged with some coarse knitting and the man smoking home-made tobacco in an old clay pipe. On a sudden the man took the pipe from his mouth, straightened his shoulders, and listened attentively. His wife noticed the movement, and hurriedly whispered:

"What is it, William?"

"Sh-h-h."

They listened a moment longer, and the man stealthily rose to his feet and gazed steadily at the door, which was barred on the inside.

"What is it, William?" the woman again whispered, having strained her hearing in vain to catch any unusual sound.

"Horses."

"Where?"

He answered by pointing in the direction of the road. The truth flashed upon the woman's mind that, beyond a doubt, a hunting party was abroad, and that their game was a deserter. She rose to her feet, very pale, and regarded her husband with an anxious look. The man glanced at his children, lying asleep on their cots, cast a loving look at his wife, stepped softly to a shelf on which was a bucket of water, and dashed its contents upon the fire. The blaze was extinguished, and the room was in profound darkness.

"Run, William!" whispered the woman in a quavering voice.

He silently clasped her in his arms, and said: "Keep a brave heart, Mary. They can't take me alive."

He pushed her away, although she unconsciously clung to him, pulled out his revolver, cocked it, and let the hammer down softly. He then put on his hat, quietly unbarred the door, and slipped out in the dark.

The sound of the horses' hoofs had ceased. The woman staggered to the open door, and saw several dark forms hurrying around the cottage. They must have seen her husband, for a stern voice called "Halt!" and she heard the click of a carbine. A shadowy figure stole crouching alongside a fence, and on hearing the command it suddenly straightened, and bounded forward like a frightened deer. There was a vivid flash and a report from the carbine, and the stealthy figure halted a moment, and returned the fire. The soldier fell as a pistol-ball crashed through his shoulder; the fugitive ran with redoubled speed, and disappeared in the darkness. There was a rapid discharge of carbines, but Martin had gained the swamp, and further pursuit was out of the question.

The hunters returned and bore the wounded man into the woman's cottage. She rekindled the fire, and assisted with trembling hands in dressing the wound.

"How long has your husband been here?" asked the captain.

"Two months."

"Where will he go?"

"I don't know."

"You do know!"

The woman made no reply.

"Do you know that you are guilty of harboring a deserter?"

"Yes," she said, firmly and proudly, looking him full in the face.

"Do you know what can be done with you?"

She said nothing.

"You can be arrested and punished for a crime."

She regarded him with intense scorn, and remained silent.

"I'm glad he got away," she said, at length, quietly.

"Did you assist him in escaping?"

"He needed no help."

"He surely told you where he was going?"

She shook her head.

"Did he say when he will come back?"

"No."

"Now, I see that you are a woman of sense and courage. If you will tell me where I can find him I will not arrest you."

She treated the proposition with contemptuous silence.

"You would not like to be handcuffed and carried to prison?"

"I wouldn't care."

"What would become of your children?"

The woman became pale, her eyes flashed, and she stammered:

"You would not leave them here to starve, would you?"

"Certainly," said the officer, as he laughed at her agony.

The mother was transformed into a tigress. She sprang across the room, seized a carbine that leaned against the wall, and leveled it at his head.

"You would! you cowardly, inhuman brute!" She screamed as she pulled the trigger.

There was a deafening report, and she fell fainting to the floor.

"Simply sheared me a little," remarked the officer, as with a certain degree of interest he felt a narrow white streak that the ball had cut through his hair. "'An inch lower, and'—what was is it old Nap said at Austerlitz? She's game, though, and quick as lightning. No use trying to get anything out of her. I just wanted to scare her a little, and she took it in dead earnest."

"What are you going to do now, Captain?" asked one of the men.

"Oh, I'll put Walker's dogs after him. They'll fetch him."

"The bloodhounds?"

"Yes."

"Will you follow them up?"

"I don't know."

"They'll never leave him alive if you don't."

"I know it."

"That would be terrible."

"Why?"

"They got that fellow, Rutherford, down, and tore him to pieces."

"Well, what's the difference? Is that any worse than calling the dogs off, and bringing him back alive to be shot?"

"But he's armed and will kill the hounds."

"Twelve dogs? Don't be uneasy. He will finish two or three of the younger dogs until his pistol is empty, and the rest will manage him. Old Tiger will be there at the finish, and will make all the final arrangements for the funeral. He hangs on closer than death, and they've never got a square blow nor a safe shot at him yet."

At daybreak the next morning an old man, smooth-shaved and stoop-shouldered, was riding in the direction of the woman's cottage. The cavalry captain accompanied him, and eleven bloodhounds—magnificent dogs—trotted along, some ahead and others on either side of the horsemen, while two hundred yards in the rear a solitary old dog jogged along as if already weary of the enterprise and disgusted with the life he was called upon to lead. This was none other than the famous Tiger, more generally called "Old Tige," the dog that never lost a trail, and never failed to run his game to earth.

"Walker," said the officer, "I think we had better skirt the woods, and not let the woman know that we've got the dogs out. She might give us trouble."

They entered the swamp in the direction the man had taken, and Walker called the dogs about him. Tiger walked leisurely up, and lay down near his master's horse.

"Heigho! get up, sir!"

The old dog slowly obeyed the command, and stood blinking and staring stupidly at his master. Walker descended from his horse, and pointing to the ground, said:

"Hie on!"

The other dogs were already scouring the ground in all directions. Old Tige put his nose to the grass, and began to hunt the scent, by systematically describing a circle which he continually widened, his master watching him closely the meanwhile, and paying no attention to the other dogs. A young hound soon sent up the well-known howl, and the other dogs chased eagerly around him, Old Tige trotting to the scene behind all the others. The dogs were greatly excited. The old dog unceremoniously pushed his way through the crowd, and sniffed the ground. The young hound, impatient that no command was given, and satisfied that he had found the trail, slowly advanced into the swamp, his nose all the time to the ground. Soon he set off on a full run, the other dogs following with yelps. Old Tige examined the spot indicated by the young hound, but was entirely unconcerned, and proceeded to smell the ground for a few yards around. Walker called the other dogs back, and Old Tige sullenly shook his head until his ragged ears flapped against his jowls, and lay down again.

"He's not satisfied," said Walker. "I will have to show him the track. He's in doubt."

Walker crept away along the fence, followed by the old dog, and when he had reached the spot opposite where the man was last seen, he saw through the fence a track indented in the soft earth, and ordered the dog to climb over. Old Tige clambered laboriously over the rails, and scented the track. He regained his master's side, and trudged with him back to the swamp.

"I think the woman heard the dogs," said Walker. "I saw her looking through the door and listening. Tiger's got the scent. Hie away, sir!"

The dog hunted for a few moments, and found the trail. With a single yelp he disappeared in the thicker part of the underbrush, and the whole pack bounded yelping after him. They pursued the trail for a mile through the swamp, and mounted a hill on the opposite side. They disappeared over the summit, and Old Tige, already far behind, reached the highest point and came to a standstill. He remained for one or two minutes surveying the surrounding country, and then struck off at a right angle from the trail, with his nose high in the air and his tail straight with his back. He went in the direction of a large plateau covered with tall pines and salamander hills. Occasionally he would stop, as if listening to the yelping of the hounds as it rapidly grew fainter in the distance. Having traversed the plateau, which was five miles in width, he came to the outskirts of a cane-brake, and bent his nose to the ground. He proceeded two miles along the edge of the dense growth of cane until he found a path which led through. The traveler would be compelled to pick his way through the mud and water by stepping carefully upon poles and cypress roots. The dog sniffed the ground attentively at the entrance to the swamp, and a sudden swishing of the tail and a loud snorting showed that he had found the trail. Before entering he looked behind him and listened for the dogs, standing the meanwhile on three legs and as still as a statue. No sound could be heard. They had followed the trail and had gone fifteen miles, while the old dog had cut across the country and headed them off.

He pulled through the mire, clambered over the slippery poles, jumped from root to root and from tuft to tuft, until he gained the opposite side. Here he found a fence that was decayed and tumbling down. It inclosed a field that had been in disuse for several years, and that was overgrown with young pines and dewberry vines. Near the opposite side of the field was an abandoned log cabin. The mud had long ago dropped from the cracks between the logs, the roof was partly gone, the chimney had fallen and was a pile of mud and sticks, the windows had lost their shutters years ago, and the hewn slabs, with which the floor was laid, were disarranged and decayed. The berries in the field were ripe, and the dog consumed considerable time in wandering around among the pines, his nose all the while close to the ground and his tail whisking fiercely. The cause is easily explained: the man had picked the berries and breakfasted in the field. The trail was hot, but the dog remained silent, every now and then raising his head and peering about him. The old house was almost hidden by young mulberries and China trees. The dog left the trail finally and trotted to the door of the cabin. He placed his fore feet upon the block that served as a step, and looked cautiously around the interior. His victim lay upon his face in a corner, sound asleep, his forehead resting upon his right arm, and the pistol clasped in his right hand. The dog pricked up his drooping ears and eyed him curiously. He noiselessly gained the doorsill, still keeping his eyes cautiously on the sleeping man. He advanced one foot upon a slab to the right, but it rocked and made a slight noise. He withdrew his foot, and tried another slab on the left. This was steadier, and bore his weight firmly. He put out his foot to try the next slab, but it was unsteady; he tried another, and it rattled. He waited a few moments, and then backed noiselessly through the door and regained the ground.

Another method of approach was left. The wily old dog crept under the sill and proceeded under the house toward the corner in which the deserter slumbered. About three feet from where he lay a slab had been displaced, leaving an opening six feet long and twelve inches wide. The dog cautiously poked his head through the hole, planted his fore paws upon a beam, and gradually brought his shoulders upward until he stood almost erect upon his hind legs. With a dextrous, noiseless spring, he brought his hind feet upon the beam, and stood a moment in this cramped position. Finding the sleeping man still undisturbed, he approached him carefully, taking his steps slowly. He smelled the man's muddy boots, drawing deep and silent inspirations, and sniffed along his entire person until he reached his head, and here he breathed with much greater caution. The man was in his shirt sleeves, and his large, strong neck presented a tempting field for attack. But the dog was old and his fangs were worn with age. He regarded the exposed neck so eagerly, and his whole frame was so rigid, that it seemed he was on the point of taking a desperate step. Had the man lain with his throat uppermost perhaps the dog would not have hesitated. As it was, while he was regarding the bait that tempted him he suddenly pricked up his ears and listened attentively. He heard the yelping of the hounds as they emerged from the canebrake. Stepping cautiously backward he disappeared through the hole, slunk into a dark corner under the cabin, and lay down.

The hounds crossed the fence, noisy, furious, and bloodthirsty. They tore wildly through the patch of berries, and their noise awakened the man. He listened, and then sprang to his feet. In a moment he realized his horrible position—alone, in a vast wilderness, with no human being to assist him in battling with a terrible death, and with a pack of infuriated bloodhounds, trained in the love of human gore, to tear out his heart and strew his entrails upon the earth. His first feeling was one of overpowering terror. He trembled in every joint and his teeth chattered with fear. He looked around wildly and despairingly, and discovered a joist above his head. Securing the pistol in his belt, he sprang upward and caught the joist with his hands. It was old and rotten, and swayed under his weight, but he pulled himself upon it and awaited the dogs.

They rushed blindly into the cabin, foaming and yelping, eagerly smelled the slabs on which the man had slept, ran around the cabin barking and hungry for blood, crawled under the house, scoured the shrubbery, went over the field again, and rushed madly back into the cabin. Knowing that they would find him sooner or later, and that every moment he lost lessened the distance between himself and the human bloodhounds, the man selected the largest and finest looking dog and sent a bullet between his eyes. The hound rolled over with quivering limbs and stiffening muscles. The dogs were thunderstruck, but not dismayed. One strong young hound made a desperate spring and fastened his fangs in the man's heel. He fell with a shot through the brain. The man had three shots left, and he must reserve at least one for a last extremity. He had killed two dogs, and counted nine remaining. With two more well-directed shots he reduced the number to seven.

By this time the fugitive had warmed to his work. The blood tingled in his hands and arms, and he felt his great strength bulging and swelling his muscles. No time was to be lost. He replaced the pistol, stood upon the joist, and pushed a few boards from the roof. Grasping the rotten rafters, he pulled himself upon the roof, and sought a bludgeon. The boards were of oak, and were weighted down with logs, which ran transversely, and which he easily pushed off with his feet. With little difficulty he secured a worm-eaten, partially decayed board, four feet long and an inch thick. By striking it over the end of a log he split it, and was thus armed with a powerful weapon. The man was naturally brave, and at this moment his strength seemed so enormous that he felt himself a match for a hundred hounds. The dogs were still in the house, howling and baffled.

Martin crawled carefully to the eaves, and prepared to give battle to the deadly enemy. He looked upon the ground, but the dogs were not visible; and, steadying himself, he dropped heavily and caught nimbly on his feet. He felt that he must finish the fight within half an hour, or he would be confronted with carbines and pistols. The dogs heard him drop, and sprang through the door. The man turned quickly and raised his weapon; the seven dogs made a furious onslaught, but a powerful blow upon the head sent the leader rolling dead upon the ground. The rotten board was strained by the blow, and he must use it more carefully. Six ferocious dogs still confronted him, and two eyes that he did not see blinked at him from under the cabin. The vigor with which the deserter met the attacks, and the threatening attitude that he maintained, disconcerted the dogs, and they ran around him at a safe distance, their teeth glistening, their tails whisking, their heads bent to the ground, the froth dripping from their protruding tongues.

The man suddenly dashed at a dog, and mortally wounded him with a heavy blow on the back of the neck. While he was in the act of striking, and before he could regain his defensive attitude, an active young dog, with fangs as sharp as knives, sprang upon his shoulders and fastened his teeth in the back of the man's neck. The other dogs, emboldened by the success of their companion, made a furious attack from behind. The man faced about, with the fangs of the hound still imbedded in his neck and his back ripped and lacerated with the sharp claws of the suspended dog, and struck about wildly and desperately, breaking the jaw of one and the leg of another. He made one terrible blow, that, in his agony, missed the mark, and his noble bludgeon was shattered against the ground.

The dog gnawed at his neck, and imbedded his fangs still deeper in the flesh, causing the blood to pour down the man's back and breast. At this moment, when the man was paralyzed with pain and frantic at the loss of his weapon, the two dogs still unhurt that confronted him sprang upon him, buried their teeth in his flesh, and bore him to the ground. He sank upon his knees, threw off the two dogs with a mighty effort, and defended his throat with all the desperation and strength that roused his every energy and sustained his failing hopes. They snapped at his hands and tore them, and completely stripped the shirt from his body. They plowed his skin with their claws, and the blood gushed from a hundred wounds. One of the dogs allowed the strong hand of the man to close upon his throat, and then he was flung stunned to the ground. Catching an idea from this manoeuvre, the man allowed the other hound to seize his arm, then took him by the leg and dashed him against the house.

The deserter was growing faint; but he staggered to his feet, grasped the hind legs of the dog that clung so tenaciously to his neck, snapped the bones as though they were reeds, and jerked him from his hold, tearing the flesh horribly.

By one of those curious eccentricities of fortuitous chance, the man found a weapon in his hands in the dog that he held by the legs, and that snapped at his legs, and writhed and squirmed and howled. The two hounds that he had succeeded in throwing off rallied their strength and returned to the attack cooler and wiser, but none the less terrible. The man backed against the wall, and met the charge by knocking down a dog with the one he held in his hands. Finding that he could not advantageously wield his heavy weapon in such close proximity to the wall, he suddenly advanced and knocked over the other dog in the act. The blows, heavy as they were, did not disable his two antagonists. Every time that he swung down his living bludgeon it became weaker and its struggles more faint. He struck rapidly and carefully, husbanding his strength, yet every now and then missing his object, as it would adroitly evade the blow, and bringing down his heavy club against the ground with a dull thud, crushing its bones and dislocating its vertebrae. In a short while it was but a lifeless mass of broken bones and bruised flesh. The wounded hounds had hidden in the thicket, and the two that remained had become bruised and crippled, and had changed their tactics into harrassing their enemy until he had expended all his strength.

The man felt himself growing sick and faint, and he recognized the necessity of immediately bringing the fight to a close by capturing his enemies with strategy. He threw aside his weapon, but the dogs simply glared at him. If he could only get them in his clutches again he would be saved, but experience had made them cunning. So he suddenly threw up his hands and fell, and they sprang for his throat. Quick as a cat he seized a throat in each hand, turned them over upon the ground with great difficulty, planted his great knees upon their breasts, and, crushing their ribs with his remaining strength, choked them until their eyes almost burst from their sockets, until their tongues swelled and hung from their mouths, and until life was extinct.

The terrible fight had lasted two hours. The man staggered to his feet and looked around. Not a soul was in sight. He drew a deep breath, and his naked, bloody chest swelled with triumph. But the loss of blood and the extreme pain of his wounds had so exhausted him that he felt the ground rising to strike him in the face, and, with a heavy lunge, he lay extended upon the ground.

Two glittering eyes, followed by the neck and shoulders of a hound, emerged from under the cabin. The Tiger crept forward softly, but darted back as the man with a desperate effort rose to his hands and knees. The deserter battled bravely with unconsciousness, but was dying of thirst. He crawled painfully along a disused path leading to a spring, while the blood streamed upon the ground. On reaching the spring he drank greedily, and bathed his face and head. The blood poured from his wounds and changed to the color of wine the little stream that flowed from the spring. The dog had followed him unseen, and was crouching behind a thick clump of shrubbery. The man, refreshed by the water, again staggered to his feet, but the pines swam before his eyes and he fell unconscious to the ground. The old dog approached cautiously, and, when within a few feet of his prey, sprang forward and closed his powerful jaws upon the throat of the fainting man.

A woman, pale and haggard, and with the wild light of insanity in her eyes, sat on the ground and held the head of her husband in her lap, and rocked, and moaned, and sang, and cried, and called him vainly. The eyes that stared at the sky were so terribly bloodshot, and the face was so black, and the features so distorted, that it is strange she recognized as her husband the disfigured, lifeless body of Martin, the deserter.

"Corporal Billee"
1891

ALBION W. TOURGÉE

Albion W. Tourgée (1838–1905) is one of the most colorful and controversial figures to come out of the Civil War. Born in Ohio, Tourgée fought in a New York regiment during the Civil War, then moved with his wife to North Carolina, where he became a radical carpetbagging lawyer who sought fervently to ensure racial equality for African-Americans and heaped scorn and disdain upon unregenerate Southerners. As a newspaper editor and, later, a judge, Tourgée evoked great hostility among North Carolinians and for a time was threatened by the Ku Klux Klan. In return, he wrote an exposé of the Klan, The Invisible Empire *(1880), as well as a novel about the Klan,* A Fool's Errand *(1874; later titled* A Royal Gentleman*). When his political and judicial career ended in the 1870s, Tourgée turned to writing, producing many novels and tales, including* Bricks without Straw *(1880), a novel that expressed his deep concern about the state of African-Americans in the South. In the short story "'Corporal Billee'" (published in* Cosmopolitan *in May 1891), Tourgée tenderly portrays the fate of a young man who joins the army because of his love of horses.*

*D*idn't know Corporal Billee?" asked the captain with a look of unfeigned surprise. "And you belonged to the old Fourteenth corps, too?"

"But there were a good many corporals who wore 'the acorn,' if I remember rightly?"

"Of course—but there was only one Billee."

The reply was greeted with a shout of laughter by the little company in the smoking compartment of the sleeping car. We were on the express bound north from Chattanooga, and had just rounded the point of Lookout mountain, looking up out of the shadow in the valley at the windows of the great hotel upon the summit, which flashed and glowed in the setting sunlight as red and fitful as the glare which some of us remembered in the centre of the white puffs of smoke in the same place so many years before. Naturally enough, our thoughts and talk were of that time which had made the region memorable as the theatre of one of the most remarkable conflicts in the history of warfare.

"Tell us about him," said one of the youngsters, with suggestive importunity.

"Well," answered the captain good-humoredly, "I don't mind. It may help pass the time and perhaps enable you young fellows to understand how the region a man has once fought over is ever after peopled with ghosts for him."

The captain shifted his cigar, drew a long whiff and, letting the smoke escape slowly from his lips, began:

Just how Billee became attached to our regiment nobody knew, and why he remained with it no one could guess. He suddenly appeared inside our lines one morning at "stable call." We had made our first march the day before, from Cincinnati into Dixie. We did not know where we were going, and it made little difference to anyone where we went. The enemy was somewhere in front of us and we were going to find him. That was about all we knew of war. We were one of those crack regiments of which so much was expected in those days—twelve troops splendidly mounted and commanded by a man who, though he had only worn an eagle for a fortnight, already had his eye upon one of the "stars" which were blazing across the firmament in such confusing splendor just at that time. He meant to be under it when it finally fell—and he was.

For offence or defence we were as yet quite harmless. Fortunately, the foe was still a good way off. Even Buell, who could see an enemy farther and conduct a retreat more expeditiously than any man we ever served under, could hardly make up his mind where his adversary was or which way he was headed. If we had stumbled across a fight we should undoubtedly have played havoc with somebody, either before or behind us, for not one in twenty could have stopped his horse, if once started on a run, to save his life.

The roads were heavy. It was late when we camped, and the raw troopers were sore and stiff when summoned the next morning to clean mud-stained horses and equipments. Billee was hanging about the tether rope of troop D, the color company, which, either because its captain was the best horseman or the shrewdest negotiator in the regiment, had received by far the finest mount. A hundred blood bays, varying hardly half a hand in height, bore the troop to which was confided the colors of the Eleventh. The men who rode them were yet unable to appreciate their good fortune. Few of them had ever laid a leg over a saddle until a week before, when we had drawn our new "McClellans," which some were yet unable to adjust without oversight. Not half of them had ever rubbed down a horse in their lives or tried to guide or control one until we had been ordered to mount and "march, march away" toward the enemy, who, whether they fought or ran, would have us at equal disadvantage.

We had had a jolly time the day before, with innumerable adventures along the way; but not a man of the whole command will ever look back to that march without the most poignant memories. Perhaps you never belonged to the cavalry? Well, you can't appreciate it then. Given a hard-bitted, hard-trotting horse, and a man who knows no more about riding than the horse does of astronomy; give him a carabine, a pistol, an iron-cased sabre, a canteen, a haversack, blanket, overcoat and everything else a new recruit considers necessary to his comfort, and put him on a hard Kentucky pike with a thousand more just like him and encumbered in the same manner, and let the orders be: "Walk!" "Trot!" "Trot!" "Walk!" for ten hours on a stretch, and then guess that man's condition the next morning if you can!

There is hardly any torture more terrible. The steady thump—thump of the saddle not only bruises but shocks and jars, until back, ribs, head, shoulders, lungs, liver—every part of the tortured torso—is shaken, strained, bruised and filled with protesting pain. Then, too, the saddle chafes the limbs, the accoutrements whack and bang in every conceivable and inconceivable way; and, long before night comes, the sufferer would welcome anything that would give a moment's relief—would count a fight, with a bullet as his share, a welcome release from his three years' enlistment. Every man in the regiment would have deserted that night but for the fact that he would rather have stayed and be killed than move a leg to get away. If the enemy had happened our way about that time there would have been a terrible fight, for everyone of us would have died where he lay rather than run a hundred yards to escape.

It was a beautiful spot where we encamped—on a slope carpeted with blue grass, a grove of oaks scattered along the crest, and a clear stream bursting out from the crevices of the flat stone wall of a spacious spring-house. We unsaddled, fed, watered and tethered the horses; made our coffee, ate our rations and got to sleep—somehow! The ground was a little moist, but we all had rubber blankets, so that didn't matter. I don't think it would have mattered if we had had no blankets at all. I would have been glad to have lain down if the mud had been a foot deep, and I really do not think the softest couch in the world would have been any more grateful to us than the bare ground that night. I never heard so many groans in my life. Men were literally rolling over the whole camp, trying to find relief from the pain which was only momentarily allayed by a change of position.

The next morning—well, words cannot do the subject justice! It was a terrible initiation, but it made us soldiers. A man who could live through that could stand anything, and when we got over it we had the consolation of knowing that the worst part of our service was behind us. That is always something.

At "stable call," as I said, Billy was found already at home among the horses of D troop. How he came there nobody knew; the guards declared that no one had passed their lines and the sentry with the horses had seen nothing of him until, a few minutes before, he had found him quietly patting the muzzle of the captain's extra mount—a dark bay stallion of magnificent appearance, the purchase of which had lightened the captain's purse of a goodly sum; but which, on the departure of his accustomed keeper, had developed such a vicious temper that as yet his new owner had not cared to attempt to ride him. This horse seemed to have caught Billy's fancy, and the animal, which the orderly declared was "all teeth and toe-corks" when he tried to approach him, submitted to the stranger's caresses, not only without remonstrance, but with apparent pleasure; but when anyone else approached the ears were laid back, the wicked eyes gleamed, and it was made evident that "Extra's" amiability was not of a promiscuous character.

Of course, being in an enemy's country, Billy was regarded with suspicion. He was of a tall, gaunt figure, with just a hint of beard upon a face singularly devoid of expression, except when lighted up with admiration for a horse. His vocabulary was curiously limited and his words were uttered in a dead monotone. To all inquiries as to his identity he answered wonderingly, "Billee;" to all questions regarding his motive for coming within the lines he replied with enthusiasm:

"Horse! Billee love horse!"

He waved one hand toward the horses of the troop as he spoke and twisted the other familiarly in the flowing mane of "Extra," which no one else dared to touch. For the rest, his ideas appeared purely mercenary.

"Gimme a thent!" he said suddenly, holding out his hand to the captain's orderly. He spoke the last word with a lisp, which did not otherwise appear in his speech.

"All right," answered the nonplussed soldier; "I'll give you a quarter if you'll clean that horse," pointing to "Extra," as the vicious stallion had been christened.

The man seemed dimly to understand what was required of him. He turned toward the horse, nodded his head slowly, spat on his hands, rubbed them together and asked, with some approach to animation:

"Gimme a thent?"

"No; I'll give you a quarter!" roared the orderly, with the habit one gets of speaking in a boisterous tone to a person who does not seem to fully understand. He threw him the curry-comb and brush as he spoke. Billy picked them up, examined them carefully, and, with a grunt of approval, laid them down at the stallion's feet. Then taking off his coat and hat, he folded the former and laid the latter carefully upon it; slipped his suspenders from his shoulders, tied them around his hips and, springing forward, caught up the brush and, grasping "Extra's" foretop, began to brush his head in a manner so furious that one looked to see the black muzzle open and the white teeth gleam through them in angry resentment. Instead of this the vicious animal bent his neck, half closed his eyes and submitted with evident enjoyment to a grooming which, though apparently rough, was executed with skill and care. When he had finished using the brush he threw it on the ground and, seizing the rubbing cloth, went over every part of the bowed head—ears, eyes and nostrils—with a swift, furious skill that woke the admiration of the raw troopers, many of whom were yet afraid of the animals they rode, and all of whom were unwilling to bestow a tithe of the energy he displayed upon their work, even if they had possessed the skill.

"That-away!" panted Billy, proudly facing the awkward squad, who had been watching the performance.

"Well, by thunder!" exclaimed the subaltern who had charge of the "stable duty," but was hardly more familiar with its performance than the men themselves.

"Lieutenant!"

The officer turned quickly and saluted awkwardly his colonel, who, despite the fact that he had ridden thirty miles the day before without once unbracing from his erect position in the saddle, was astir fresh and alert to see that his men performed their new duties faithfully if not satisfactorily. He was a regular army officer, who had undertaken to put the crude material of the Eleventh into shape, with the fixed determination to make it the best cavalry regiment in the volunteer service. He was an ambitious as well as a thoroughly trained soldier, who meant that his new command should win him promotion, and knew that, to do so, it must first be well disciplined—taught to do its work well, to obey implicitly and endure fatigue and discomfort patiently. These qualities he fully realized were infinitely more valuable than tactical proficiency.

It was a hard task. How well he accomplished it the world knows. He never forgot the means by which he had won his way to renown, and when he had two stars upon his shoulders, came the very first day he wore them to tell the men of his old regiment that he owed to them the honors he had received.

They idolized him then, but he was a terribly hard master in those early days and was far from popular with the men or officers under his command. His idea of the best way to train men to be soldiers was to compel them to march, and, if occasion served, to give them a chance to fight.

"A month in the field is worth a year in camp," was the keynote of his method of making raw troops the most effective soldiers in the world.

So, as soon as his men were mounted, the Eleventh started on their first march; in a month they saw their first fight, and in three months felt themselves to be veterans, as indeed they were.

The colonel was inspecting men and officers at their "stable duty," after their first day in the saddle. What he had seen thus far had not tended to put him in a good humor. He was what was called "a born horseman" himself, and knew that half the efficiency of a cavalry regiment lay in the care bestowed upon its horses. He could not only ride and fight, but he could groom and shoe a horse as well.

"Lieutenant!" he repeated, answering the salute, "what's that man's name?"

He indicated Billy with a glance.

"I—I don't know, sir," stammered the lieutenant.

"You don't? Never let me hear you say that again. Learn the names of your men, if you don't learn anything else."

"But, colonel—"

"Not a word, sir. Make him take off that white shirt and tell your captain my orders are that he be made a corporal—at once. A man who knows how to groom a horse deserves promotion in such company."

"All right, sir," answered the lieutenant, and the colonel strode away muttering angrily to himself.

"Here, you man," said the puzzled officer, turning to Billy, who had resumed his occupation. "You!" he repeated, taking a step nearer. The stallion laid back his ears threateningly. "I say, you!" roared the lieutenant.

"Name Billee," said the stranger vacantly. As he turned and faced the officer his head showed a symmetrical dome in which it seemed the most powerful intellect might be fitly throned, yet one saw at a glance that he was only a simple original.

"Well, Billy," said the officer soothingly.

"Gimme a thent," interrupted Billy.

The men laughed. The officer grew red in the face.

"You must go to the captain, Billy."

"Him?" asked Billy, indicating the colonel with a gesture.

"Yes; it's the colonel's orders. Come along."

Billy shook his head.

"Bad man!" he said, spitting on the ground and glancing at the retreating colonel. "Bad man! Billee clean horse!"

He resumed his work, the stallion standing guard over him, and as the mountain would not go to Mahomet, Mahomet must come to the mountain. So reasoned the lieutenant, and went for Captain Ellerton, to whom he communicated the colonel's order.

Billy had just finished grooming the vicious bay when the captain arrived. It was evident that he was well pleased to find some one who could handle his extra horse. Billy, however, paid no attention to the captain's presence, but after stepping back to admire the shining coat and returning to give it another and yet another touch, he walked up to the orderly who had agreed to pay for his services, and extending his hand said in his accustomed monotone:

"Gimme a thent."

The soldier handed him the quarter he had promised—one of the paper postal-notes of the time. Billy turned it over questioningly, and handed it back.

"Gimme a thent," he repeated.

"Opposed to paper currency, are you?" interposed the captain. "Here's a silver quarter; how'll that do?"

Billy looked at the captain solemnly, took the coin, bit it, and apparently satisifed with his inspection, put it in his pocket.

"White thent," he said gravely. "Thank ye, sir."

He bowed his head by thrusting his chin out and then drawing it in two or three times, without moving his body.

Then he turned to a trooper who was having trouble with his horse and said, cheerfully:

"Rub him for ye, gimme a thent!"

Without waiting for a reply he began upon the restive animal, which at once ceased kicking and biting and submitted patiently to his manipulation.

"Well, I vow!" exclaimed the captain, "he'd be worth something to the troop, wouldn't he? I think, boys, we'd better chip in a cent apiece and keep him. What do you say?"

As usual, the official jest was received with approval by the men, and more than one, responding to the captain's familiarity, offered some amendment.

"Tell you what, lieutenant," said the captain, "I'm afraid he'd make a sorry corporal, but as it's the colonel's orders we'll have an extra one. I'll pay him myself and keep him to look after that brute and help around the 'shebang' generally. Billy," he continued, advancing toward the new arrival, "how would you like to go with me and take care of this horse?" pointing toward the extra mount.

"Your horse?" asked Billy admiringly. "Nice horse!"

He left his work to go and straighten out the stallion's mane.

"Will you go?"

"Way off?" indicated Billy with a wave of his arm.

"Yes; all over Dixie."

"Ride horse?" patting the stallion.

"Yes; whenever I don't want him," answered the captain; adding humorously, "and that's likely to be the bigger part of the time."

The captain was a handsome, genial fellow whom the men all liked. Billy felt the charm of his manner, and in a little while was installed as general assistant in the mess tent of the officers of troop D, whose especial duty it was to look after the captain's horse, "Extra." From that time he was known sometimes as "Extra Billy," but more generally as "Corporal Billee." Instead of a worsted chevron the men furnished him with a set made of yellow silk cord with tassels at the ends, to show the "extra" character of his rank.

It was a foolish, almost a wicked thing to do. Billy was evidently the unfortunate child of some family who would mourn his absence even more than his death, because of the uncertainty attaching to it. He had no doubt followed the regiment, attracted by the horses, and perhaps by the music, for which he displayed great fondness. It was a thoughtless act to take the poor fellow into the maelstrom of war toward which we were headed, and away from the home that had protected his incapacity; yet perhaps it was better after all than to have put him outside the lines and left him to wander wherever his weak fancy might dictate, which was the only alternative.

He was kindly and obliging, except to those to whom he took a dislike or from whom he received harsh treatment. For them he manifested his repugnance in approved oriental fashion by turning away and spitting on the ground. With the officers and men of troop D he soon became a prime favorite and could not do too much for them. He had a natural gift as a horse-tamer, and Captain Ellerton was soon able to use his extra horse, but both pride and discretion led him to do so only on particular occasions. On review and parade, and sometimes at the outset of a march, he made his humble attendant happy by riding the bay stallion. At other times the horse was left in Billy's charge, who would walk by his side all day long rather than see a hair wet with sweat upon his favorite.

He was of immense strength and never seemed to feel fatigue. One day, after a hard march, he thrashed the bully of the regiment, who had picked at him for a month, to the infinite satisfaction of everyone, especially the colonel, who for once looked on approvingly at a fight.

"Isn't that my corporal, Ellerton?" he asked when it was over. On being informed that it was, he said: "It's a pity his wits are not brighter. He's got good qualities. He's a good horseman, a gentleman, and knows how to resent an insult. You did just right, my man," he added as Billy, grimy and bloody, passed by him toward his company's limits.

"Thank ye, sir," said Billy, with his usual comical bow, as he paused to dust his hat. Then looking timidly at the officer, he added in his customary monotone: "Gimme a thent."

The colonel laughed, fished a silver quarter out of his pocket, and with another bow and thanks Billy went on. Up to that time the colonel had been an object of particular aversion to him. After this incident his admiration for that officer was only second to his devotion to troop D.

He was mortally afraid of guns, but having been ordered to hold the captain's horse once during an engagement, he did not attempt to leave his post though the bullets whistled around him and he was trembling in every limb; and one sultry day, during a long, hot fight, he won a cheer by appearing upon the scene loaded down with canteens full of cold water, and having first handed one to the colonel, distributed the others along the line unmindful of the danger.

His constant inquiry for a cent would seem to indicate a covetous disposition, but nothing could be farther from Billy's nature. He would give a cent as readily as ask for one, provided always it was not his last. He had no idea of the value of money and very little of its use. When the captain became a major Billy still remained with him, and, being sent now and then to the sutler's, learned that the purchasing power of a "thent"—every coin was a cent to him—was considerably increased by a statement of his employer's rank. After that, when he laid down his money, he always said, "Major," and I am bound to admit that the kind-hearted dealer rarely failed to give him what he asked for whether his cent was "white" or not.

One thing which Billy would have, if possible, was a clean collar and cuffs—or, at least, white ones—and no presentation was ever made by admiring friends that was more heartily appreciated than when troop D chipped in and bought a set of enamelled steel cuffs and collar of the same character for the patient fellow who had curried their horses, brought their water, cut their wood, and done a thousand other kindnesses in addition to the duties he owed his employer.

Three years afterward the Eleventh were indeed "veterans"—what were left of them, that is. Their exploits had become historical. They had won "stars" for two colonels; one had been killed in battle and another lived, the victim of wounds which fame could never heal. Three hundred and seventy-six: that was the number of reënlistments out of our twelve companies! Yet we were still the "fighting Eleventh." Ellerton was the colonel now. Those left of us after the reënlistment furloughs were granted were ordered into camp to wait for recruits, fresh horses and repairs generally. We needed a rest and it was admitted that we deserved it. Only once or twice had we passed a fortnight in one place since we had first answered to "Boot and Saddle."

The post to which we were assigned was Shell Mound, a little station on the railroad twenty miles below Chattanooga, just opposite the mouth of the Sequatchie, where there was a ferry, and a road leading across the Sand mountain to Pond Spring, Georgia, by which we had flanked Bragg out of his stronghold—Chattanooga—a year before. The cantonment was the pleasantest I ever saw. The little stream running down from Nickajack cave—the mouth of which yawns dark and grim against the mountain side—divides the plateau, which has been the scene of so many savage conflicts, in its course to the river half a mile away. A hospital, a small convalescent camp, a stockade held by a company of colored troops, and quite a cluster of buildings filled with forage and stores constituted the post of which Colonel Ellerton was commandant. The garrison numbered about 1000 men, but hardly half of them were "effectives," and there were not horses enough to mount all of the cavalry.

Our camp soon became very homelike. The wives of several of the officers and of some of the enlisted men came to visit them; friends and relatives were coming and going, for we were so far in the rear of the army as to be considered almost beyond the seat of war. We were presently to be in its very vortex, but did not know it.

Among the ladies who became denizens of our camp was the wife of the colonel and their little daughter Maggie, a winsome child not yet five years old. "Corporal Billee" had remained the faithful servitor of Colonel Ellerton, though "Extra" had long since ceased to be what his name implied, but was a war-horse, worn and scarred, though still a favorite, and as ill-tempered as ever.

On the arrival of the colonel's wife and daughter Billy at once transferred his allegiance to them. Very naturally the young wife found much to engage her attention in her new and delightful surroundings, and was not unwilling the faithful fellow should often relieve her of the care of the child. Mounted on a snow-white mule, which had somehow become the property of the regiment, with "Corporal Billee" carefully holding the leading rein, sometimes riding and sometimes running beside her, the bright-eyed child explored the camp and the surrounding valley almost at her own sweet will.

But if Billy was the faithful guardian of little Maggie, his devotion to the colonel's wife was something marvellous. He was always deferential to ladies. Never was he known to pass even the most shabbily dressed woman without removing his hat. He had evidently been tenderly reared, and his gentle, decorous manner, as well perhaps as gratitude for his devotion to her husband, led the fair young wife to treat him with a consideration he had probably never before received except from his mother, of whom it is likely that her kindness brought some dim suggestion. His eyes followed her movements with the wistfulness of a pet dog. He read her thought almost before she was aware of it herself; studied her wishes and anticipated her desires.

I am sorry to say that Billy had grown very profane since he joined the regiment; and profanity uttered in his habitual monotone was far more horrible than if varied by the emphasis which fuller intelligence gives. It was enough to make the wickedest man's blood run cold to hear him pour out in even, unvaried accents the uncomprehended anathemas he had picked up around the campfire. More than one chaplain had reproved him, but they had too frequently done so in harsh or angry tones. Billy did not like to be "hollered at," as the boys said. Even if pleasantly done it was apt to make him lose his head. He did not mind being bantered or teased, so long as it was done in a moderate tone of voice, but he would not be scolded in any tone. It made him angry and sometimes vicious to be blamed. So when the chaplains reproved him he would turn away, spit on the ground and treat them to choice specimens from his vocabulary of profanity. Once was enough. No chaplain ever tried it a second time. It was like hearing a corpse swear.

It would only have needed a hint from the colonel's wife, I believe, to have sealed his lips forever from any profane expression. But this was not enough; the good woman tried to teach him its wickedness, and explain to him the idea of salvation. She read the Scriptures to him, explaining the words in soft, low tones. Billy listened with rapt attention. He preferred the New Testament narrative, and she read, over and over again, the story of the Christ and the incidents of His childhood and death until the poor fellow became thoroughly imbued with these features of the Gospel, and would repeat them to curious listeners beside the campfires with laughable inconsequence but with the utmost seriousness and a curious dramatic power. He liked best of all the story of Herod's unsuccessful search for "the child Jesus." Herod was a "bad man," for whom Billy showed a most unchristian hate, spitting and stamping his feet with angry vehemence whenever he mentioned the name. The climax of his enjoyment came, however, with the flight into Egypt: "Take the young child and flee—into—into Egypt—into Egypt!" he would exclaim. "Stay there until I come; so bad man—bad man—can't get baby!"

This scene he acted over and over again with little Maggie, until both child and man performed it with the utmost relish. At the words, "Take the young child," she would fling her arms about Billy's neck and he would run across the parade and through the guard line—no one thought of stopping Billy or the colonel's daughter—while they both shouted, "Flee away! flee away!" It was a bit of sacred drama of his own adaptation which he greatly enjoyed enacting. Sometimes they returned after a short absence, and sometimes it would be hours before they came back.

One day the colonel received orders to patrol the east bank of the river to and below Bridgeport for the purpose of breaking up the haunts of bushwhackers, some of whom were reported to have fired upon our trains; and it was decided to give the ladies a picnic, with just enough of real war about it to enable them to comprehend its dangers. All the mounted men of the Eleventh were detailed for this duty. The colonel himself took command, leaving the post in my charge, I being the only captain who was not blessed with a wife to go with him on this novel pleasuring.

It was a gay cavalcade that filed out of our post the next morning. Little Maggie was left in charge of her colored nurse and "Corporal Billee" was especially enjoined not to take her outside of the guard lines, unless "the bad man" should come for her. This allusion to the Herodian episode awakened all the enthusiasm of his sluggish nature, and he repeated over and over again how he would "flee away" with her, if any harm should threaten. As she could not leave the lines, however, it suited the pretty tyrant's whim to order her faithful drudge to bring her some of the golden hickory leaves, growing far up on the mountain side, which had attracted her attention in their ramble of the day before.

The uneasy feeling an officer is apt to experience when placed in a position of unusual responsibility was just beginning to take hold of me when I saw him start to perform her bidding. Of course, the officers of the post had often talked of what should be done in the event of an attack. We had no artillery, though the colonel had several times asked for a couple of guns, that we might not be quite without means of defence should we be shelled from across the river. Of course, such a thing was not at all probable, but, in war especially, it is the unexpected that happens. Though no specific plan had been adopted, it was tacitly understood that, if compelled to abandon the stockade, the unmounted part of the command would retreat to the cave, which was easily defensible and would accommodate many times our number. With this possibility in view a supply of arms, ammunition and some quartermaster's stores had been deposited just within the cave, a guard set over them and a low earthwork thrown up near the entrance. Unless cut off from this there was little, if any, fear of capture. The Indians had long ago demonstrated its capacity for defence.

Do what I might I could not shake off the impression that I ought to prepare to carry this plan into execution at any moment. Summoning my subordinates, therefore, I directed everything to be made ready to repel an attack. The officer in command of the convalescent camp was ordered to send a detail at once to occupy the cave, and direct his men on the first alarm to rally on this force without waiting for orders, while the rest of the garrison were to be so disposed as to hold the palisade as long as was prudent and fall back on this stronghold when necessary. It was not the first time that Nickajack had been made a strategic point in a mortal conflict, and war, whether savage or civilized, is waged on the same principles. The old Indian chiefs who are buried on the plateau must have smiled complacently if they heard me echoing the orders they had no doubt given their braves when this wonderful subterranean chasm was the impregnable stronghold of their tribe.

Hardly had these orders been carried into effect when the crack of rifles was heard upon the hillside, and a moment after Billy came rushing down the road waving his hat and shouting, "Rebs! Rebs!" The long roll had scarcely begun to sound when a six-pounder opened fire across the river. It all flashed upon me in an instant!

A raiding party of the enemy had come down the Sequatchie intending to seize the post, destroy the stores collected there, cut the railroad and retreat over the mountain. In order to accomplish this I guessed that a part of their force had crossed the river during the night, with orders to seize the mouth of the cave when the signal should be given. With regard to this I felt no apprehension. I could see that the convalescents were already in line, and knew that they could hold the position at the mouth of the cave against ten times their number. I judged that the force Billy had discovered was not a large one, and concluded that the enemy, having witnessed the departure of the cavalry, would seek to cross more of their men and carry the place by storm before the main part of the garrison could return. I therefore directed a lieutenant to take the unmounted men of the Eleventh, creep along under cover of the railroad embankment to the bend of the river above, and prevent the enemy from landing at that point. As they were armed with the Spencer carabine and would have good cover, I did not doubt their ability to do this for a considerable time. As the bed of the little stream flowing out of the cave offered a fairly safe line of retreat, if we should be obliged to abandon the palisade, I determined to hold this as long as possible, knowing that an hour, or two hours at farthest, would bring reinforcements; and realizing that the public stores were perhaps even more important than the lives of the garrison.

While these things were taking place and despite the confusion that prevailed I had not failed to give some thought to Billy and his charge. I have said there were two things of which he stood in mortal fear—a gun and a scolding. There was also another—the cave. No persuasion had ever been sufficient to induce him to venture more than a few steps into it. But his anxiety for the child's safety overcame this fear. As he flew past me, his face was lit up with a glow of intelligence I had never seen in it before.

"Rebs! Rebs!" he repeated. "Nick-um-jack! Nick-um-jack! Take the young child and flee away—flee away!"

He dashed into the tent where little Maggie and the nurse were cowering in affright; snatched the child in his arms and started across the plateau toward the mouth of the cave. Satisfied of their safety, I turned my attention to the palisade, where a company of colored troops were standing to their work bravely, though the splinters flew thick about them every time the enemy's six-pounders sent their spiteful greetings through the sheltering piles. There were but two of these guns, and as they had to run up on the river bank to fire, our rifles interfered with their aim and the shots very often went wide of the mark. Enough were well-directed, however, to be troublesome, and those which missed played havoc with the quarters and the convalescent camp beyond. After a time some piles of forage caught fire and it began to look as if we should have to take to our heels and make for the cover of the cave. I have often thought it would have been a quaint parallel with barbaric times if I had been compelled to stand a siege in the cave. Of course the stores outside would have been lost, but I think we could have held Nickajack a long time. It was well provisioned, there was abundance of water and we had plenty of ammunition. I do not see how we could have been dislodged. Perhaps I might have distinguished myself.

Just at this time I heard the rattle of musketry around the point and knew the enemy were trying to cross. Then came the roar of a rifled gun and a shell howled past us and over the heads of the gunners on the other bank. A cheer went up from our men. All knew what it was—the armored car with its two twelve-pounders had steamed up from Bridgeport to our relief. A few minutes after the shouts of the Eleventh were heard as they dashed across the plateau and engaged the force on the hillside. It was all over then in a moment. Colonel Ellerton rode up to me where I stood just outside the palisade, his face pale as ashes and the bay stallion all in a lather.

"My daughter!" he exclaimed, hoarsely.

It was all he could say.

I assured the agitated father of his child's safety, telling him what I had seen; but nothing would relieve his anxiety except the actual sight of her whose danger had filled his heart with agony during his ride to our relief— the hardest ride, by the way, as I afterward learned, that even the Eleventh had ever known. I remember it struck me, when they first appeared, as a curious thing, that so experienced a cavalry officer should come into action with the horses so badly blown. I had no idea then that our men had ridden at top speed for a longer distance at that gait than had ever before been attempted by us. I suppose, if there had been a superior officer on the ground, the colonel would probably have been reprimanded for having hopelessly winded so many of Uncle Sam's valuable horses. It seems a curious thing, but there are times when horses are worth more than men—that is, they are more difficult to provide at the precise point where they are wanted—and this was one of the times, and our camp the particular spot where horses were especially valuable. The truth is, the father had wholly usurped the officer in Colonel Ellerton's breast, and he would have killed every horse in the regiment rather than delay a moment in reaching the spot where he believed his child to be imperilled.

"Come!" he said impatiently, "we must find her."

Calling an officer to relieve me, he dismounted and we walked together to the cave. No one there had seen anything of Billy or the little girl. I felt sure they had entered the cave, and procuring torches, we started to find them. Pursuing the course of the stream that flows through the chasm, we found that the dugout which was used for traversing the narrower portions, where the stream was deepest, was missing, and I was sure then that the half-witted fellow, crazed by the noise of the fight and frenzied with anxiety for his charge, must have taken it and paddled up the stream on his way to the more hidden portions of the cave. So we pressed on, sometimes wading, sometimes swimming from side to side to find a foothold. At length we came upon the dugout lodged against the bank, under a rock overhung with stalactites. The father gazed with a shudder at the deep pool beyond, but by flashing our torches over it the reflection of the bottom, covered with fragments broken from the roof, showed him that his fear was groundless.

We passed this place with difficulty. On the farther bank we found a little shoe. There were only a half-dozen of us, but we made the deep, dark chasm ring with hearty cheers as the colonel pressed it to his lips. Then we shouted the names of the fugitives, but no answer came back to us. At length we came upon the paddle. The man who picked it up, happening to hold his hand to the light, found there was blood upon it.

"That must be the reason he left the canoe," said the colonel. "He is wounded in the arm and could not paddle further. He will probably turn off from the direct route as soon as he can find a hiding place which he thinks entirely secure."

"But he has no torch," I suggested.

"He always carries one or two candles in his breast pocket," was the reply. "You know he is afraid to be alone in the dark."

We soon found traces of melted stearine where it had dropped upon the gray rocks, which confirmed this view. The frightened imbecile had evidently lighted a candle and pressed on into the heart of the mountain. Guided by the white, glistening drops we followed his trail until it finally disappeared. Turning back we found he had abandoned the main passage, and pursuing a narrow and difficult way to the left, finally entered a low opening, through which we crawled, until at length it spread out into a gallery of vast height which none of us had ever seen before.

"Hush!" whispered the colonel, as we rose to our feet. "I thought I heard a child cry."

We held our breath to listen. Then the colonel called.

No answer, only deafening echoes.

We followed a narrow path that ran along one side of the chamber. To the right, the rocks fallen from the roof above were heaped up, forming an uneven slope which reached—we could not guess how high. We halted and called again.

"They are up there," said the colonel, pointing to the rugged pile. "Let us climb the slope."

We ascended cautiously, taking care to disturb none of the loose rocks. The bats were in a state of strange activity. They flew about us and against us in swarms. This satisfied us that they had been disturbed before our entrance. The air was full of that yellow, impalpable dust which is nowhere found but in great caverns—the undisturbed deposit of unnumbered ages. Finally we reached the top of the heap of fallen rocks, where the other wall of the chamber rose sheer into impenetrable darkness. It must have been a hundred feet or more from the bottom of the pile on the side from which we had started.

The colonel called again. No one could recognize word or voice three steps away. The echoes came back, mocking, distorted, horrible, as only such sealed-up galleries of the underworld can distort human speech. We went on, clinging to the gray wall on our right and peering down into the murky gloom on our left and up into the darkness above, while the count-less army of yellow-winged bats circled and squealed above us like demons of destruction. My foot struck something that had a curious feeling. I low-ered my torch and found that I had trodden on a skeleton. The bones were bare and yellow. There was a little heap of dust about it. We shuddered and passed on.

Suddenly a tall figure leaped from a recess of the wall before us.

"Billy!" we all shouted at once. He turned a frightened, uncomprehending look upon us and leaped swiftly down the sharp, rocky slope. The father would have followed, but I held him back. It was well I did so, for at that moment occurred the most terrible thing I have ever experienced. For an instant a curious, rumbling sound seemed to echo through the mass of heaped-up rocks on which we stood. We felt it grate and tremble under our feet. A terrible grinding roar swelled and echoed through the gloom with deafening force. The whole vast pile was in motion! It was as if the earth had broken into fragments and was sinking down—down into impenetrable darkness beneath our feet. Now and then great masses seemed to break away near the summit of the pile and start a granite avalanche that rolled and thundered down the slope. Masses fell from the unseen ceiling—we knew not how many feet above—and echoed like bursting shells as they struck the moving heap below.

Never shall I forget the sickly pallor of the faces about me, seen for a moment through the clouds of yellow dust which soon hid us from each other's eyes, leaving only the fitful glare of the torches visible in the choking waves. Soon these began to disappear. Despite all we could do, we were thrown dazed and deafened down the groaning declivity. I remember being tossed as on a rocky wave, and thinking the end of the world had come. I suppose I must have been insensible for a time, though the echoes were still reverberating through the boundless chamber when I revived.

I could not at once recall what had occurred. All was dark, and my first idea was that the earth had gone back to chaos and that I was alone, buried in its gloom. I heard my name spoken in a whisper; reached out my hand and touched another hand. Then a third voice came out of the darkness— a fourth and a fifth! Our party were all alive, though bruised and terrified. The torches had fallen and been extinguished. The adjutant had a wax taper in his pocket and my matchbox fortunately was watertight. We lighted the taper and found one of the torches.

Was the passage by which we entered still open, or were we buried alive? That was the question each one read in the other faces, but no one uttered it.

"We must find the—the others," said the colonel huskily. He could not bring himself to say "the bodies," though we all knew that was in his thought. No one on the slope of that rolling wave could possibly have lived through that terrible convulsion. This was the conviction each read in the others' eyes.

We climbed the slope and examined the wall to get our bearings; found the niche where the frightened imbecile had hidden, and then started, slowly and carefully, to descend the treacherous incline. Half way down it, as we judged, we found the child unconscious but seemingly unharmed. The rocky torrent had tossed her about on its jagged granite surface; had bruised and beaten her into insensibility, but spared life and limb. A little spirits, rubbed on lips and wrists and temples, revived her so that she began to moan and weep, calling incessantly for "Billee! Billee!"

She did not seem to recognize her father. The poor silly boy who had been her friend and protector in that black and terrible underworld now crowded all other thoughts from her mind.

A sob came up out of the darkness in answer to her cry. We followed the sound and soon found the poor fellow, his limbs wedged beneath a mass of rock that left no hope that he could be rescued alive. He was muttering, brokenly:

"Take—take—the young child—and flee—flee away—into—into Egypt—into Egypt!"

It was soon over. Neither the child's kisses nor the father's entreaties could call back the poor shattered brain to even a moment's consciousness. After some hours of cautious clambering we found our way out.

When we returned the next day the roof had fallen down, and "Corporal Billee" was buried in a sepulchre which will not give up its dead until the angel rolls away the stone and breaks the seals thereof. Facing the setting sun on the plateau before the yawning mouth of Nickajack we set up a white stone, inscribed "Corporal Billee." I wonder if it is there yet!

No one spoke when the story ended. The roar of the train came up through the darkness, harsh and grinding, as we sped on over historic ground. We had not noticed it before, so absorbed had our interest been in the narrative. The captain lighted a fresh cigar, but in a moment threw it away. There were several attempts at conversation, but they were futile, as no one seemed to care to talk; and one by one the little party withdrew, said "good night" and retired each one to his berth. I do not know whether the captain's story kept the others awake or not, but "Corporal Billee" and his tragic death in the Nickajack cave had a large place in my dreams that night.

"Little Lamkin's Battery"
1898

GEORGE CARY EGGLESTON

*George Cary Eggleston (1839–1911), younger brother of the
better-known writer Edward Eggleston, was born in Indiana and
worked there as a schoolteacher, but during the Civil War he fought
in the Confederate army; he later wrote of his service in* A Rebel's
Recollections *(1874). After the war he returned north and had a
distinguished career as a journalist, becoming literary editor of the*
New York Evening Post *and, later, an editorial writer for Joseph
Pulitzer's* New York World. *He also wrote novels and historical
works.* Southern Soldier Stories *(1898) is a collection of tales
and sketches that includes many fine specimens, including the following tale of a deserter's experiences during and after the war.*

For twenty-four hours I had had a man on my mind.

He had been court-martialled and was sentenced to be shot. He
was in the guardhouse.

I know of no good reason why I should have objected to his execution;
he certainly deserved all that he was to get. But I had been his counsel
before the court-martial, and it is never a pleasant thing for a lawyer to
have his client executed.

He belonged officially to me. I had assumed a responsibility for him, and
I felt that it would not be fully discharged if he should be led out and shot.

I had known Beavers for a very brief time; but as his counsel I had learned
much from him in confidence as to his career. He was a person of elective
affinities. It was his habit to desert. He had served on both sides and in many
capacities. He always fought well on whichever side he might happen to be
serving. As a gambler, he always "played his game for all it was worth."

Why he had deserted back and forth in this way without any cogent reason, I never knew. I used to think sometimes that he had done so at first just to try how a new style and color of uniform might suit his particular kind of beauty. His beauty was not in itself conspicuous.

I learned from him incidentally that his various reasons for desertion from one side to the other had not been of a kind that would have controlled the action of a less fastidious man.

On one occasion he had deserted because he smelt mutton from the camp-kettles of the enemy. He had a predilection for mutton.

I learned that he returned to us once, because one night, when he was not quite himself, a comrade had put him to bed and reversed the order of his blankets. Beavers explained to me with great particularity that a certain gray blanket had been placed on top of a certain brown one. He could not be expected to remain with a regiment under such conditions.

At last he had been caught in the act of deserting. He had been tried, and, in spite of such legal acumen as I could bring to bear, had been convicted, sentenced, and the next day but one was to be shot.

Now that he was sure to die, he seemed to make no more of the fact than of any other indifferent thing. I do not mean that he was careless of his fate. He took everything seriously. But facts were to him facts, and he did not worry over them. He did not think it worth while.

So when he was sentenced to death, he adjusted his blankets in the proper order so that he might not have a nightmare, and slept the sleep of the contented.

With all my contempt for Beavers I was sorry that he was to die. There was something in the reckless character of the man that appealed to me. Something that made me feel that it was a pity that this abundant life should be extinguished by a rifle shot.

I had been thinking all night. I had thought of every argument in his favor. I had searched my mind to see if any point had been neglected. Early in the night I had gone to Beavers, and asked him for the aid of suggestion—suggestion that might lead to information. But here again his habits balked me. He said: "I'm gambling in this case on your brains."

I might myself have been willing to do that, but I was gambling with Beaver's life for a stake.

Beavers was of course just that kind of man, whom a self-respecting person feels it his duty to despise; but somehow I could not quite despise Beavers. His coolness appealed to me strongly. His bravado seemed a sort of bravery. His readiness to meet the consequences, and pay the penalties of his own misdeeds, was a thing hard to distinguish from heroism.

He had no principles, of course. He did not pretend to have any. But he had certain methods of thought which seemed to serve him in lieu of principles.

It was just before dawn. I had not slept. As I lay in my tent with the flaps thrown back, all that was discernible was the rather spectral-looking tented city with its precise white rows. I had become so nervous, staring through the dark at the place where I knew the tent pole to be, that at last I turned out for good. I tightened my belt. It was our habit to sleep in our clothes — for reasons.

The first gray of the morning touched the camp, and looking down the row I saw a fragile figure moving from one tent to another, and pausing occasionally in uncertainty. At first I could not be certain whether it was a woman or not. Finally the figure straightened up and stood looking towards the guardhouse; it was that of a woman.

I had not seen a woman in two months.

The camp was silent with that quietude that is so impressive just before the dawn.

After staring at the guardhouse for a moment, while I stood staring at her, the woman turned her eyes and we stood looking at each other. After halting a moment she came staggering up the narrow lane between the two rows of tents, making a peculiar, nervous movement with her hands, but saying nothing. She stood for a few moments a little way from the tent door, clasping and unclasping her hands.

I saw that she was ill. She reeled up against the tent pole, and would have fallen had I not caught her by the arm. I seated her on a log, all the seat there was. After a moment she revived a little, and said in a faint voice, "Beavers."

At that moment reveille sounded. The woman was too evidently ill for me to leave her. I sent a sergeant to attend the roll-call. I directed our cook to provide the woman with coffee and food.

Then I questioned her a little. She had walked twenty-two miles over railroad ties.

She was Beavers's wife.

She said to me: "You are his counsel, I believe?"

"Yes," I replied, "and I have done everything I could to save him."

"No, you have not," she answered. "You have not made the point that he was never legally enlisted as a soldier, I'll warrant! He's over forty-five and can't be conscripted. He was pardoned out of the penitentiary on condition that he should enlist, but the court-martial had no proof of that. There's nothing whatever to show that he's a soldier; and if he ain't a soldier, he can't be punished for desertion. I've come to tell you, for he would never think of it."

I jumped to my feet. I called a sentinel, and told him to take the woman to the guardhouse and make her as comfortable as possible. I mounted my horse and galloped to the station. I roused the telegraph operator two hours before his time. He was a sleepy fellow, but he was accustomed to taking imperative messages out of hours. I gave him this one to the war department: —

> Beavers to be shot to-morrow morning. No proof whatever he was ever soldier. If not soldier, could not have deserted. Too old for conscript law, and no proof of enlistment except Governor Letcher's telegram. Telegram not under oath, not legal testimony. Witness not subjected to cross-examination. As counsel, I demand stay in this man's case.

I rode back to the guardhouse, and found that a new member had been added to the battery. The company was known as Lamkin's Battery.

We named the new member "*Little* Lamkin's Battery," to distinguish it, I suppose, from the big one.

Beavers sat all that morning with his wife's hand in his, and Little Lamkin's Battery in his arms.

He said it looked like its mother. He'd "gamble on that."

Not until within an hour of the time appointed for Beavers's execution did there come a reply from the war department. But when it came it was thoroughly satisfactory. It read thus: —

> Legal points conclusive. Release Beavers and restore him to duty. Duplicate sent to General Walker.

Soon after that Beavers deserted, blankets and all, to "the other enemy" —that was his form of speech, not mine.

The next time I saw him was under peculiar circumstances.

In July, 1865, I went on board the steamer *Morning Star*, at Portland, four miles below Louisville, Kentucky.

I was two or three hours in advance of the sailing of the boat. Only a few people were scattered about the front of the cabin. I went to the clerk, paid for my room and passage, and pocketed thirty dollars in change. A moment later the porter came in with my trunk. I put my hand in my vest pocket to get the dollar due him, but found my thirty dollars gone.

I had all the feelings which a man always has when he finds that his pocket has been picked — which include the feeling of helplessness.

There was on board a brigade of troops going South. They were late enlisters, who had seen none of the fighting. The men were on the deck below, of course. The officers, though their transportation orders called only for deck passage, were by courtesy permitted in the cabin. There were a dozen or twenty of them, mainly rough lumbermen, or something of that kind. They evidently wanted to see a fight. So they concluded to pick that fight with me.

One of them came up to me where I was reading a novel, and began the trouble by saying: "You're a rebel."

"No," I replied. "I was a rebel while the rebellion lasted, but I have taken the oath of allegiance, and am at present a loyal citizen of the United States."

"Well, you *were* a rebel," he said, with more offence in his tone than in his words; "and I want to know what you are doing here in the North."

"I'm not in the North," I replied; "but in the middle of the river that separates the North from the South."

By this time half a dozen others of the crowd had gathered in front of me with angry faces. It was manifestly their purpose to make trouble, and I saw no use in trying to ward it off. They were planning a fight; and whether it was to be a safe one or not, it seemed to me a good time to begin it.

I sprang to my feet and faced them. I was utterly unarmed, while they carried their weapons. I grasped a chair as the only means of defence at hand, and with remarks which are better not repeated, perhaps, told them to come on.

Just at that moment a stateroom door opened behind me, and two warm hands thrust two pistols into my grasp. The next moment a stalwart figure, armed in the same way, stood beside me, and, presenting two pistols, called out: "Hands up, gentlemen! The first man that moves dies. You're twenty to two of us, but —"

Some language followed.

The men threw up their hands.

Without taking his eyes off his adversaries or lowering his weapons, my comrade called out: "Mr. Clerk, send for the captain."

When the captain came, my comrade reported that these men had made an unwarranted assault upon an inoffensive passenger, and said: "They have no business in the cabin, anyway. As a first-class passenger, I call on you to send 'em below, where they belong."

The captain was willing enough. He had been three times arrested during the war for aiding "rebel sympathizers." A minute later these officers had become deck passengers.

Then I turned to my deliverer, and to my astonishment he was Beavers. He had grown stout, and was resplendent in a suit of clothes with checks so broad that it might easily have taken two persons to show the pattern; otherwise he was the same old nonchalant, reckless Beavers, ready to gamble upon any chance and to pay his losses though the payment might be with his life.

I made my identity known to him of course. He replied immediately: "Why, of course, I reckonized you long before this thing occurred, and I have been trying to get an excuse for speaking to you. Because you see when you came aboard in mufti I didn't know who you was, and so I lifted thirty dollars out of your clothes. I wouldn't have done it if I'd a' known it was you, and now I want to hand it back. I could just as easily have picked that other fellow's pocket—the one that picked the quarrel with you. I never go back on my friends, never! And I've never forgot how you got me out of that scrape."

He handed me back the thirty dollars and I thanked him. He said: "Don't mention it." He added, though I never knew what he meant by it: "I'll square the whole thing with that other feller. He's got more'n thirty dollars in *his* wad."

I naturally felt a little warm towards Beavers. I owed him my life. Therefore when he suggested some alcoholic celebration of the incident I compromised on a cigar. However little you may esteem a man, it is difficult to snub him a few minutes after he has saved your life.

Beavers went to the baggage-master and said something to him which I didn't hear. The baggage-master shook his head in dissent.

"Oh, that's all right," said Beavers; "it's five dollars to you, old man."

"Oh, well, that's different," said the baggage-master, and two minutes later Beavers was searching one of his trunks. Presently he came up with a wad of papers in his hand and we returned to the cabin. There he spread out some architectural designs for a gorgeous monument, and said: "Look at that. That's the design of the monument I've just put up over that wife of mine. She was a mighty good sort, and I've spent good money to give her a proper send-off. I've paid five thousand dollars to the architect for the design, and fifteen thousand dollars to have it built. You see business is good with me just now. I've got a faro bank at Louisville and another at Evansville and two at Cairo, and another at St. Louis, and three at

Memphis and one at Vicksburg, and two at New Orleans. As for me *I run the river and make what there is in it.*"

Suddenly a thought occurred to him.

"By the way," he said, "you remember about Little Lamkin's Battery? Well, he's on board." Beckoning to a negro nurse, he said: "Bring that little rascal here."

A few minutes later the nurse returned, having a peculiarly bright, three-year-old boy in charge, whom I greeted as an old friend. After talking with the little chap for a few moments I turned to Beavers and said: "What are you going to make out of him, Beavers?"

"Something better than his father is," he replied, "for his mother's sake; and that reminds me you're just out of the war and you've got your way to make. It won't do for you to know *me.* If you ever meet me goin' up and down the river, I'll cut you dead and don't you say nothing."

Part III

The Home Front

Lucretia Smith's Soldier
1864

MARK TWAIN

Born in Hannibal, Missouri, Samuel Langhorne Clemens (1835–1910) found himself in the late 1850s in New Orleans, where he became the pilot of a riverboat freighter. His sympathy for the South led him, it is believed, to join the Louisiana Guards in 1860–61 (an experience reflected in his "Quintus Curtius Snodgrass" letters published in the New Orleans Crescent *in early 1861). Then, in June 1861, he returned to Missouri and helped to organize a small Confederate battalion; this adventure would serve as the basis of his celebrated Civil War tale "The Private History of a Campaign That Failed" (1865). Shortly thereafter Clemens joined his brother Orion in Nevada, gaining spectacular celebrity as "Mark Twain." Twain did not write many other works about the Civil War, but the brief sketch "Lucretia Smith's Soldier"—first published in the* Californian *on December 3, 1864, and collected in Twain's first story collection,* The Celebrated Jumping Frog of Calaveras County *(1867)—reveals the tart satire that would characterize much of his later work.*

I am an ardent admirer of those nice, sickly war stories which have lately been so popular, and for the last three months I have been at work upon one of that character, which is now completed. It can be relied upon as true in every particular, inasmuch as the facts it contains were compiled from the official record in the War Department at Washington. It is but just, also, that I should confess that I have drawn largely on *Jomini's Art of War,* the *Message of the President and Accompanying Documents,* and sundry maps and military works, so necessary for reference in building a novel like this. To the accommodating Directors of the Overland Telegraph Company I take pleasure in returning my thanks for tendering me the use of their wires at the customary rates. And finally, to all those kind friends who have, by good deeds or encouraging words, assisted me in my labors upon this story of "Lucretia Smith's Soldier," during the past three months, and whose names are too numerous for special mention, I take this method of tendering my sincerest gratitude.

Chapter I

On a balmy May morning in 1861, the little village of Bluemass, in Massachusetts, lay wrapped in the splendor of the newly-risen sun. Reginald de Whittaker, confidential and only clerk in the house of Bushrod & Ferguson, general drygoods and grocery dealers and keepers of the post-office, rose from his bunk under the counter, and shook himself. After yawning and stretching comfortably, he sprinkled the floor and proceeded to sweep it. He had only half finished his task, however, when he sat down on a keg of nails and fell into a reverie. "This is my last day in this shanty," said he. "How it will surprise Lucretia when she hears I am going for a soldier! How proud she will be, the little darling!" He pictured himself in all manner of warlike situations; the hero of a thousand extraordinary adventures; the man of rising fame; the pet of Fortune at last; and beheld himself, finally, returning to his own home, a bronzed and scarred brigadier-general, to cast his honors and his matured and perfect love at the feet of his Lucretia Borgia Smith.

At this point a thrill of joy and pride suffused his system; but he looked down and saw his broom, and blushed. He came toppling down from the clouds he had been soaring among, and was an obscure clerk again, on a salary of two dollars and a half a week.

Chapter II

At eight o'clock that evening, with a heart palpitating with the proud news he had brought for his beloved, Reginald sat in Mr. Smith's parlor awaiting Lucretia's appearance. The moment she entered, he sprang to meet her, his face lighted by the torch of love that was blazing in his head somewhere and shining through, and ejaculated, "Mine own!" as he opened his arms to receive her.

"Sir!" said she, and drew herself up like an offended queen.

Poor Reginald was stricken dumb with astonishment. This chilling demeanor, this angry rebuff, where he had expected the old, tender welcome, banished the gladness from his heart as the cheerful brightness is swept from the landscape when a dark cloud drifts athwart the face of the sun. He stood bewildered a moment, with a sense of goneness on him like one who finds himself suddenly overboard upon a midnight sea, and beholds the ship pass into shrouding gloom, while the dreadful conviction falls upon his soul that he has not been missed. He tried to speak, but his pallid lips refused their office. At last he murmured:

"O Lucretia! what have I done; what is the matter; why this cruel coldness? Don't you love your Reginald any more?"

Her lips curled in bitter scorn, and she replied, in mocking tones:

"Don't I love my Reginald any more? No, I *don't* love my Reginald any more! Go back to your pitiful junk-shop and grab your pitiful yard-stick, and stuff cotton in your ears, so that you can't hear your country shout to you to fall in and shoulder arms. Go!" And then, unheeding the new light that flashed from his eyes, she fled from the room and slammed the door behind her.

Only a moment more! Only a single moment more, he thought, and he could have told her how he had already answered the summons and signed his name to the muster-roll, and all would have been well; his lost bride would have come back to his arms with words of praise and thanksgiving upon her lips. He made a step forward, once, to recall her, but he remembered that he was no longer an effeminate drygoods student, and his warrior soul scorned to sue for quarter. He strode from the place with martial firmness, and never looked behind him.

Chapter III

When Lucretia awoke next morning, the faint music of fife and the roll of a distant drum came floating upon the soft spring breeze, and as she listened the sounds grew more subdued, and finally passed out of hearing. She lay absorbed in thought for many minutes, and then she sighed and said: "Oh! if he were only with that band of fellows, how I could love him!"

In the course of the day a neighbor dropped in, and when the conversation turned upon the soldiers, the visitor said:

"Reginald de Whittaker looked rather down-hearted, and didn't shout when he marched along with the other boys this morning. I expect it's owing to you, Miss Loo, though when I met him coming here yesterday evening to tell you he'd enlisted, he thought you'd like it and be proud of— Mercy! what in the nation's the matter with the girl?"

Nothing, only a sudden misery had fallen like a blight upon her heart, and a deadly pallor telegraphed it to her countenance. She rose up without a word and walked with a firm step out of the room; but once within the sacred seclusion of her own chamber, her strong will gave way and she burst into a flood of passionate tears. Bitterly she upbraided herself for her foolish haste of the night before, and her harsh treatment of her lover at the very moment that he had come to anticipate the proudest wish of her heart, and to tell her that he had enrolled himself under the battle-flag, and was going forth to fight as *her* soldier. Alas! other maidens would have soldiers in those glorious fields, and be entitled to the sweet pain of feeling a tender solicitude for them, but she would be unrepresented. No soldier in all the vast armies would breathe her name as he breasted the crimson tide of war! She wept again—or, rather, she went on weeping where she left off a moment before. In her bitterness of spirit she almost cursed the precipitancy that had brought all this sorrow upon her young life. "Drat it!" The words were in her bosom, but she locked them there, and closed her lips against their utterance.

For weeks she nursed her grief in silence, while the roses faded from her cheeks. And through it all she clung to the hope that some day the old love would bloom again in Reginald's heart, and he would write to her; but the long summer days dragged wearily along, and still no letter came. The newspapers teemed with stories of battle and carnage, and eagerly she read them, but always with the same result: the tears welled up and blurred the closing lines—the name she sought was looked for in vain, and the dull aching returned to her sinking heart. Letters to the other girls sometimes contained brief mention of him, and presented always the same picture of him—a morose, unsmiling, desperate man, always in the thickest of the fight, begrimed with powder, and moving calm and unscathed through tempests of shot and shell, as if he bore a charmed life.

But at last, in a long list of maimed and killed, poor Lucretia read these terrible words, and fell fainting to the floor: "*R. D. Whittaker, private soldier, desperately wounded!*"

Chapter IV

On a couch in one of the wards of a hospital at Washington lay a wounded soldier; his head was so profusely bandaged that his features were not visible; but there was no mistaking the happy face of the young girl who sat beside him—it was Lucretia Borgia Smith's. She had hunted him out several weeks before, and since that time she had patiently watched by him and nursed him, coming in the morning as soon as the surgeon had finished dressing his wounds, and never leaving him until relieved at nightfall. A ball had shattered his lower jaw, and he could not utter a syllable; through all her weary vigils she had never once been blessed with a grateful word from his dear lips; yet she stood to her post bravely and without a murmur, feeling that when he did get well again she would hear that which would more than reward her for all her devotion.

At the hour we have chosen for the opening of this chapter, Lucretia was in a tumult of happy excitement; for the surgeon had told her that at last her Whittaker had recovered sufficiently to admit of the removal of the bandages from his head, and she was now waiting with feverish impatience for the doctor to come and disclose the loved features to her view. At last he came, and Lucretia, with beaming eyes and fluttering heart, bent over the couch with anxious expectancy. One bandage was removed, then another and another, and lo! the poor wounded face was revealed to the light of day.

"O my own dar—"

What have we here! What is the matter! Alas! it was the face of a stranger!

Poor Lucretia! With one hand covering her upturned eyes, she staggered back with a moan of anguish. Then a spasm of fury distorted her countenance as she brought her fist down with a crash that made the medicine bottles on the table dance again, and exclaimed:

"Oh! confound my cats, if I haven't gone and fooled away three mortal weeks here, snuffling and slobbering over the wrong soldier!"

It was a sad, sad truth. The wretched but innocent and unwitting impostor was R. D., or Richard Dilworthy Whittaker, of Wisconsin, the soldier of dear little Eugenie Le Mulligan, of that State, and utterly unknown to our unhappy Lucretia B. Smith.

Such is life, and the tail of the serpent is over us all. Let us draw the curtain over this melancholy history—for melancholy it must still remain, during a season at least, for the real Reginald de Whittaker has not turned up yet.

The Story of a Year
1865

HENRY JAMES

The cosmopolitan Henry James (1843–1916) had little direct involvement in the Civil War, serving only as a volunteer fireman in Newport, Rhode Island, some months after the outbreak of the war. It was at this time that James suffered what he later termed an "obscure hurt" (probably a back injury). He spent much of the rest of the war at Harvard Law School. However, some of James's earliest tales deal with the conflict; among them are "The Story of a Year" (his first signed story), "Poor Richard" (1867), and "A Most Extraordinary Case" (1868). The first of these, appearing in the Atlantic Monthly *of March 1865, depicts the interrupted romance of a man who leaves his fiancée to fight in the war, and is typically Jamesian in its loving and delicate portrayal of character.*

I

My story begins as a great many stories have begun within the last three years, and indeed as a great many have ended; for, when the hero is despatched, does not the romance come to a stop?

In early May, two years ago, a young couple I wot of strolled homeward from an evening walk, a long ramble among the peaceful hills which inclosed their rustic home. Into these peaceful hills the young man had brought, not the rumor, (which was an old inhabitant,) but some of the reality of war, —a little whiff of gunpowder, the clanking of a sword; for, although Mr John Ford had his campaign still before him, he wore a certain comely air of camp-life which stamped him a very Hector to the steady-going villagers, and a very pretty fellow to Miss Elizabeth Crowe, his companion in this sentimental stroll. And was he not attired in the great brightness of blue and gold which befits a freshly made lieutenant? This was a strange sight for these happy Northern glades; for, although the first Revolution had boomed awhile in their midst, the honest yeomen who defended them were clad in sober homespun, and it is well known that His Majesty's troops wore red.

These young people, I say, had been roaming. It was plain that they had wandered into spots where the brambles were thick and the dews heavy,—nay, into swamps and puddles where the April rains were still undried. Ford's boots and trousers had imbibed a deep foretaste of the Virginia mud; his companion's skirts were fearfully bedraggled. What great enthusiasm had made our friends so unmindful of their steps? What blinding ardor had kindled these strange phenomena: a young lieutenant scornful of his first uniform, a well-bred young lady reckless of her stockings?

Good reader, this narrative is averse to retrospect.

Elizabeth (as I shall not scruple to call her outright) was leaning upon her companion's arm, half moving in concert with him, and half allowing herself to be led, with that instinctive acknowledgment of dependence natural to a young girl who has just received the assurance of lifelong protection. Ford was lounging along with that calm, swinging stride which often bespeaks, when you can read it aright, the answering consciousness of a sudden rush of manhood. A spectator might have thought him at this moment profoundly conceited. The young girl's blue veil was dangling from his pocket; he had shouldered her sun-umbrella after the fashion of a musket on march: he might carry these trifles. Was there not a vague longing expressed in the strong expansion of his stalwart shoulders, in the fond accommodation of his pace to hers,—her pace so submissive and slow, that, when he tried to match it, they almost came to a delightful standstill,—a silent desire for the whole fair burden?

They made their way up a long swelling mound, whose top commanded the sunset. The dim landscape which had been brightening all day to the green of spring was now darkening to the gray of evening. The lesser hills, the farms, the brooks, the fields, orchards, and woods, made a dusky gulf before the great splendor of the west. As Ford looked at the clouds, it seemed to him that their imagery was all of war, their great uneven masses were marshalled into the semblance of a battle. There were columns charging and columns flying and standards floating,—tatters of the reflected purple; and great captains on colossal horses, and a rolling canopy of cannon-smoke and fire and blood. The background of the clouds, indeed, was like a land on fire, or a battle-ground illumined by another sunset, a country of blackened villages and crimsoned pastures. The tumult of the clouds increased; it was hard to believe them inanimate. You might have fancied them an army of gigantic souls playing at football with the sun. They seemed to sway in confused splendor; the opposing squadrons bore each other down; and then suddenly they scattered, bowling with equal velocity towards north and south, and gradually fading into the pale evening sky. The purple pennons sailed away and sank out of sight, caught, doubtless, upon the brambles of the intervening plain. Day contracted itself into a fiery ball and vanished.

Ford and Elizabeth had quietly watched this great mystery of the heavens.

"That is an allegory," said the young man, as the sun went under, looking into his companion's face, where a pink flush seemed still to linger: "it means the end of the war. The forces on both sides are withdrawn. The blood that has been shed gathers itself into a vast globule and drops into the ocean."

"I'm afraid it means a shabby compromise," said Elizabeth. "Light disappears, too, and the land is in darkness."

"Only for a season," answered the other. "We mourn our dead. Then light comes again, stronger and brighter than ever. Perhaps you'll be crying for me, Lizzie, at that distant day."

"Oh, Jack, didn't you promise not to talk about that?" says Lizzie, threatening to anticipate the performance in question.

Jack took this rebuke in silence, gazing soberly at the empty sky. Soon the young girl's eyes stole up to his face. If he had been looking at anything in particular, I think she would have followed the direction of his glance; but as it seemed to be a very vacant one, she let her eyes rest.

"Jack," said she, after a pause, "I wonder how you'll look when you get back."

Ford's soberness gave way to a laugh.

"Uglier than ever. I shall be all incrusted with mud and gore. And then I shall be magnificently sunburnt, and I shall have a beard."

"Oh, you dreadful!" and Lizzie gave a little shout. "Really, Jack, if you have a beard, you'll not look like a gentleman."

"Shall I look like a lady, pray?" says Jack.

"Are you serious?" asked Lizzie.

"To be sure. I mean to alter my face as you do your misfitting garments,—take in on one side and let out the other. Isn't that the process? I shall crop my head and cultivate my chin."

"You've a very nice chin, my dear, and I think it's a shame to hide it."

"Yes, I know my chin's handsome; but wait till you see my beard."

"Oh, the vanity!" cried Lizzie, "the vanity of men in their faces! Talk of women!" and the silly creature looked up at her lover with most inconsistent satisfaction.

"Oh, the pride of women in their husbands!" said Jack, who of course knew what she was about.

"You're not my husband, Sir. There's many a slip"— But the young girl stopped short.

"Twixt the cup and the lip," said Jack. "Go on. I can match your proverb with another. 'There's many a true word,' and so forth. No, my darling: I'm not your husband. Perhaps I never shall be. But if anything happens to me, you'll take comfort, won't you?"

"Never!" said Lizzie, tremulously.

"Oh, but you must; otherwise, Lizzie, I should think our engagement inexcusable. Stuff! who am I that you should cry for me?"

"You are the best and wisest of men. I don't care; you *are.*"

"Thank you for your great love, my dear. That's a delightful illusion. But I hope Time will kill it, in his own good way, before it hurts any one. I know so many men who are worth infinitely more than I—men wise, generous, and brave—that I shall not feel as if I were leaving you in an empty world."

"Oh, my dear friend!" said Lizzie, after a pause, "I wish you could advise me all my life."

"Take care, take care," laughed Jack; "you don't know what you are bargaining for. But will you let me say a word now? If by chance I'm taken out of the world, I want you to beware of that tawdry sentiment which enjoins you to be 'constant to my memory.' My memory be hanged! Remember me at my best,—that is, fullest of the desire of humility. Don't inflict me on people. There are some widows and bereaved sweethearts who remind me of the peddler in that horrible murder-story, who carried a corpse in his pack. Really, it's their stock in trade. The only justification of a man's personality is his rights. What rights has a dead man?—Let's go down."

They turned southward and went jolting down the hill.

"Do you mind this talk, Lizzie?" asked Ford.

"No," said Lizzie, swallowing a sob, unnoticed by her companion in the sublime egotism of protection; "I like it."

"Very well," said the young man, "I want my memory to help you. When I am down in Virginia, I expect to get a vast deal of good from thinking of you,—to do my work better, and to keep straighter altogether. Like all lovers, I'm horribly selfish. I expect to see a vast deal of shabbiness and baseness and turmoil, and in the midst of it all I'm sure the inspiration of patriotism will sometimes fail. Then I'll think of you. I love you a thousand times better than my country, Liz.—Wicked? So much the worse. It's the truth. But if I find your memory makes a milksop of me, I shall thrust you out of the way without ceremony,—I shall clap you into my box or between the leaves of my Bible, and only look at you on Sunday."

"I shall be very glad, Sir, if that makes you open your Bible frequently," says Elizabeth, rather demurely.

"I shall put one of your photographs against every page," cried Ford; "and then I think I shall not lack a text for my meditations. Don't you know how Catholics keep little pictures of their adored Lady in their prayer-books?"

"Yes, indeed," said Lizzie; "I should think it would be a very soul-stirring picture, when you are marching to the front, the night before a battle,— a poor, stupid girl, knitting stupid socks, in a stupid Yankee village."

Oh, the craft of artless tongues! Jack strode along in silence a few moments, splashing straight through a puddle; then, ere he was quite clear of it, he stretched out his arm and gave his companion a long embrace.

"And pray what am I to do," resumed Lizzie, wondering, rather proudly perhaps, at Jack's averted face, "while you are marching and counter-marching in Virginia?"

"Your duty, of course," said Jack, in a steady voice, which belied a certain little conjecture of Lizzie's. "I think you will find the sun will rise in the east, my dear, just as it did before you were engaged."

"I'm sure I didn't suppose it wouldn't," says Lizzie.

"By duty I don't mean anything disagreeable, Liz," pursued the young man. "I hope you'll take your pleasure, too. I wish you might go to Boston, or even to Leatherborough, for a month or two."

"What for, pray?"

"What for? Why, for the fun of it: to 'go out,' as they say."

"Jack, do you think me capable of going to parties while you are in danger?"

"Why not? Why should I have all the fun?"

"Fun? I'm sure you're welcome to it all. As for me, I mean to make a new beginning."

"Of what?"

"Oh, of everything. In the first place, I shall begin to improve my mind. But don't you think it's horrid for women to be reasonable?"

"Hard, say you?"

"Horrid,—yes, and hard too. But I mean to become so. Oh, girls are such fools, Jack! I mean to learn to like boiled mutton and history and plain sewing, and all that. Yet, when a girl's engaged, she's not expected to do anything in particular."

Jack laughed, and said nothing; and Lizzie went on.

"I wonder what your mother will say to the news. I think I know."

"What?"

"She'll say you've been very unwise. No, she won't: she never speaks so to you. She'll say I've been very dishonest or indelicate, or something of that kind. No, she won't either: she doesn't say such things, though I'm sure she thinks them. I don't know what she'll say."

"No, I think not, Lizzie, if you indulge in such conjectures. My mother never speaks without thinking. Let us hope that she may think favorably of our plan. Even if she doesn't"—

Jack did not finish his sentence, nor did Lizzie urge him. She had a great respect for his hesitations. But in a moment he began again.

"I was going to say this, Lizzie: I think for the present our engagement had better be kept quiet."

Lizzie's heart sank with a sudden disappointment. Imagine the feelings of the damsel in the fairy-tale, whom the disguised enchantress had just empowered to utter diamonds and pearls, should the old beldame have straightway added that for the present mademoiselle had better hold her tongue. Yet the disappointment was brief. I think this enviable young lady would have tripped home talking very hard to herself, and have been not ill pleased to find her little mouth turning into a tightly clasped jewel-casket. Nay, would she not on this occasion have been thankful for a large mouth,—a mouth huge and unnatural,—stretching from ear to ear? Who wish to cast their pearls before swine? The young lady of the pearls was, after all, but a barnyard miss. Lizzie was too proud of Jack to be vain. It's well enough to wear our own hearts upon our sleeves; but for those of others, when intrusted to our keeping, I think we had better find a more secluded lodging.

"You see, I think secrecy would leave us much freer," said Jack,—"leave *you* much freer."

"Oh, Jack, how can you?" cried Lizzie. "Yes, of course; I shall be falling in love with someone else. Freer! Thank you, Sir!"

"Nay, Lizzie, what I'm saying is really kinder than it sounds. Perhaps you *will* thank me one of these days."

"Doubtless! I've already taken a great fancy to George Mackenzie."

"Will you let me enlarge on my suggestion?"

"Oh, certainly! You seem to have your mind quite made up."

"I confess I like to take account of possibilities. Don't you know mathematics are my hobby? Did you ever study algebra? I always have an eye on the unknown quantity."

"No, I never studied algebra. I agree with you, that we had better not speak of our engagement."

"That's right, my dear. You're always right. But mind, I don't want to bind you to secrecy. Hang it, do as you please! Do what comes easiest to you, and you'll do the best thing. What made me speak is my dread of the horrible publicity which clings to all this business. Nowadays, when a girl's engaged, it's no long, 'Ask mamma,' simply; but 'Ask Mrs Brown, and Mrs Jones, and my large circle of acquaintance,—Mrs Grundy, in short.' I say nowadays, but I suppose it's always been so."

"Very well, we'll keep it all nice and quiet," said Lizzie, who would have been ready to celebrate her nuptials according to the rites of the Esquimaux, had Jack seen fit to suggest it.

"I know it doesn't look well for a lover to be so cautious," pursued Jack; "but you understand me, Lizzie, don't you?"

"I don't entirely understand you, but I quite trust you."

"God bless you! My prudence, you see, is my best strength. Now, if ever, I need my strength. When a man's a-wooing, Lizzie, he is all feeling, or he ought to be; when he's accepted, then he begins to think."

"And to repent, I suppose you mean."

"Nay, to devise means to keep his sweetheart from repenting. Let me be frank. Is it the greatest fools only that are the best lovers? There's no telling what may happen, Lizzie. I want you to marry me with your eyes open. I don't want you to feel tied down or taken in. You're very young, you know. You're responsible to yourself of a year hence. You're at an age when no girl can count safely from year's end to year's end."

"And you, Sir!" cries Lizzie; "one would think you were a grandfather."

"Well, I'm on the way to it. I'm a pretty old boy. I mean what I say. I may not be entirely frank, but I think I'm sincere. It seems to me as if I'd been fibbing all my life before I told you that your affection was necessary to my happiness. I mean it out and out. I never loved anyone before, and I never will again. If you had refused me half an hour ago, I should have died a bachelor. I have no fear for myself. But I have for you. You said a few minutes ago that you wanted me to be your adviser. Now you know the function of an adviser is to perfect his victim in the art of walking with his eyes shut. I sha'n't be so cruel."

Lizzie saw fit to view these remarks in a humorous light. "How disinterested!" quoth she: "how very self-sacrificing! Bachelor indeed! For my part, I think I shall become a Mormon!"—I verily believe the poor misinformed creature fancied that in Utah it is the ladies who are guilty of polygamy.

Before many minutes they drew near home. There stood Mrs Ford at the garden gate, looking up and down the road, with a letter in her hand.

"Something for you, John," said his mother, as they approached. "It looks as if it came from camp.—Why, Elizabeth, look at your skirts!"

"I know it," says Lizzie, giving the articles in question a shake. "What is it, Jack?"

"Marching orders!" cried the young man. "The regiment leaves day after to-morrow. I must leave by the early train in the morning. Hurray!" And he diverted a sudden gleeful kiss into a filial salute.

They went in. The two women were silent, after the manner of women who suffer. But Jack did little else than laugh and talk and circumnavigate the parlor, sitting first here and then there,—close beside Lizzie and on the opposite side of the room. After a while Miss Crowe joined in his laughter, but I think her mirth might have been resolved into articulate heartbeats. After tea she went to bed, to give Jack opportunity for his last filial *épanchements*. How generous a man's intervention makes women! But Lizzie promised to see her lover off in the morning.

"Nonsense!" said Mrs Ford. "You'll not be up. John will want to breakfast quietly."

"I shall see you off, Jack," repeated the young lady, from the threshold.

Elizabeth went upstairs buoyant with her young love. It had dawned upon her like a new life,—a life positively worth the living. Hereby she would subsist and cost nobody anything. In it she was boundlessly rich. She would make it the hidden spring of a hundred praiseworthy deeds. She would begin the career of duty: she would enjoy boundless equanimity: she would raise her whole being to the level of her sublime passion. She would practise charity, humility, piety,—in fine, all the virtues: together with certain *morceaux* of Beethoven and Chopin. She would walk the earth like one glorified. She would do homage to the best of men by inviolate secrecy. Here, by I know not what gentle transition, as she lay in the quiet darkness, Elizabeth covered her pillow with a flood of tears.

Meanwhile Ford, downstairs, began in this fashion. He was lounging at his manly length on the sofa, in his slippers.

"May I light a pipe, mother?"

"Yes, my love. But please be careful of your ashes. There's a newspaper."

"Pipes don't make ashes.—Mother, what do you think?" he continued between the puffs of his smoking; "I've got a piece of news."

"Ah?" said Mrs Ford, fumbling for her scissors; "I hope it's good news."

"I hope you'll think it so. I've been engaging myself"—puff,—puff—"to Lizzie Crowe." A cloud of puffs between his mother's face and his own. When they had cleared away Jack felt his mother's eyes. Her work was in her lap. "To be married, you know," he added.

In Mrs Ford's view, like the king in that of the British Constitution, her only son could do no wrong. Prejudice is a stout bulwark against surprise. Moreover, Mrs Ford's motherly instinct had not been entirely at fault. Still, it had by no means kept pace with fact. She had been silent, partly from doubt, partly out of respect for her son. As long as John did not doubt of himself, he was right. Should he come to do so, she was sure he would speak. And now, when he told her the matter was settled, she persuaded herself that he was asking her advice.

"I've been expecting it," she said, at last.

"You have? Why didn't you speak?"

"Well, John, I can't say I've been hoping it."

"Why not?"

"I am not sure of Lizzie's heart," said Mrs Ford, who, it may be well to add, was very sure of her own.

Jack began to laugh. "What's the matter with her heart?"

"I think Lizzie's shallow," said Mrs Ford; and there was that in her tone which betokened some satisfaction with this adjective.

"Hang it! she is shallow," said Jack. "But when a thing's shallow, you can see to the bottom. Lizzie doesn't pretend to be deep. I want a wife, mother, that I can understand. That's the only wife I can love. Lizzie's the only girl I ever understood, and the first I ever loved. I love her very much,—more than I can explain to you."

"Yes, I confess it's inexplicable. It seems to me," she added, with a bad smile, "like infatuation."

Jack did not like the smile; he liked it even less than the remark. He smoked steadily for a few moments, and then he said,—

"Well, mother, love is notoriously obstinate, you know. We shall not be able to take the same view of this subject: suppose we drop it."

"Remember that this is your last evening at home, my son," said Mrs Ford.

"I do remember. Therefore I wish to avoid disagreement."

There was a pause. The young man smoked, and his mother sewed, in silence.

"I think my position, as Lizzie's guardian," resumed Mrs Ford, "entitles me to an interest in the matter."

"Certainly, I acknowledged your interest by telling you of our engagement."

Further pause.

"Will you allow me to say," said Mrs Ford, after a while, "that I think this a little selfish?"

"Allow you? Certainly, if you particularly desire it. Though I confess it isn't very pleasant for a man to sit and hear his future wife pitched into,— by his own mother, too."

"John, I am surprised at your language."

"I beg your pardon," and John spoke more gently. "You mustn't be surprised at anything from an accepted lover.—I'm sure you misconceive her. In fact, mother, I don't believe you know her."

Mrs Ford nodded, with an infinite depth of meaning; and from the grimness with which she bit off the end of her thread it might have seemed that she fancied herself to be executing a human vengeance.

"Ah, I know her only too well!"

"And you don't like her?"

Mrs Ford performed another decapitation of her thread.

"Well, I'm glad Lizzie has one friend in the world," said Jack.

"Her best friend," said Mrs Ford, "is the one who flatters her least. I see it all, John. Her pretty face has done the business."

The young man flushed impatiently.

"Mother," said he, "you are very much mistaken. I'm not a boy nor a fool. You trust me in a great many things; why not trust me in this?"

"My dear son, you are throwing yourself away. You deserve for your companion in life a higher character than that girl."

I think Mrs Ford, who had been an excellent mother, would like to give her son a wife fashioned on her own model.

"Oh, come, mother," said he, "that's twaddle. I should be thankful if I were half as good as Lizzie."

"It's the truth, John, and your conduct—not only the step you've taken, but your talk about it—is a great disappointment to me. If I have cherished any wish of late, it is that my darling boy should get a wife worthy of him. The household governed by Elizabeth Crowe is not the home I should desire for anyone I love."

"It's one to which you should always be welcome, Ma'am," said Jack.

"It's not a place I should feel at home in," replied his mother.

"I'm sorry," said Jack. And he got up and began to walk about the room. "Well, well, mother," he said at last, stopping in front of Mrs Ford, "we don't understand each other. One of these days we shall. For the present let us have done with discussion. I'm half sorry I told you."

"I'm glad of such proof of your confidence. But if you hadn't, of course Elizabeth would have done so."

"No, Ma'am, I think not."

"Then she is even more reckless of her obligations than I thought her."

"I advised her to say nothing about it."

Mrs Ford made no answer. She began slowly to fold up her work.

"I think we had better let the matter stand," continued her son. "I'm not afraid of time. But I wish to make a request of you: you won't mention this conversation to Lizzie, will you? or allow her to suppose that you know of our engagement? I have a particular reason."

Mrs Ford went on smoothing out her work. Then she suddenly looked up.

"No, my dear, I'll keep your secret. Give me a kiss."

II

I have no intention of following Lieutenant Ford to the seat of war. The exploits of his campaign are recorded in the public journals of the day, where the curious may still peruse them. My own taste has always been for unwritten history, and my present business is with the reverse of the picture.

After Jack went off, the two ladies resumed their old homely life. But the homeliest life had now ceased to be repulsive to Elizabeth. Her common duties were no longer wearisome: for the first time, she experienced the delicious companionship of thought. Her chief task was still to sit by the window knitting soldiers' socks; but even Mrs Ford could not help owning that she worked with a much greater diligence, yawned, rubbed her eyes, gazed up and down the road less, and indeed produced a much more comely article. Ah, me! if half the lovesome fancies that flitted through Lizzie's spirit in those busy hours could have found their way into the texture of the dingy yarn, as it was slowly wrought into shape, the eventual wearer of the socks would have been as light-footed as Mercury. I am afraid I should make the reader sneer, were I to rehearse some of this little fool's diversions. She passed several hours daily in Jack's old chamber: it was in this sanctuary, indeed, at the sunny south window, overlooking the long road, the wood-crowned heights, the gleaming river, that she worked with most pleasure and profit. Here she was removed from the untiring glance of the elder lady, from her jarring questions and commonplaces; here she was alone with her love,—that greatest commonplace in life. Lizzie felt in Jack's room a certain impress of his personality. The idle fancies of her mood were bodied forth in a dozen sacred relics. Some of these articles Elizabeth carefully cherished. It was rather late in the day for her to assert a literary taste,—her reading having begun and ended (naturally enough) with the ancient fiction of the "Scottish Chiefs." So she could hardly help smiling, herself, sometimes, at her interest in Jack's old college tomes. She carried several of them to her own apartment, and placed them at the foot of her little bed, on a book-shelf adorned, besides, with a pot of spring violets, a portrait of General McClellan, and a likeness of Lieutenant Ford. She had a vague belief that a loving study of their well-thumbed verses would remedy, in some degree, her sad intellectual deficiencies. She was sorry she knew so little: as sorry, that is, as she might be, for we know that she was shallow. Jack's omniscience was one of his most awful attributes. And yet she comforted herself with the thought that, as he had forgiven her ignorance, she herself might surely forget it. Happy Lizzie, I envy you this easy path to knowledge! The volume she most frequently consulted was an old German "Faust," over which she used to fumble with a battered lexicon. The secret of this preference was in certain marginal notes in pencil, signed "J." I hope they were really of Jack's making.

Lizzie was always a small walker. Until she knew Jack, this had been quite an unsuspected pleasure. She was afraid, too, of the cows, geese, and sheep,—all the agricultural *spectra* of the feminine imagination. But now her terrors were over. Might she not play the soldier, too, in her own humble way? Often with a beating heart, I fear, but still with resolute, elastic steps, she revisited Jack's old haunts; she tried to love Nature as he had seemed to love it; she gazed at his old sunsets; she fathomed his old pools with bright plummet glances, as if seeking some lingering trace of his features in their brown depths, stamped there as on a fond human heart; she sought out his dear name, scratched on the rocks and trees,—and when night came on, she studied, in her simple way, the great starlit canopy, under which, perhaps, her warrior lay sleeping; she wandered through the green glades, singing snatches of his old ballads in a clear voice, made tuneful with love,—and as she sang, there mingled with the everlasting murmur of the trees the faint sound of a muffled bass, borne upon the south wind like a distant drum-beat, responsive to a bugle. So she led for some months a very pleasant idyllic life, face to face with a strong, vivid memory, which gave everything and asked nothing. These were doubtless to be (and she half knew it) the happiest days of her life. Has life any bliss so great as this pensive ecstasy? To know that the golden sands are dropping one by one makes servitude freedom, and poverty riches.

In spite of a certain sense of loss, Lizzie passed a very blissful summer. She enjoyed the deep repose which, it is to be hoped, sanctifies all honest betrothals. Possible calamity weighed lightly upon her. We know that when the columns of battle-smoke leave the field, they journey through the heavy air to a thousand quiet homes, and play about the crackling blaze of as many firesides. But Lizzie's vision was never clouded. Mrs Ford might gaze into the thickening summer dusk and wipe her spectacles; but her companion hummed her old ballad-ends with an unbroken voice. She no more ceased to smile under evil tidings than the brooklet ceases to ripple beneath the projected shadow of the roadside willow. The self-given promises of that tearful night of parting were forgotten. Vigilance had no place in Lizzie's scheme of heavenly idleness. The idea of moralizing in Elysium!

It must not be supposed that Mrs Ford was indifferent to Lizzie's mood. She studied it watchfully, and kept note of all its variations. And among the things she learned was, that her companion knew of her scrutiny, and was, on the whole, indifferent to it. Of the full extent of Mrs Ford's observation, however, I think Lizzie was hardly aware. She was like a reveler in a brilliantly lighted room, with a curtainless window, conscious, and yet heedless, of passers-by. And Mrs Ford may not inaptly be compared to the chilly spectator on the dark side of the pane. Very few words passed on the topic of their common thoughts. From the first, as we have seen, Lizzie guessed at her guardian's probable view of her engagement: an abasement incurred by John. Lizzie lacked what is called a sense of duty; and, unlike the majority of such temperaments, which contrive to be buoyant on the glistening bubble of Dignity, she had likewise a modest estimate of her dues. Alack, my poor heroine had no pride! Mrs Ford's silent censure awakened no resentment. It sounded in her ears like a dull, soporific hum. Lizzie was deeply enamoured of what a French book terms her *aises intellectuelles*. Her mental comfort lay in the ignoring of problems. She possessed a certain native insight which revealed many of the horrent inequalities of her pathway; but she found it so cruel and disenchanting a faculty, that blindness was infinitely preferable. She preferred repose to order, and mercy to justice. She was speculative, without being critical. She was continually wondering, but she never inquired. This world was the riddle; the next alone would be the answer.

So she never felt any desire to have an "understanding" with Mrs Ford. Did the old lady misconceive her? it was her own business. Mrs Ford apparently felt no desire to set herself right. You see, Lizzie was ignorant of her friend's promise. There were moments when Mrs Ford's tongue itched to speak. There were others, it is true, when she dreaded any explanation which would compel her to forfeit her displeasure. Lizzie's happy self-sufficiency was most irritating. She grudged the young girl the dignity of her secret; her own actual knowledge of it rather increased her jealousy, by showing her the importance of the scheme from which she was excluded. Lizzie, being in perfect good-humor with the world and with herself, abated no jot of her personal deference to Mrs Ford. Of Jack, as a good friend and her guardian's son, she spoke very freely. But Mrs Ford was mistrustful of this semi-confidence. She would not, she often said to herself, be wheedled against her principles. Her principles! Oh for some shining blade of purpose to hew down such stubborn stakes! Lizzie had no thought of flattering her companion. She never deceived anyone but herself. She could not bring herself to value Mrs Ford's goodwill. She knew that Jack often suffered from his mother's obstinacy. So her unbroken humility shielded no unavowed purpose. She was patient and kindly from nature, from habit. Yet I think, that, if Mrs Ford could have measured her benignity, she would have preferred, on the whole, the most open defiance. "Of all things," she would sometimes mutter, "to be patronized by that little piece!" It was very disagreeable, for instance, to have to listen to *portions* of her own son's letters.

These letters came week by week, flying out of the South like white-winged carrier-doves. Many and many a time, for very pride, Lizzie would have liked a larger audience. Portions of them certainly deserved publicity. They were far too good for her. Were they not better than that stupid war-correspondence in the "Times," which she so often tried to read in vain? They contained long details of movements, plans of campaigns, military opinions and conjectures, expressed with the emphasis habitual to young sub-lieutenants. I doubt whether General Halleck's despatches laid down the law more absolutely than Lieutenant Ford's. Lizzie answered in her own fashion. It must be owned that hers was a dull pen. She told her dearest, dearest Jack how much she loved and honored him, and how much she missed him, and how delightful his last letter was, (with those beautifully drawn diagrams,) and the village gossip, and how stout and strong his mother continued to be,—and again, how she loved, etc., etc., and that she remained his loving L. Jack read these effusions as became one so beloved. I should not wonder if he thought them very brilliant.

The summer waned to its close, and through myriad silent stages began to darken into autumn. Who can tell the story of those red months? I have to chronicle another silent transition. But as I can find no words delicate and fine enough to describe the multifold changes of Nature, so, too, I must be content to give you the spiritual facts in gross.

John Ford became a veteran down by the Potomac. And, to tell the truth, Lizzie became a veteran at home. That is, her love and hope grew to be an old story. She gave way, as the strongest must, as the wisest will, to time. The passion which in her simple, shallow way, she had confided to the woods and waters reflected their outward variations; she thought of her lover less, and with less positive pleasure. The golden sands had run out. Perfect rest was over. Mrs Ford's tacit protest began to be annoying. In a rather resentful spirit, Lizzie forbore to read any more letters aloud. These were as regular as ever. One of them contained a rough camp-photograph of Jack's newly bearded visage. Lizzie declared it was "too ugly for anything," and thrust it out of sight. She found herself skipping his military dissertations, which were still as long and written in as handsome a hand as ever. The "too good," which used to be uttered rather proudly, was now rather a wearisome truth. When Lizzie in certain critical moods tried to qualify Jack's temperament, she said to herself that he was too literal. Once he gave her a little scolding for not writing oftener. "Jack can make no allowances," murmured Lizzie. "He can understand no feelings but his own. I remember he used to say that moods were diseases. His mind is too healthy for such things; his heart is too stout for ache or pain. The night before he went off he told me that Reason, as he calls it, was the rule of life. I suppose he thinks it the rule of love, too. But his heart is younger than mine,—younger and better. He has lived through awful scenes of danger and bloodshed and cruelty, yet his heart is purer." Lizzie had a horrible feeling of being *blasée* of this one affection. "Oh, God bless him!" she cried. She felt much better for the tears in which this soliloquy ended. I fear she had begun to doubt her ability to cry about Jack.

III

Christmas came. The Army of the Potomac had stacked its muskets and gone into winter-quarters. Miss Crowe received an invitation to pass the second fortnight in February at the great manufacturing town of

Leatherborough. Leatherborough is on the railroad, two hours south of Glenham, at the mouth of the great river Tan, where this noble stream expands into its broadest smile, or gapes in too huge a fashion to be disguised by a bridge.

"Mrs Littlefield kindly invites you for the last of the month," said Mrs Ford, reading a letter behind the tea-urn.

It suited Mrs Ford's purpose—a purpose which I have not space to elaborate—that her young charge should now go forth into society and pick up acquaintances.

Two sparks of pleasure gleamed in Elizabeth's eyes. But, as she had taught herself to do of late with her protectress, she mused before answering.

"It is my desire that you should go," said Mrs Ford, taking silence for dissent.

The sparks went out.

"I intend to go," said Lizzie, rather grimly. "I am much obliged to Mrs Littlefield."

Her companion looked up.

"I intend you shall. You will please to write this morning."

For the rest of the week the two stitched together over muslins and silks, and were very good friends. Lizzie could scarcely help wondering at Mrs Ford's zeal on her behalf. Might she not have referred it to her guardian's principles? Her wardrobe, hitherto fashioned on the Glenham notion of elegance, was gradually raised to the Leatherborough standard of fitness. As she took up her bedroom candle the night before she left home, she said,—

"I thank you very much, Mrs Ford, for having worked so hard for me,—for having taken so much interest in my outfit. If they ask me at Leatherborough who made my things, I shall certainly say it was you."

Mrs Littlefield treated her young friend with great kindness. She was a good-natured, childless matron. She found Lizzie very ignorant and very pretty. She was glad to have so great a beauty and so many lions to show.

One evening Lizzie went to her room with one of the maids, carrying half a dozen candles between them. Heaven forbid that I should cross that virgin threshold—for the present! But we will wait. We will allow them two hours. At the end of that time, having gently knocked, we will enter the sanctuary. Glory of glories! The faithful attendant has done her work. Our lady is robed, crowned, ready for worshippers.

I trust I shall not be held to a minute description of our dear Lizzie's person and costume. Who is so great a recluse as never to have beheld young ladyhood in full dress? Many of us have sisters and daughters. Not a few of us, I hope, have female connections of another degree, yet no less dear. Others have looking-glasses. I give you my word for it that Elizabeth made as pretty a show as it is possible to see. She was of course well-dressed. Her skirt was of voluminous white, puffed and trimmed in wondrous sort. Her hair was profusely ornamented with curls and braids of its own rich substance. From her waist depended a ribbon, broad and blue. White with coral ornaments, as she wrote to Jack in the course of the week. Coral ornaments, forsooth! And pray, Miss, what of the other jewels with which your person was decorated,—the rubies, pearls, and sapphires? One by one Lizzie assumes her modest gimcracks: her bracelet, her gloves, her handkerchief, her fan, and then—her smile. Ah, that strange crowning smile!

An hour later, in Mrs Littlefield's pretty drawing-room, amid music, lights, and talk, Miss Crowe was sweeping a grand curtsy before a tall, sallow man, whose name she caught from her hostess's redundant murmur as Bruce. Five minutes later, when the honest matron gave a glance at her newly started enterprise from the other side of the room, she said to herself that really, for a plain country-girl, Miss Crowe did this kind of thing very well. Her next glimpse of the couple showed them whirling round the room to the crashing thrum of the piano. At eleven o'clock she beheld them linked by their fingertips in the dazzling mazes of the reel. At half-past eleven she discerned them charging shoulder to shoulder in the serried columns of the Lancers. At midnight she tapped her young friend gently with her fan.

"Your sash is unpinned, my dear.—I think you have danced often enough with Mr Bruce. If he asks you again, you had better refuse. It's not quite the thing.—Yes, my dear, I know. —Mr Simpson, will you be so good as to take Miss Crowe down to supper?"

I'm afraid young Simpson had rather a snappish partner.

After the proper interval, Mr Bruce called to pay his respects to Mrs Littlefield. He found Miss Crowe also in the drawing-room. Lizzie and he met like old friends. Mrs Littlefield was a willing listener; but it seemed to her that she had come in at the second act of the play. Bruce went off with Miss Crowe's promise to drive with him in the afternoon. In the afternoon he swept up to the door in a prancing, tinkling sleigh. After some minutes of hoarse jesting and silvery laughter in the keen wintry air, he swept away again with Lizzie curled up in the buffalo-robe beside him, like a kitten in a rug. It was dark when they returned. When Lizzie came in to the sitting-room fire, she was congratulated by her hostess upon having made a "conquest."

"I think he's a most gentlemanly man," says Lizzie.

"So he is, my dear," said Mrs Littlefield; "Mr Bruce is a perfect gentleman. He's one of the finest young men I know. He's not so young either. He's a little too yellow for my taste; but he's beautifully educated. I wish you could hear his French accent. He has been abroad I don't know how many years. The firm of Bruce and Robertson does an immense business."

"And I'm so glad," cries Lizzie, "he's coming to Glenham in March! He's going to take his sister to the water-cure."

"Really?—poor thing! She has very good manners."

"What do you think of his looks?" asked Lizzie, smoothing her feather.

"I was speaking of Jane Bruce. I think Mr Bruce has fine eyes."

"I must say I like tall men," says Miss Crowe.

"Then Robert Bruce is your man," laughs Mr Littlefield. "He's as tall as a bell-tower. And he's got a bell-clapper in his head, too."

"I believe I will go and take off my things," remarks Miss Crowe, flinging up her curls.

Of course it behoved Mr Bruce to call next day and see how Miss Crowe had stood her drive. He set a veto upon her intended departure, and presented an invitation from his sister for the following week. At Mrs Littlefield's instance, Lizzie accepted the invitation, despatched a laconic note to Mrs Ford, and stayed over for Miss Bruce's party. It was a grand affair. Miss Bruce was a very great lady: she treated Miss Crowe with every attention. Lizzie was thought by some persons to look prettier than ever. The vaporous gauze, the sunny hair, the coral, the sapphires, the smile, were displayed with renewed success. The master of the house was unable to dance; he was summoned to sterner duties. Nor could Miss Crowe be induced to perform, having hurt her foot on the ice. This was of course a disappointment; let us hope that her entertainers made it up to her.

On the second day after the party, Lizzie returned to Glenham. Good Mr Littlefield took her to the station, stealing a moment from his precious business-hours.

"There are your checks," said he; "be sure you don't lose them. Put them in your glove."

Lizzie gave a little scream of merriment.

"Mr Littlefield, how can you? I've a reticule, Sir. But I really don't want you to stay."

"Well, I confess," said her companion.—"Hullo! there's your Scottish chief! I'll get him to stay with you till the train leaves. He may be going. Bruce!"

"Oh, Mr Littlefield, don't!" cries Lizzie. "Perhaps Mr Bruce is engaged."

Bruce's tall figure came striding towards them. He was astounded to find that Miss Crowe was going by this train. Delightful! He had come to meet a friend who had not arrived.

"Littlefield," said he, "you can't be spared from your business. I will see Miss Crowe off."

When the elder gentleman had departed, Mr Bruce conducted his companion into the car, and found her a comfortable seat, equidistant from the torrid stove and the frigid door. Then he stowed away her shawls, umbrella, and reticule. She would keep her muff? She did well. What a pretty fur!

"It's just like your collar," said Lizzie. "I wish I had a muff for my feet," she pursued, tapping the floor.

"Why not use some of those shawls?" said Bruce; "let's see what we can make of them."

And he stooped down and arranged them as a rug, very neatly and kindly. And then he called himself a fool for not having used the next seat, which was empty; and the wrapping was done over again.

"I'm so afraid you'll be carried off!" said Lizzie. "What would you do?"

"I think I should make the best of it. And you?"

"I would tell you to sit down *there*"; and she indicated the seat facing her. He took it. "Now you'll be sure to," said Elizabeth.

"I'm afraid I shall, unless I put the newspaper between us." And he took it out of his pocket. "Have you seen the news?"

"No," says Lizzie, elongating her bonnet-ribbons. "What is it? Just look at that party."

"There's not much news. There's been a scrimmage on the Rappahannock. Two of our regiments engaged,—the Fifteenth and the Twenty-Eighth. Didn't you tell me you had a cousin or something in the Fifteenth?"

"Not a cousin, no relation, but an intimate friend,—my guardian's son. What does the paper say, please?" inquires Lizzie, very pale.

Bruce cast his eye over the report. "It doesn't seem to have amounted to much; we drove back the enemy, and recrossed the river at our ease. Our loss only fifty. There are no names," he added, catching a glimpse of Lizzie's pallor,—"none in this paper at least."

In a few moments appeared a newsboy crying the New York journals.

"Do you think the New York papers would have any names?" asked Lizzie.

"We can try," said Bruce. And he bought a "Herald," and unfolded it.

"Yes, there *is* a list," he continued, some time after he had opened out the sheet. "What's your friend's name?" he asked, from behind the paper.

"Ford,—John Ford, second lieutenant," said Lizzie.

There was a long pause.

At last Bruce lowered the sheet, and showed a face in which Lizzie's pallor seemed faintly reflected.

"There *is* such a name among the wounded," he said; and, folding the paper down, he held it out, and gently crossed to the seat beside her.

Lizzie took the paper, and held it close to her eyes. But Bruce could not help seeing that her temples had turned from white to crimson.

"Do you see it?" he asked; "I sincerely hope it's nothing very bad."

"*Severely*," whispered Lizzie.

"Yes, but that proves nothing. Those things are most unreliable. *Do* hope for the best."

Lizzie made no answer. Meanwhile passengers had been brushing in, and the car was full. The engine began to puff, and the conductor to shout. The train gave a jog.

"You'd better go, Sir, or you'll be carried off," said Lizzie, holding out her hand, with her face still hidden.

"May I go on to the next station with you?" said Bruce.

Lizzie gave him a rapid look, with a deepened flush. He had fancied that she was shedding tears. But those eyes were dry; they held fire rather than water.

"No, no, Sir; you must not. I insist. Good bye."

Bruce's offer had cost him a blush, too. He had been prepared to back it with the assurance that he had business ahead, and, indeed, to make a little business in order to satisfy his conscience. But Lizzie's answer was final.

"Very well," said he, "*good* bye. You have my real sympathy, Miss Crowe. Don't despair. We shall meet again."

The train rattled away. Lizzie caught a glimpse of a tall figure with lifted hat on the platform. But she sat motionless, with her head against the windowframe, her veil down, and her hands idle.

She had enough to do to think, or rather to feel. It is fortunate that the utmost shock of evil tidings often comes first. After that everything is for the better. Jack's name stood printed in the fatal column like a stern signal for despair. Lizzie felt conscious of a crisis which almost arrested her breath. Night had fallen at midday: what was the hour? A tragedy had stepped into her life: was she spectator or actor? She found herself face to face with death: was it not her own soul masquerading in a shroud? She sat in a half-stupor. She had been aroused from a dream into a waking nightmare. It was like hearing a murder-shriek while you turn the page of your novel. But I cannot describe these things. In time the crushing sense of calamity loosened its grasp. Feeling lashed her pinions. Thought struggled to rise. Passion was still, stunned, floored. She had recoiled like a receding wave for a stronger onset. A hundred ghastly fears and fancies strutted a moment, pecking at the young girl's naked heart, like sandpipers on the weltering beach. Then, as with a great murmurous rush, came the meaning of her grief. The flood-gates of emotion were opened.

At last passion exhausted itself, and Lizzie thought. Bruce's parting words rang in her ears. She did her best to hope. She reflected that wounds, even severe wounds, did not necessarily mean death. Death might easily be warded off. She would go to Jack; she would nurse him; she would watch by him; she would cure him. Even if Death had already beckoned, she would strike down his hand: if Life had already obeyed, she would issue the stronger mandate of Love. She would stanch his wounds; she would unseal his eyes with her kisses; she would call till he answered her.

Lizzie reached home and walked up the garden path. Mrs Ford stood in the parlor as she entered, upright, pale, and rigid. Each read the other's countenance. Lizzie went towards her slowly and giddily. She must of course kiss her patroness. She took her listless hand and bent towards her stern lips. Habitually Mrs Ford was the most undemonstrative of women. But as Lizzie looked closer into her face, she read signs of a grief infinitely more potent than her own. The formal kiss gave way: the young girl leaned her head on the old woman's shoulder and burst into sobs. Mrs Ford acknowledged those tears with a slow inclination of the head, full of a certain grim pathos: she put out her arms and pressed them closer to her heart.

At last Lizzie disengaged herself and sat down.

"I am going to him," said Mrs Ford.

Lizzie's dizziness returned. Mrs Ford was going,—and she, she?

"I am going to nurse him, and with God's help to save him."

"How did you hear?"

"I have a telegram from the surgeon of the regiment"; and Mrs Ford held out a paper.

Lizzie took it and read: "Lieutenant Ford dangerously wounded in the action of yesterday. You had better come on."

"I should like to go myself," said Lizzie: "I think Jack would like to have me."

"Nonsense! A pretty place for a young girl! I am not going for sentiment; I am going for use."

Lizzie leaned her head back in her chair, and closed her eyes. From the moment they had fallen upon Mrs Ford, she had felt a certain quiescence. And now it was a relief to have responsibility denied her. Like most weak persons, she was glad to step out of the current of life, now that it had begun to quicken into action. In emergencies, such persons are tacitly counted out; and they as tacitly consent to the arrangement. Even to the sensitive spirit there is a certain meditative rapture in standing on the quiet shore, (beside the ruminating cattle,) and watching the hurrying, eddying flood, which makes up for the loss of dignity. Lizzie's heart resumed its peaceful throbs. She sat, almost dreamily, with her eyes shut.

"I leave in an hour," said Mrs Ford. "I am going to get ready.—Do you hear?"

The young girl's silence was deeper consent than her companion supposed.

IV

It was a week before Lizzie heard from Mrs Ford. The letter, when it came, was very brief. Jack still lived. The wounds were three in number, and very serious; he was unconscious; he had not recognized her; but still the chances either way were thought equal. They would be much greater for his recovery nearer home; but it was impossible to move him. "I write from the midst of horrible scenes," said the poor lady. Subjoined was a list of necessary medicines, comforts, and delicacies, to be boxed up and sent.

For a while Lizzie found occupation in writing a letter to Jack, to be read in his first lucid moment, as she told Mrs Ford. This lady's man-of-business came up from the village to superintend the packing of the boxes. Her directions were strictly followed; and in no point were they found wanting. Mr Mackenzie bespoke Lizzie's admiration for their friend's wonderful clearness of memory and judgment. "I wish we had that woman at the head of affairs," said he. "'Gad, I'd apply for a Brigadier-Generalship."— "I'd apply to be sent South," thought Lizzie. When the boxes and letters were despatched, she sat down to await more news. Sat down, say I? Sat down, and rose, and wondered, and sat down again. These were lonely, weary days. Very different are the idleness of love and the idleness of grief. Very different it is to be alone with your hope and alone with your despair. Lizzie failed to rally her musings. I do not mean to say that her sorrow was very poignant, although she fancied it was. Habit was a great force in her simple nature; and her chief trouble now was that habit refused to work. Lizzie had to grapple with the stern tribulation of a decision to make, a problem to solve. She felt that there was some spiritual barrier between herself and repose. So she began in her usual fashion to build up a false repose on the hither side of belief. She might as well have tried to float on the Dead Sea. Peace eluding her, she tried to resign herself to tumult. She drank deep at the well of self-pity, but found its waters brackish. People are apt to think that they may temper the penalties of misconduct by self-commiseration, just as they season the long aftertaste of beneficence by a little spice of self-applause. But the Power of Good is a more grateful master than the Devil. What bliss to gaze into the smooth gurgling wake of a good deed, while the comely bark sails on with floating pennon! What horror to look into the muddy sediment which floats round the piratic keel! Go, sinner, and dissolve it with your tears! And you, scoffing friend, there is a way out! Or would you prefer the window? I'm an honest man forevermore.

One night Lizzie had a dream,—a rather disagreeable one,—which haunted her during many waking hours. It seemed to her that she was walking in a lonely place, with a tall, dark-eyed man who called her wife. Suddenly, in the shadow of a tree, they came upon an unburied corpse. Lizzie proposed to dig him a grave. They dug a great hole and took hold the corpse to lift him in; when suddenly he opened his eyes. Then they saw that he was covered with wounds. He looked at them intently for some time, turning his eyes from one to the other. At last he solemnly said, "Amen!" and closed his eyes. Then she and her companion placed him in the grave, and shovelled the earth over him, and stamped it down with their feet.

He of the dark eyes and he of the wounds were the two constantly recurring figures of Lizzie's reveries. She could never think of John without thinking of the courteous Leatherborough gentleman, too. These were the *data* of her problem. These two figures stood like opposing knights, (the black and the white,) foremost on the great chess-board of fate. Lizzie was the wearied, puzzled player. She would idly finger the other pieces, and shift them carelessly hither and thither; but it was of no avail: the game lay between the two knights. She would shut her eyes and long for some kind hand to come and tamper with the board; she would open them and see the two knights standing immovable, face to face. It was nothing new. A fancy had come in and offered defiance to a fact; they must fight it out. Lizzie generously inclined to the fancy, the unknown champion, with a reputation to make. Call her *blasée*, if you like, this little girl, whose record told of a couple of dances and a single lover, heartless, old before her time. Perhaps she deserves your scorn. I confess she thought herself ill-used. By whom? by what? wherein? These were questions Miss Crowe was not prepared to answer. Her intellect was unequal to the stern logic of human events. She expected two and two to make five: as why should they not for the nonce? She was like an actor who finds himself on the stage with a half-learned part and without sufficient wit to extemporize. Pray, where is the prompter? Alas, Elizabeth, that you had no mother! Young girls are prone to fancy that when once they have a lover, they have everything they need: a conclusion inconsistent with the belief entertained by many persons, that life begins with love. Lizzie's fortunes became old stories to her before she had half read them through. Jack's wounds and danger were an old story. Do not suppose that she had exhausted the lessons, the suggestions of these awful events, their inspirations, exhortations,—that she had wept as became the horror of the tragedy. No: the curtain had not yet fallen, yet our young lady had begun to yawn. To yawn? Aye, and to long for the afterpiece. Since the tragedy dragged, might she not divert herself with that well-bred man beside her?

Elizabeth was far from owning to herself that she had fallen away from her love. For my own part, I need no better proof of the fact than the dull persistency with which she denied it. What accusing voice broke out of the stillness? Jack's nobleness and magnanimity were the hourly theme of her clogged fancy. Again and again she declared to herself that she was unworthy of them, but that, if he would only recover and come home, she would be his eternal bond-slave. So she passed a very miserable month. Let us hope that her childish spirit was being tempered to some useful purpose. Let us hope so.

She roamed about the empty house with her footsteps tracked by an unlaid ghost. She cried aloud and said that she was very unhappy; she groaned and called herself wicked. Then, sometimes, appalled at her moral perplexities, she declared that she was neither wicked nor unhappy; she was contented, patient, and wise. Other girls had lost their lovers: it was the present way of life. Was she weaker than most women? Nay, but Jack was the best of men. If he would only come back directly, without delay, as he was, senseless, dying even, that she might look at him, touch him, speak to him! Then she would say that she could no longer answer for herself, and wonder (or pretend to wonder) whether she were not going mad. Suppose Mrs Ford should come back and find her in an unswept room, pallid and insane? or suppose she should die of her troubles? What if she should kill herself?—dismiss the servants, and close the house, and lock herself up with a knife? Then she would cut her arm to escape from dismay at what she had already done; and then her courage would ebb away with her blood, and, having so far pledged herself to despair, her life would ebb away with her courage: and then, alone, in darkness, with none to help her, she would vainly scream, and thrust the knife into her temple, and swoon to death. And Jack would come back, and burst into the house, and wander through the empty rooms, calling her name, and for all answer get a deathscent! These imaginings were the more creditable or discreditable to Lizzie, that she had never read "Romeo and Juliet." At any rate, they served to dissipate time,—heavy, weary time,—the more heavy and weary as it bore dark foreshadowings of some momentous event. If that event would only come, whatever it was, and sever this Gordian knot of doubt!

The days passed slowly: the leaden sands dropped one by one. The roads were too bad for walking; so Lizzie was obliged to confine her restlessness to the narrow bounds of the empty house, or to an occasional journey to the village, where people sickened her by their dull indifference to her spiritual agony. Still they could not fail to remark how poorly Miss Crowe was looking. This was true, and Lizzie knew it. I think she even took a certain comfort in her pallor and in her failing interest in her dress. There was some satisfaction in displaying her white roses amid the apple-cheeked prosperity of Main Street. At last Miss Cooper, the Doctor's sister, spoke to her:—

"How is it, Elizabeth, you look so pale, and thin, and worn out? What you been doing with yourself? Falling in love, eh? It isn't right to be so much alone. Come down and stay with us awhile,—till Mrs Ford and John come back," added Miss Cooper, who wished to put a cheerful face on the matter.

For Miss Cooper, indeed, any other face would have been difficult. Lizzie agreed to come. Her hostess was a busy, unbeautiful old maid, sister and housekeeper of the village physician. Her occupation here below was to perform the forgotten tasks of her fellowmen,—to pick up their dropped stitches, as she herself declared. She was never idle, for her general cleverness was commensurate with mortal needs. Her own story was, that she kept moving, so that folks couldn't see how ugly she was. And, in fact, her existence was manifest through her long train of good deeds,— just as the presence of a comet is shown by its tail. It was doubtless on the above principle that her visage was agitated by a perpetual laugh.

Meanwhile more news had been coming from Virginia. "What an absurdly long letter you sent John," wrote Mrs Ford, in acknowledging the receipt of the boxes. "His first lucid moment would be very short, if he were to take upon himself to read your effusions. Pray keep your long stories till he gets well." For a fortnight the young soldier remained the same,—feverish, conscious only at intervals. Then came a change for the worse, which, for many weary days, however, resulted in nothing decisive. "If he could only be moved to Glenham, home, and old sights," said his mother, "I should have hope. But think of the journey!" By this time Lizzie had stayed out ten days of her visit.

One day Miss Cooper came in from a walk, radiant with tidings. Her face, as I have observed, wore a continual smile, being dimpled and punctured all over with merriment,—so that, when an unusual cheerfulness was super-diffused, it resembled a tempestuous little pool into which a great stone has been cast.

"Guess who's come," said she, going up to the piano, which Lizzie was carelessly fingering, and putting her hands on the young girl's shoulders. "Just guess!"

Lizzie looked up.

"Jack," she half gasped.

"Oh, dear, no, not that! How stupid of me! I mean Mr Bruce, your Leatherborough admirer."

"Mr Bruce! Mr Bruce!" said Lizzie. "Really?"

"True as I live. He's come to bring his sister to the Water-Cure. I met them at the post-office."

Lizzie felt a strange sensation of good news. Her finger-tips were on fire. She was deaf to her companion's rattling chronicle. She broke into the midst of it with a fragment of some triumphant, jubilant melody. The keys rang beneath her flashing hands. And then she suddenly stopped, and Miss Cooper, who was taking off her bonnet at the mirror, saw that her face was covered with a burning flush.

That evening, Mr Bruce presented himself at Doctor Cooper's, with whom he had a slight acquaintance. To Lizzie he was infinitely courteous and tender. He assured her, in very pretty terms, of his profound sympathy with her in her cousin's danger,—her cousin he still called him,—and it seemed to Lizzie that until that moment no one had begun to be kind. And then he began to rebuke her, playfully and in excellent taste, for her pale cheeks.

"Isn't it dreadful?" said Miss Cooper. "She looks like a ghost. I guess she's in love."

"He must be a good-for-nothing lover to make his mistress look so sad. If I were you, I'd give him up, Miss Crowe."

162

"I didn't know I looked sad," said Lizzie.

"You don't now," said Miss Cooper. "You're smiling and blushing. A'n't she blushing, Mr Bruce?"

"I think Miss Crowe has no more than her natural color," said Bruce, dropping his eye-glass. "What have you been doing all this while since we parted?"

"All this while? It's only six weeks. I don't know. Nothing. What have you?"

"I've been doing nothing, too. It's hard work."

"Have you been to any more parties?"

"Not one."

"Any more sleigh-rides?"

"Yes. I took one more dreary drive all alone,—over that same road, you know. And I stopped at the farm-house again, and saw the old woman we had the talk with. She remembered us, and asked me what had become of the young lady who was with me before. I told her you were gone home, but that I hoped soon to go and see you. So she sent you her love"—

"Oh, how nice!" exclaimed Lizzie.

"Wasn't it? And then she made a certain little speech; I won't repeat it, or we shall have Miss Cooper talking about your blushes again."

"I know," cried the lady in question: "she said she was very"—

"Very what?" said Lizzie.

"Very h-a-n-d—what everyone says."

"Very handy?" asked Lizzie. "I'm sure no one ever said that."

"Of course," said Bruce; "and I answered what everyone answers."

"Have you seen Mrs Littlefield lately?"

"Several times. I called on her the day before I left town, to see if she had any messages for you."

"Oh, thank you! I hope she's well."

"Oh, she's as jolly as ever. She sent you her love, and hoped you would come back to Leatherborough very soon again. I told her, that, however it might be with the first message, the second should be a joint one from both of us."

"You're very kind. I should like very much to go again.—Do you like Mrs Littlefield?"

"Like her? Yes. Don't you? She's thought a very pleasing woman."

"Oh, she's very nice.—I don't think she has much conversation."

"Ah, I'm afraid you mean she doesn't backbite. We've always found plenty to talk about."

"That's a very significant tone. What, for instance?"

"Well, we *have* talked about Miss Crowe."

"Oh, you have? Do you call that having plenty to talk about?"

"We *have* talked about Mr Bruce,—haven't we, Elizabeth?" said Miss Cooper, who had her own notion of being agreeable.

It was not an altogether bad notion, perhaps; but Bruce found her interruptions rather annoying, and insensibly allowed them to shorten his visit. Yet, as it was, he sat till eleven o'clock,—a stay quite unprecedented at Glenham.

When he left the house, he went splashing down the road with a very elastic tread, springing over the starlit puddles, and trolling out some sentimental ditty. He reached the inn, and went up to his sister's sitting-room.

"Why, Robert, where have you been all this while?" said Miss Bruce.

"At Dr Cooper's."

"Dr Cooper's? I should think you had! Who's Dr Cooper?"

"Where Miss Crowe's staying."

"Miss Crowe? Ah, Mrs Littlefield's friend! Is she as pretty as ever?"

"Prettier,—prettier,—prettier. *Ta-ra-ta! tara-ta!*"

"Oh, Robert, do stop that singing! You'll rouse the whole house."

V

Late one afternoon, at dusk, about three weeks after Mr Bruce's arrival, Lizzie was sitting alone by the fire, in Miss Cooper's parlor, musing, as became the place and hour. The Doctor and his sister came in, dressed for a lecture.

"I'm sorry you won't go, my dear," said Miss Cooper. "It's a most interesting subject: 'A Year of the War.' All the battles and things described, you know."

"I'm tired of war," said Lizzie.

"Well, well, if you're tired of the war, we'll leave you in peace. Kiss me good-bye. What's the matter? You look sick. You are homesick, a'n't you?"

"No, no,—I'm very well."

"Would you like me to stay at home with you?"

"Oh, no! pray, don't!"

"Well, we'll tell you all about it. Will they have programmes, James? I'll bring her a programme.—But you really feel as if you were going to be ill. Feel of her skin, James."

"No, you needn't, Sir," said Lizzie. "How queer of you, Miss Cooper! I'm perfectly well."

And at last her friends departed. Before long the servant came with the lamp, ushering Mr Mackenzie.

"Good evening, Miss," said he. "Bad news from Mrs Ford."

"Bad news?"

"Yes, Miss. I've just got a letter stating that Mr John is growing worse and worse, and that they look for his death from hour to hour.—It's very sad," he added, as Elizabeth was silent.

"Yes, it's very sad," said Lizzie.

"I thought you'd like to hear it."

"Thank you."

"He was a very noble young fellow," pursued Mr Mackenzie.

Lizzie made no response.

"There's the letter," said Mr Mackenzie, handing it over to her.

Lizzie opened it.

"How long she is reading it!" thought her visitor. "You can't see so far from the light, can you, Miss?"

"Yes," said Lizzie.—"His poor mother! Poor woman!"

"Aye, indeed, Miss,—she's the one to be pitied."

"Yes, she's the one to be pitied," said Lizzie. "Well!" and she gave him back the letter.

"I thought you'd like to see it," said Mackenzie, drawing on his gloves; and then, after a pause,—"I'll call again, Miss, if I hear anything more. Good night!"

Lizzie got up and lowered the light, and then went back to her sofa by the fire.

Half an hour passed; it went slowly; but it passed. Still lying there in the dark room on the sofa, Lizzie heard a ring at the door-bell, a man's voice and a man's tread in the hall. She rose and went to the lamp. As she turned it up, the parlor door opened. Bruce came in.

"I was sitting in the dark," said Lizzie; "but when I heard you coming, I raised the light."

"Are you afraid of me?" said Bruce.

"Oh, no! I'll put it down again. Sit down."

"I saw your friends going out," pursued Bruce; "so I knew I should find you alone.—What are you doing here in the dark?"

"I've just received very bad news from Mrs Ford about her son. He's much worse, and will probably not live."

"Is it possible?"

"I was thinking about that."

"Dear me! Well, that's a sad subject. I'm told he was a very fine young man."

"He was,—very," said Lizzie.

Bruce was silent awhile. He was a stranger to the young officer, and felt that he had nothing to offer beyond the commonplace expressions of sympathy and surprise. Nor had he exactly the measure of his companion's interest in him.

"If he dies," said Lizzie, "it will be under great injustice."

"Ah! what do you mean?"

"There wasn't a braver man in the army."

"I suppose not."

"And, oh, Mr Bruce," continued Lizzie, "he was so clever and good and generous! I wish you had known him."

"I wish I had. But what do you mean by injustice? Were these qualities denied him?"

"No indeed! Everyone that looked at him could see that he was perfect."

"Where's the injustice, then? It ought to be enough for him that you should think so highly of him."

"Oh, he knew that," said Lizzie.

Bruce was a little puzzled by his companion's manner. He watched her, as she sat with her cheek on her hand, looking at the fire. There was a long pause. Either they were too friendly or too thoughtful for the silence to be embarrassing. Bruce broke it at last.

"Miss Crowe," said he, "on a certain occasion, some time ago, when you first heard of Mr Ford's wounds, I offered you my company, with the wish to console you as far as I might for what seemed a considerable shock. It was, perhaps, a bold offer for so new a friend; but, nevertheless, in it even then my heart spoke. You turned me off. Will you let me repeat it? Now, with a better right, will you let me speak out all my heart?"

Lizzie heard this speech, which was delivered in a slow and hesitating tone, without looking up or moving her head, except, perhaps, at the words, "turned me off." After Bruce had ceased, she still kept her position.

"You'll not turn me off now?" added her companion.

She dropped her hand, raised her head, and looked at him a moment: he thought he saw the glow of tears in her eyes. Then she sank back upon the sofa with her face in the shadow of the mantelpiece.

"I don't understand you, Mr Bruce," said she.

"Ah, Elizabeth! am I such a poor speaker. How shall I make it plain? When I saw your friends leave home half an hour ago, and reflected that you would probably be alone, I determined to go right in and have a talk with you that I've long been wanting to have. But first I walked half a mile up the road, thinking hard,—thinking how I should say what I had to say. I made up my mind to nothing, but that somehow or other I should say it. I would trust,—I *do* trust your frankness, kindness, and sympathy, to a feeling corresponding to my own. Do you understand that feeling? Do you know that I love you? I do, I do, I do! You *must* know it. If you don't, I solemnly swear it. I solemnly ask you, Elizabeth, to take me for your husband."

While Bruce said these words, he rose, with their rising passion, and came and stood before Lizzie. Again she was motionless.

"Does it take you so long to think?" said he, trying to read her indistinct features; and he sat down on the sofa beside her and took her hand.

At last Lizzie spoke.

"Are you sure," said she, "that you love me?"

"As sure as that I breathe. Now, Elizabeth, make me as sure that I am loved in return."

"It seems very strange, Mr Bruce," said Lizzie.

"What seems strange? Why should it? For a month I've been trying, in a hundred dumb ways, to make it plain: and now, when I swear it, it only seems strange!"

"What do you love me for?"

"For? For yourself, Elizabeth."

"Myself? I am nothing."

"I love you for what you are,—for your deep, kind heart,—for being so perfectly a woman."

Lizzie drew away her hand, and her lover rose and stood before her again. But now she looked up into his face, questioning when she should have answered, drinking strength from his entreaties for her replies. There he stood before her, in the glow of the firelight, in all his gentlemanhood, for her to accept or reject. She slowly rose and gave him the hand she had withdrawn.

"Mr Bruce, I shall be very proud to love you," she said.

And then, as if this effort was beyond her strength, she half staggered back to the sofa again. And still holding her hand, he sat down beside her. And there they were still sitting when they heard the Doctor and his sister come in.

For three days Elizabeth saw nothing of Mr Mackenzie. At last, on the fourth day, passing his office in the village, she went in and asked for him. He came out of his little back parlour with his mouth full and a beaming face.

"Good-day, Miss Crowe, and good news!"

"*Good* news?" cried Lizzie.

"Capital!" said he, looking hard at her, while he put on his spectacles. "She writes that Mr John—won't you take a seat?—has taken a sudden and unexpected turn for the better. Now's the moment to save him; it's an equal risk. They were to start for the North the second day after date. The surgeon comes with them. So they'll be home—of course they'll travel slowly—in four or five days. Yes, Miss, it's a remarkable Providence. And that noble young man will be spared to the country, and to those who love him, as I do."

"I had better go back to the house and have it got ready," said Lizzie, for an answer.

"Yes, Miss, I think you had. In fact, Mrs Ford made that request."

The request was obeyed. That same day Lizzie went home. For two days she found it her interest to overlook, assiduously, a general sweeping, scrubbing, and provisioning. She allowed herself no idle moment until bed-time. Then—But I would rather not be the chamberlain of her agony. It was the easier to work, as Mr Bruce had gone to Leatherborough on business.

On the fourth evening, at twilight, John Ford was borne up to the door on his stretcher, with his mother stalking beside him in rigid grief, and kind, silent friends pressing about with helping hands.

"Home they brought her warrior dead,
She nor swooned nor uttered cry."

It was, indeed, almost a question, whether Jack was not dead. Death is not thinner, paler, stiller. Lizzie moved about like one in a dream. Of course, when there are so many sympathetic friends, a man's family has nothing to do,—except exercise a little self-control. The women huddled Mrs Ford to bed; rest was imperative; she was killing herself. And it was significant of her weakness that she did not resent this advice. In greeting her, Lizzie felt as if she were embracing the stone image on the top of a sepulchre. She, too, had her cares anticipated. Good Doctor Cooper and his sister stationed themselves at the young man's couch.

The Doctor prophesied wondrous things of the change of climate; he was certain of a recovery. Lizzie found herself very shortly dealt with as an obstacle to this consummation. Access to John was prohibited. "Perfect stillness, you know, my dear," whispered Miss Cooper, opening his chamber door on a crack, in a pair of very creaking shoes. So for the first evening that her old friend was at home Lizzie caught but a glimpse of his pale, senseless face, as she hovered outside the long train of his attendants. If we may suppose any of these kind people to have had eyes for aught but the sufferer, we may be sure that they saw another visage equally sad and white. The sufferer? It was hardly Jack, after all.

When Lizzie was turned from Jack's door, she took a covering from a heap of draperies that had been hurriedly tossed down in the hall: it was an old army blanket. She wrapped it round her, and went out on the verandah. It was nine o'clock; but the darkness was filled with light. A great wanton wind—the ghost of the raw blast which travels by day—had arisen, bearing long, soft gusts of inland spring. Scattered clouds were hurrying across the white sky. The bright moon, careering in their midst, seemed to have wandered forth in frantic quest of the hidden stars.

Lizzie nestled her head in the blanket, and sat down on the steps. A strange earthy smell lingered in that faded old rug, and with it a faint perfume of tobacco. Instantly the young girl's senses were transported as they had never been before to those far-off Southern battlefields. She saw men lying in swamps, puffing their kindly pipes, drawing their blankets closer, canopied with the same luminous dusk that shone down upon her comfortable weakness. Her mind wandered amid these scenes till recalled to the present by the swinging of the garden gate. She heard a firm, well-known tread crunching the gravel. Mr Bruce came up the path. As he drew near the steps, Lizzie arose. The blanket fell back from her head, and Bruce started at recognizing her.

"Hullo! You, Elizabeth? What's the matter?"

Lizzie made no answer.

"Are you one of Mr Ford's watchers?" he continued, coming up the steps; "how is he?"

Still she was silent. Bruce put out his hands to take hers, and bent forward as if to kiss her. She half shook him off, and retreated toward the door.

"Good heavens!" cried Bruce; "what's the matter? Are you moonstruck? Can't you speak?"

"No,—no,—not to-night," said Lizzie, in a choking voice. "Go away,—go away!"

She stood holding the door-handle, and motioning him off. He hesitated a moment, and then advanced. She opened the door rapidly, and went in. He heard her lock it. He stood looking at it stupidly for some time, and then slowly turned round and walked down the steps.

The next morning Lizzie arose with the early dawn, and came downstairs. She went to the room where Jack lay, and gently opened the door. Miss Cooper was dozing in her chair. Lizzie crossed the threshold, and stole up to the bed. Poor Ford lay peacefully sleeping. There was his old face, after all,—his strong, honest features refined, but not weakened, by pain. Lizzie softly drew up a low chair, and sat down beside him. She gazed into his face,—the dear honored face into which she had so often gazed in health. It was strangely handsomer: body stood for less. It seemed to Lizzie, that, as the fabric of her lover's soul was more clearly revealed,—the veil of the temple rent wellnigh in twain,—she could read the justification of all her old worship. One of Jack's hands lay outside the sheets,—those strong, supple fingers, once so cunning in workmanship, so frank in friendship, now thinner and whiter than her own. After looking at it for some time, Lizzie gently grasped it. Jack slowly opened his eyes. Lizzie's heart began to throb; it was as if the stillness of the sanctuary had given a sign. At first there was no recognition in the young man's gaze. Then the dull pupils began visibly to brighten. There came to his lips the commencement of that strange moribund smile which seems so ineffably satirical of the things of this world. O imposing spectacle of death! O blessed soul, marked for promotion! What earthly favor is like thine? Lizzie sank down on her knees, and, still clasping John's hand, bent closer over him.

"Jack,—dear, dear Jack," she whispered, "do you know me?"

The smile grew more intense. The poor fellow drew out his other hand, and slowly, feebly placed it on Lizzie's head, stroking down her hair with his fingers.

"Yes, yes," she murmured; "you know me, don't you? I am Lizzie, Jack. Don't you remember Lizzie?"

Ford moved his lips inaudibly, and went on patting her head.

"This is home, you know," said Lizzie; "this is Glenham. You haven't forgotten Glenham? You are with your mother and me and your friends. Dear, darling Jack!"

Still he went on, stroking her head; and his feeble lips tried to emit some sound. Lizzie laid her head down on the pillow beside his own, and still his hand lingered caressingly on her hair.

"Yes, you know me," she pursued; "you are with your friends now forever,—with those who will love and take care of you, oh, forever!"

"I'm very badly wounded," murmured Jack, close to her ear.

"Yes, yes, my dear boy, but your wounds are healing. I will love you and nurse you forever."

"Yes, Lizzie, our old promise," said Jack: and his hand fell upon her neck, and with its feeble pressure he drew her closer, and she wet his face with her tears.

Then Miss Cooper, awakening, rose and drew Lizzie away.

"I am sure you excite him, my dear. It is best he should have none of his family near him,—persons with whom he has associations, you know."

Here the Doctor was heard gently tapping on the window, and Lizzie went round to the door to admit him.

She did not see Jack again all day. Two or three times she ventured into the room, but she was banished by a frown, or a finger raised to the lips. She waylaid the Doctor frequently. He was blithe and cheerful, certain of Jack's recovery. This good man used to exhibit as much moral elation at the prospect of a cure as an orthodox believer at that of a new convert: it was one more body gained from the Devil. He assured Lizzie that the change of scene and climate had already begun to tell: the fever was lessening, the worst symptoms disappearing. He answered Lizzie's reiterated desire to do something by directions to keep the house quiet and the sick-room empty.

Soon after breakfast, Miss Dawes, a neighbor, came in to relieve Miss Cooper, and this indefatigable lady transferred her attention to Mrs Ford. Action was forbidden her. Miss Cooper was delighted for once to be able to lay down the law to her vigorous neighbor, of whose fine judgment she had always stood in awe. Having bullied Mrs Ford into taking her breakfast in the little sitting-room, she closed the doors, and prepared for "a good long talk." Lizzie was careful not to break in upon this interview. She had bidden her patroness good morning, asked after her health, and received one of her temperate osculations. As she passed the invalid's door, Doctor Cooper came out and asked her to go and look for a certain roll of bandages, in Mr John's trunk, which had been carried into another room. Lizzie hastened to perform this task. In fumbling through the contents of the trunk, she came across a packet of letters in a well-known feminine handwriting. She pocketed it, and, after disposing of the bandages, went to her own room, locked the door, and sat down to examine the letters. Between reading and thinking and sighing and (in spite of herself) smiling, this process took the whole morning. As she came down to dinner, she encountered Mrs Ford and Miss Cooper, emerging from the sitting-room, the good long talk being only just concluded.

"How do you feel, Ma'am?" she asked the elder lady,—"rested?"

For all answer, Mrs Ford gave a look—I had almost said a scowl—so hard, so cold, so reproachful, that Lizzie was transfixed. But suddenly its sickening meaning was revealed to her. She turned to Miss Cooper, who stood pale and fluttering beside the mistress, her everlasting smile glazed over with a piteous, deprecating glance; and I fear her eyes flashed out the same message of angry scorn they had just received. These telegraphic operations are very rapid. The ladies hardly halted: the next moment found them seated at the dinner-table with Miss Cooper scrutinising her napkin-mark and Mrs Ford saying grace.

Dinner was eaten in silence. When it was over, Lizzie returned to her own room. Miss Cooper went home, and Mrs Ford went to her son. Lizzie heard the firm low click of the lock as she closed the door. Why did she lock it? There was something fatal in the silence that followed. The plot of her little tragedy thickened. Be it so: she would act her part with the rest. For the second time in her experience, her mind was lightened by the intervention of Mrs Ford. Before the scorn of her own conscience, (which never came), before Jack's deepest reproach, she was ready to bow down,—but not before that long-faced Nemesis in black silk. The leaven of resentment began to work. She leaned back in her chair, and folded her arms, brave to await results. But before long she fell asleep. She was roused by a knock at her chamber-door. The afternoon was far gone. Miss Dawes stood without.

"Elizabeth, Mr John wants very much to see you, with his love. Come down very gently: his mother is lying down. Will you sit with him while I take my dinner?—Better? Yes, ever so much."

Lizzie betook herself with trembling haste to Jack's bedside.

He was propped up with pillows. His pale cheeks were slightly flushed. His eyes were bright. He raised himself, and, for such feeble arms, gave Lizzie a long, strong embrace.

"I've not seen you all day, Lizzie," said he. "Where have you been?"

"Dear Jack, they wouldn't let me come near you. I begged and prayed. And I wanted so to go to you in the army; but I couldn't. I wish, I wish I had!"

"You wouldn't have liked it, Lizzie. I'm glad you didn't. It's a bad, bad place."

He lay quietly, holding her hands and gazing at her.

"Can I do anything for you, dear?" asked the young girl. "I would work my life out. I'm so glad you're better!"

It was some time before Jack answered,—

"Lizzie," said he, at last, "I sent for you to look at you.—You are more wondrously beautiful than ever. Your hair is brown,—like—like nothing; your eyes are blue; your neck is white. Well, well!"

He lay perfectly motionless, but for his eyes. They wandered over her with a kind of peaceful glee, like sunbeams playing on a statue. Poor Ford lay, indeed, not unlike an old wounded Greek, who at falling dusk has crawled into a temple to die, steeping the last dull interval in idle admiration of sculptured Artemis.

"Ah, Lizzie, this is already heaven!" he murmured.

"It will be heaven when you get well," whispered Lizzie.

He smiled into her eyes:—

"You say more than you mean. There should be perfect truth between us. Dear Lizzie, I am not going to get well. They are all very much mistaken. I am going to die. I've done my work. Death makes up for everything. My great pain is in leaving you. But you, too, will die one of these days; remember that. In all pain and sorrow, remember that."

Lizzie was able to reply only by the tightening grasp of her hands.

"But there is something more," pursued Jack. "Life *is* as good as death. Your heart has found its true keeper; so we shall all three be happy. Tell him I bless him and honor him. Tell him God, too, blesses him. Shake hands with him for me," said Jack, feebly moving his pale fingers. "My mother," he went on—"be very kind to her. She will have great grief, but she will not die of it. She'll live to great age. Now, Lizzie, I can't talk any more; I wanted to say farewell. You'll keep me farewell,—you'll stay with me awhile,—won't you? I'll look at you till the last. For a little while you'll be mine, holding my hands—so—until death parts us."

Jack kept his promise. His eyes were fixed in a firm gaze long after the sense had left them.

In the early dawn of the next day, Elizabeth left her sleepless bed, opened the window, and looked out on the wide prospect, still cool and dim with departing night. It offered freshness and peace to her hot head and restless heart. She dressed herself hastily, crept downstairs, passed the death-chamber, and stole out of the quiet house. She turned away from the still sleeping village and walked towards the open country. She went a long way without knowing it. The sun had risen high when she bethought herself to turn. As she came back along the brightening highway, and drew near home, she saw a tall figure standing beneath the budding trees of the garden, hesitating, apparently, whether to open the gate. Lizzie came upon him almost before he had seen her. Bruce's first movement was to put out his hands, as any lover might; but as Lizzie raised her veil, he dropped them.

"Yes, Mr Bruce," said Lizzie, "I'll give you my hand once more,—in farewell."

"Elizabeth!" cried Bruce, half stupefied, "in God's name, what do you mean by these crazy speeches?"

"I mean well. I mean kindly and humanely to you. And I mean justice to my old—old love."

She went to him, took his listless hand, without looking into his wild, smitten face, shook it passionately, and then, wrenching her own from his grasp, opened the gate and let it swing behind her.

"No! no! no!" she almost shrieked, turning about in the path. "I forbid you to follow me!"

But for all that, he went in.

Bayou L'Ombre
1892

GRACE E. KING

Grace E. King (1852–1932) was born in New Orleans, where, at the age of ten, she witnessed the Federal occupation of the city— an event recounted in her Memories of a Southern Woman of Letters *(1932), published shortly after her death. By the 1880s she had begun to write short stories, many of them drawing upon her Southern roots and upbringing. "Bayou L'Ombre," included in King's collection* Tales of a Time and Place *(1892), is clearly autobiographical in its account of three sisters undergoing the trauma of a siege at their New Orleans plantation.*

Of course they knew all about war—soldiers, flags, music, generals on horseback brandishing swords, knights in armor escalading walls, cannons booming through clouds of smoke. They were familiarized with it pictorially and by narrative long before the alphabet made its appearance in the nursery with rudimentary accounts of the world they were born into, the simple juvenile world of primary sensations and colors. Their great men, and great women, too, were all fighters; the great events of their histories, battles; the great places of their geography, where they were fought (and generally the more bloody the battle, the more glorious the place); while their little chronology—the pink-covered one— stepped briskly over the centuries solely on the names of kings and sanguinary saliencies. Sunday added the sabbatical supplement to weekday lessons, symbolizing religion, concreting sin, incorporating evil, for their better comprehension, putting Jehovah himself in armor, to please their childish faculties—the omnipotent Intervener of the Old Testament, for whom they waved banners, sang hymns, and by the brevet title, "little *soldiers* of the cross," felt committed as by baptism to an attitude of expectant hostility. Mademoiselle Couper, their governess, eased the cross-stitching in their samplers during the evenings, after supper, with traditions of "le grand Napoleon," in whose army her grandfather was a terrible and distinguished officer, le Capitaine Césaire Paul Picquet de Montignac; and although Mademoiselle Couper was most unlovable and exacting at times, and very homely, such were their powers of sympathetic enthusiasm even then that they often went to bed envious of the possessor of so glorious an ancestor, and dreamed fairy tales of him whose gray hair, enshrined in a brooch, reposed comfortably under the folds of mademoiselle's fat chin—the hair that Napoleon had looked upon!

When a war broke out in their own country they could hardly credit their good-fortune; that is, Christine and Régina, for Lolotte was still a baby. A wonderful panorama was suddenly unfolded before them. It was their first intimation of the identity of the world they lived in with the world they learned about, their first perception of the existence of an entirely novel sentiment in their hearts—patriotism, the *amour sacré de la patrie,* over which they had seen mademoiselle shed tears as copiously as her grandfather had blood. It made them and all their little companions feel very proud, this war; but it gave them a heavy sense of responsibility, turning their youthful precocity incontinently away from books, slates, and pianos towards the martial considerations that befitted the hour. State rights, Federal limits, monitors and fortresses, proclamations, Presidents, recognitions, and declarations, they acquired them all with facility, taxing, as in other lessons, their tongue to repeat the unintelligible on trust for future intelligence. As their father fired his huge after-dinner bombs, so they shot their diminutive ammunition; as he lighted brands in the great conflagration, they lighted tapers; and the two contending Presidents themselves did not get on their knees with more fervor before their colossal sphinxes than these little girls did before their doll-baby presentment of "Country." It was very hard to realize at times that histories and story-books and poetry would indeed be written about them; that little flags would mark battles all over the map of their country—the country Mademoiselle Couper despised as so hopelessly, warlessly insignificant; that men would do great things and women say them, teachers and copy-books reiterate them, and children learn them, just as they did of the Greeks and Romans, the English and French. The great advantage was having God on their side, as the children of Israel had; the next best thing was having the finest country, the most noble men, and the bravest soldiers. The only fear was that the enemy would be beaten too easily, and the war cease too soon to be glorious; for, characteristic of their sex, they demanded nothing less than that their war should be the longest, bloodiest, and most glorious of all wars ever heard of, in comparison with which even "le grand Napoleon" and his Capitaine Picquet would be effaced from memory. For this were exercised their first attempts at extempore prayer. God, the dispenser of inexhaustible supplies of munitions of war, became quite a different power, a nearer and dearer personality, than "Our Father," the giver of simple daily bread, and He did not lack reminding of the existence of the young Confederacy, nor of the hearsay exigencies they gathered from the dinner-table talk.

Titine was about thirteen, Gina twelve, and Lolotte barely eight years old, when this, to them, happy break in their lives occurred. It was easily comprehensible to them that their city should be captured, and that to escape that grim ultimatum of Mademoiselle Couper, *"passées au fil de l'épée,"* they should be bundled up very hurriedly one night, carried out of their home, and journey in troublesome roundabout ways to the plantation on Bayou l'Ombre.

That was all four years ago. School and play and city life, dolls and fêtes and Santa Claus, had become the property of memory. Peace for them hovered in that obscurity which had once enveloped war, while "'61," "'62," "'63," "'64," filled immeasurable spaces in their short past. Four times had Christine and Régina changed the date in their diaries—the last token of remembrance from Mademoiselle Couper—altering the numerals with naïve solemnity, as if under the direction of the Almighty himself, closing with conventional ceremony the record of the lived-out twelve months, opening with appropriate aspirations the year to come. The laboriously careful chronicle that followed was not, however, of the growth of their bodies advancing by inches, nor the expansion of their minds, nor of the vague forms that began to people the shadow-land of their sixteen and seventeen year old hearts. Their own budding and leafing and growing was as unnoted as that of the trees and weeds about them. The progress of the war, the growth of their hatred of the enemy, the expansion of the *amour sacré* germ—these were the confidences that filled the neatly-stitched foolscap volumes. If on comparison one sister was found to have been happier in the rendition of the common sentiment, the coveted fervor and eloquence were plagiarized or imitated the next day by the other, a generous emulation thus keeping the original flame not only alight, but burning, while from assimilating each other's sentiments the two girls grew with identity of purpose into identity of mind, and effaced the slight difference of age between them.

Little Lolotte responded as well as she could to the enthusiastic exactions of her sisters. She gave her rag dolls patriotic names, obediently hated and loved as they required, and learned to recite all the war songs procurable, even to the teeming quantities of the stirring "Men of the South, our foes are up!" But as long as the squirrels gambolled on the fences, the blackbirds flocked in the fields, and the ditches filled with fish; as long as the seasons imported such constant variety of attractions—persimmons, dewberries, blackberries, acorns, wild plums, grapes, and muscadines; as long as the cows had calves, the dogs puppies, the hogs pigs, and the quarters new babies to be named; as long as the exasperating negro children needed daily subjugation, regulation, and discipline—the day's measure was too well filled and the night's slumber too short to admit of her carrying on a very vigorous warfare for a country so far away from Bayou l'Ombre—a country whose grievances she could not understand.

But—there were no soldiers, flags, music, parades, battles, or sieges. This war was altogether distinct from the wars contained in books or in Mademoiselle Couper's memory. There was an absence of the simplest requirements of war. They kept awaiting the familiar events for which they had been prepared; but after four years the only shots fired on Bayou l'Ombre were at game in the forest, the only blood shed was from the tottering herds of Texas beeves driven across the swamps to them, barely escaping by timely butchery the starvation they came to relieve, and the only heroism they had been called upon to display was still going to bed in the dark. Indeed, were it not that they knew there was a war they might have supposed that some malignant fairy had transported them from a state of wealth and luxury to the condition of those miserable Hathorns, the pariahs of their childhood, who lived just around the corner from them in the city, with whom they had never been allowed to associate. If they had not so industriously fostered the proper feelings in their hearts, they might almost have forgotten it, or, like Lolotte, been diverted from it by the generous overtures of nature all around them. But they kept on reminding each other that it was not the degrading want of money, as in the Hathorns' case, that forced them to live on salt meat, corn-bread, and sassafras tea, to dress like the negro women in the quarters, that deprived them of education and society, and imprisoned them in a swamp-encircled plantation, the prey of chills and fever; but it was for love of country, and being little women now, they loved their country more, the more they suffered for her. Disillusion might have supervened to disappointment and bitterness have quenched hope, experience might at last have sharpened their vision, but for the imagination, that ethereal parasite which fattens on the stagnant forces of youth and garnishes with tropical luxuriance the abnormal source of its nourishment. Soaring aloft, above the prosaic actualities of the present, beyond the rebutting evidence of earth, was a fanciful stage where the drama of war such as they craved was unfolded; where neither homespun, starvation, overflows, nor illness were allowed to enter; where the heroes and heroines they loved acted roles in all the conventional glitter of costume and conduct, amid the dazzling pomps and circumstances immortalized in history and romance. Their hearts would bound and leap after these phantasms, like babes in nurses' arms after the moon, and would almost burst with longing, their ripe little hearts, Pandora-boxes packed with passions and pleasures for a lifetime, ready to spring open at a touch! On moonlit nights in summer, or under the low gray clouds of winter days, in the monotony of nothingness about them, the yearning in their breasts was like that of hunting dogs howling for the unseen game. Sometimes a rumor of a battle "out in the Confederacy" would find its way across the swamps to them, and months afterwards a newspaper would be thrown to them from a passing skiff, some old, useless, tattered, disreputable, journalistic tramp, garrulous with mendacities; but it was all true to them, if to no one else in the world—the factitious triumphs, the lurid glories, the pyrotechnical promises, prophecies, calculations, and Victory with the laurel wreath always in the future, never out of sight for an instant. They would con the fraudulent evangel, entranced; their eyes would sparkle, the blood color their cheeks, their voices vibrate, and a strange strength excite and nerve their bodies. Then would follow wakeful nights and restless days; Black Margarets, Jeanne d'Arcs, Maids of Saragossa, Katherine Douglases, Charlotte Cordays, would haunt them like the goblins of a delirium; then their prayers would become imperious demands upon Heaven, their diaries would almost break into spontaneous combustion from the incendiary material enmagazined in their pages, and the South would have conquered the world then and there could their hands but have pointed the guns and their hearts have recruited the armies. They would with mingled pride and envy read all the names, barely decipherable in the travel-stained record, from the President and Generals in big print to the diminishing insignificance of smallest-type privates; and they would shed tears, when the reaction would come a few days later, at the thought that in the whole area of typography, from the officers gaining immortality to the privates losing lives, there was not one name belonging to them; and they would ask why, of all the families in the

South, precisely their father and mother should have no relations, why, of all the women in the South, they should be brotherless.

There was Beau, a too notorious guerrilla captain; but what glory was to be won by raiding towns, wrecking trains, plundering transports, capturing couriers, disobeying orders, defying regulations? He was almost as obnoxious to his own as to the enemy's flag.

Besides, Beau at most was only a kind of a cousin, the son of a deceased step-sister of their father's; the most they could expect from him was to keep his undisciplined crew of "'Cadians," Indians, and swampers away from Bayou l'Ombre.

"Ah, if we were only men!" But no! They who could grip daggers and shed blood, they who teemed with all the possibilities of romance or poetry, they were selected for a passive, paltry contest against their own necessities; the endurance that would have laughed a siege to scorn ebbing away in a never-ceasing wrangle with fever and ague—willow-bark tea at odds with a malarious swamp!

It was now early summer; the foliage of spring was lusty and strong, fast outgrowing tenderness and delicacy of shade, with hints of maturity already swelling the shape. The day was cloudless and warm, the dinner-hour was long past, and supper still far off. There were no appetizing varieties of menu to make meals objects of pleasant anticipation; on the contrary, they had become mournful effigies of a convivial institution of which they served at most only to recall the hours, monotonously measuring off the recurring days which passed like unlettered mileposts in a desert, with no information to give except that of transition. To-day the meal-times were so far apart as to make one believe that the sun had given up all forward motion, and intended prolonging the present into eternity. The plantation was quiet and still; not the dewy hush of early dawn trembling before the rising sun, nor the mysterious muteness of midnight, nor yet the lethargic dulness of summer when the vertical sun-rays pin sense and motion to the earth. It was the motionless, voiceless state of unnatural quietude, the oppressive consciousness of abstracted activity, which characterized those days when the whole force of Bayou l'Ombre went off into the swamps to cut timber. Days that began shortly after one midnight and lasted to the other; rare days, when neither horn nor bell was heard for summons; when not a skiff, flat-boat, nor pirogue was left at the "gunnels;"[1] when old Uncle John alone remained to represent both master and men in the cares and responsibilities devolving upon his sex. The bayou lived and moved as usual,

[1] "Gunnels," floating wharf.

carrying its deceptive depths of brackish water unceasingly onward through the shadow and sunshine, rippling over the opposite low, soft banks, which seemed slowly sinking out of sight under the weight of the huge cypress-trees growing upon it. The long stretch of untilled fields back of the house, feebly kept in symmetrical proportion by crumbling fences, bared their rigid, seedless furrows in despairing barrenness to the sun, except in corner spots where a rank growth of weeds had inaugurated a reclamation in favor of barbarism. The sugar-house, superannuated and decrepit from unwhole-some idleness, tottered against its own massive, smokeless chimney; the sur-rounding sheds, stables, and smithy looked forsaken and neglected; the old blind mule peacefully slept in the shade of his once flagellated course under the corn-mill. Afar off against the woods the huge wheel of the draining-machine rose from the underbrush in the big ditch. The patient buzzards, roosting on the branches of the gaunt, blasted gum-tree by the bayou, would raise their heads from time to time to question the loitering sun, or, slowly flapping their heavy wings, circle up into the blue sky, to fall again in lazy spirals to their watch-tower, or they would take short flights by twos and threes over the moribund plantation to see if dissolution had not yet set in, and then all would settle themselves again to brood and sleep and dream, and wait in tranquil certainty the striking of their banqueting hour.

The three girls were in the open hall-way of the plantation house, Christine reading, Régina knitting, both listlessly occupied. Like every-thing else, they were passively quiet, and, like everything else, their appearance advertised an unwholesome lack of vitality, an insidious anamorphosis from an unexplained dearth or constraint. Their meagre maturity and scant development clashed abnormally with the surrounding prodigality of insensible nature. Though tall, they were thin; they were fair, but sallow; their gentle deep eyes were reproachful and deprived-look-ing. If their secluded hearts ventured even in thought towards the plum-ings natural to their age, their coarse, homely, ill-fitting garments anathematized any coquettish effort or naïve expression of a desire to find favor. Like the fields, they seemed hesitating on the backward path from cultivation. Lolotte stood before the cherry-wood armoire that held the hunting and fishing tackle, the wholesome receptacle of useful odds and ends. Not old enough to have come into the war with preconceptions, Lolotte had no reconciliations or compromises to effect between the ideal and the real, no compensations to solicit from an obliging imagination, which so far never rose beyond the possibilities of perch, blackbirds, and turtle eggs. The first of these occupied her thoughts at the present moment. She had made a tryst with the negro children at the draining-machine this afternoon. If she could, unperceived, abstract enough tackle from the armoire for the crowd, and if they could slip away from the quarters, and she evade the surveillance of Uncle John, there would be a diminished number of "brim" and "goggle-eye" in the ditch out yonder, and such a notable addition to the plantation supper to-night as would crown the exploit a success, and establish for herself a reputation above all annoying recollections of recent mishaps and failures. As she tied the hooks on to the lines she saw herself surrounded by the acclaiming infantile populace, pulling the struggling perch up one after the other; she saw them strung on palmetto thongs, long strings of them; she walked home at the head of her procession; heard Peggy's exclamations of surprise, smelt them frying, and finally was sitting at the table, a plate of bones before her, the radiant hostess of an imperial feast.

"Listen!" Like wood-ducks from under the water, the three heads rose simultaneously above their abstractions. "Rowlock! Rowlock!" The eyes might become dull, the tongue inert, and the heart languid on Bayou l'Ombre, but the ears were ever assiduous, ever on duty. Quivering and nervous, they listened even through sleep for that one blessed echo of travel, the signal from another and a distant world. Faint, shadowy, delusive, the whispering forerunner of on-coming news, it overrode the rippling of the current, the hooting of the owls, the barking of dogs, the splash of the gar-fish, the grunting of the alligator, the croaking of frogs, penetrating all turmoil, silencing all other sounds. "Rowlock! Rowlock!" Slow, deliberate, hard, and strenuous, coming up-stream; easy, soft, and musical, gliding down. "Rowlock! Rowlock!" Every stroke a very universe of hope, every oar frothing a sea of expectation! Was it the bayou or the secret stream of their longing that suggested the sound today? "Rowlock! Rowlock!" The smouldering glances brightened in their eyes, they hollowed their hands behind their ears and held their breath for greater surety. "Rowlock! Rowlock!" In clear, distinct reiteration. It resolved the moment of doubt.

"Can it be papa coming back?"

"No; it's against stream."

"It must be swampers."

"Or hunters, perhaps."

"Or Indians from the mound."

"Indians in a skiff?"

"Well, they sometimes come in a skiff."

The contingencies were soon exhausted, a cut-off leading travellers far around Bayou l'Ombre, whose snaggy, rafted, convoluted course was by universal avoidance relegated to an isolation almost insulting. The girls, listening, not to lose a single vibration, quit their places and advanced to the edge of the gallery, then out under the trees, then to the levee, then to the "gunnels," where they stretched their long, thin, white necks out of their blue and brown check gowns, and shaded their eyes and gazed downstream for the first glimpse of the skiff—their patience which had lasted months fretting now over the delay of a few moments.

"At last we shall get some news again."

"If they only leave a newspaper!"

"Or a letter," said Lolotte.

"A letter! From whom?"

"Ah, that's it!"

"What a pity papa isn't here!"

"Lolotte, don't shake the gunnels so; you are wetting our feet."

"How long is it since the last one passed?"

"I can tell you," said Lolotte—"I can tell you exactly: it was the day Lou Ann fell in the bayou and nearly got drowned."

"You mean when you both fell in."

"I didn't fall in at all; I held on to the pirogue."

The weeping-willow on the point below veiled the view; stretching straight out from the bank, it dropped its shock of long, green, pliant branches into the water, titillating and dimpling the surface. The rising bayou bore a freight of logs and drift from the swamps above; rudely pushing their way through the willow boughs, they tore and bruised the fragile tendrils that clung to the rough bark, scattering the tiny leaves which followed hopelessly after in their wake or danced up and down in the hollow eddies behind them. Each time the willow screen moved, the gunnels swayed under the forward motion of the eager bodies of the girls.

"At last!"

They turned their eyes to the shaft of sunlight that fell through the plantation clearing, bridging the stream. The skiff touched, entered, and passed through it with a marvellous revelation of form and color, the oars silvering and dripping diamonds, arrows and lances of light scintillating from polished steel, golden stars rising like dust from tassels, cordons, buttons, and epaulets, while the blue clouds themselves seemed to have fallen from their empyrean heights to uniform the rowers with their own celestial hue—blue, not gray!

"Rowlock! Rowlock!" What loud, frightful, threatening reverberations of the oars! And the bayou flowed on the same, and the cypress-trees gazed stolidly and steadfastly up to the heavens, and the heavens were serenely blue and white! But the earth was sympathetic, the ground shook and swayed under their feet; or was it the rush of thoughts that made their heads so giddy? They tried to arrest one and hold it for guidance, but on they sped, leaving only wild confusion of conjecture behind.

"Rowlock! Rowlock!" The rudder headed the bow for the gunnels.

"Titine! Gina! Will they kill us all?" whispered Lolotte, with anxious horror.

The agile Lou Ann, Lolotte's most efficient coadjutor and Uncle John's most successful tormentor, dropped her bundle of fishing-poles (which he had carefully spread on his roof to "cure"), and while they rolled and rattled over the dry shingles she scrambled with inconceivable haste to her corner of descent. Holding to the eaves while her excited black feet searched and found the top of the window that served as a step, she dropped into the ash-hopper below. Without pausing, as usual, to efface betraying evidences of her enterprise from her person, or to cover her tracks in the wet ashes, she jumped to the ground, and ignoring all secreting offers of bush, fence, or ditch, contrary to her custom, she ran with all the speed of her thin legs down the shortest road to the quarters. They were, as she knew, deserted. The doors of the cabins were all shut, with logs of wood or chairs propped against them. The chickens and dogs were making free of the galleries, and the hogs wallowed in peaceful immunity underneath. A waking baby from a lonely imprisoned cradle sent cries for relief through an open window. Lou Ann, looking neither to the right nor the left, slackened not her steps, but passed straight on through the little avenue to the great white-oak which stood just outside the levee on the bank of the bayou.

Under the wide-spreading, moss-hung branches, upon the broad flat slope, a grand general washing of the clothes of the small community was in busy progress by the women, a proper feminine consecration of this purely feminine day. The daily irksome routine was broken, the men were all away, the sun was bright and warm, the air soft and sweet. The vague recesses of the opposite forest were dim and silent, the bayou played under the gunnels in caressing modulations. All furthered the hearkening and the yielding to a debonair mood, with disregard of concealment, license of pose, freedom of limb, hilarity, conviviality, audacities of heart and tongue, joyous indulgence in freak and impulse, banishment of thought, a return, indeed, for one brief moment to the wild, sweet ways of nature, to the festal days of ancestral golden age (a short retrogression for them), when the body still had claims, and the mind concessions, and the heart owed no allegiance, and when god and satyr eyes still might be caught peeping and glistening from leafy covert on feminine midsummer gambols. Their skirts were girt high around their broad full hips, their dark arms and necks came naked out of their low, sleeveless, white chemise bodies, and glistened with perspiration in the sun as if frosted with silver. Little clouds of steam rose from the kettles standing around them over heaps of burning chips. The splay-legged battling-boards sank firmer and firmer into the earth under the blows of the bats, pounding and thumping the wet clothes, squirting the warm suds in all directions, up into the laughing faces, down into the panting bosoms, against the shortened, clinging skirts, over the bare legs, out in frothy runners over the soft red clay corrugated with innumerable toe-prints. Out upon the gunnels the water swished and foamed under the vigorous movements of the rinsers, endlessly bending and raising their flexible, muscular bodies, burying their arms to the shoulders in the cool, green depths, piling higher and higher the heaps of tightly-wrung clothes at their sides. The water-carriers, passing up and down the narrow, slippery plank-way, held the evenly filled pails with the ease of coronets upon their heads. The children, under compulsion of continuous threats and occasional chastisement, fed the fire with chips from distant wood-piles, squabbling for the possession of the one cane-knife to split kindlers, imitating the noise and echoing with absurd fidelity the full-throated laughter that interrupted from time to time the work around the wash-kettles.

High above the slop and tumult sat old Aunt Mary, the official sick-nurse of the plantation, commonly credited with conjuring powers. She held a corn-cob pipe between her yellow protruding teeth, and her little restless eyes travelled inquisitively from person to person as if in quest of professional information, twinkling with amusement at notable efforts of wit, and with malice at the general discomfiture expressed under their gaze. Heelen sat near, nursing her baby. She had taken off her kerchief, and leaned her uncovered head back against the trunk of the tree; the long wisps of wool, tightly wrapped in white knitting-cotton, rose from irregular sections all over her elongated narrow skull, and encircled her wrinkled, nervous, toothless face like some ghastly serpentine chevelure.

"De Yankees! de Yankees! I seed 'em—at de big house! Little mistus she come for Uncle John. He fotched his gun—for to shoot 'em."

Lou Ann struggled to make her exhausted breath carry all her tidings. After each item she closed her mouth and swallowed violently, working her muscles until her little horns of hair rose and moved with the contortions of her face.

"An' dey locked a passel o' men up in de smoke-house—Cornfedrits."

The bats paused in the air, the women on the gunnels lifted their arms out of the water, those on the gang-plank stopped where they were; only the kettles simmered on audibly.

Lou Ann recommenced, this time finishing in one breath, with the added emphasis of raising her arm and pointing in the direction from whence she came, her voice getting shriller and shriller to the end:

"I seed 'em. Dey was Yankees. Little mistus she come for Uncle John; he fotched his gun for to shoot 'em; and they locked a passel o' men up in de smoke-house—Cornfedrits."

The Yankees! What did it mean to them? How much from the world outside had penetrated into the unlettered fastnesses of their ignorance? What did the war mean to them? Had Bayou l'Ombre indeed isolated both mind and body? Had the subtle time-spirit itself been diverted from them by the cut-off? Could their rude minds draw no inferences from the gradual loosening of authority and relaxing of discipline? Did they neither guess nor divine their share in the shock of battle out there? Could their ghost-seeing eyes not discern the martyr-spirits rising from two opposing armies, pointing at, beckoning to them? If, indeed, the water-shed of their destiny was forming without their knowledge as without their assistance, could not maternal instinct spell it out of the heart-throbs pulsing into life under their bosoms, or read from the dumb faces of the children at their breast the triumphant secret of their superiority over others born and nourished before them?

Had they, indeed, no gratifications beyond the physical, no yearnings, no secret burden of a secret prayer to God, these bonded wives and mothers? Was this careless, happy, indolent existence genuine, or only a fool's motley to disguise a tragedy of suffering? What to them was the difference between themselves and their mistresses? their condition? or their skin, that opaque black skin which hid so well the secrets of life, which could feel but not own the blush of shame, the pallor of weakness.

If their husbands had brought only rum from their stealthy midnight excursions to distant towns, how could the child repeat it so glibly— "Yankees—Cornfedrits?" The women stood still and silent, but their eyes began to creep around furtively, as if seeking degrees of complicity in a common guilt, each waiting for the other to confess comprehension, to assume the responsibility of knowledge.

The clear-headed children, profiting by the distraction of attention from them, stole away for their fishing engagement, leaving cane-knife and chips scattered on the ground behind them. The murmuring of the bayou seemed to rise louder and louder; the cries of the forsaken baby, clamorous and hoarse, fell distinctly on the air.

"My Gord A'mighty!"

The exclamation was uncompromising; it relieved the tension and encouraged rejoinder.

"My Lord!—humph!"

One bat slowly and deliberately began to beat again—Black Maria's. Her tall, straight back was to them, but, as if they saw it, they knew that her face was settling into that cold, stern rigidity of hers, the keen eyes beginning to glisten, the long, thin nostrils nervously to twitch, the lips to open over her fine white teeth—the expression they hated and feared.

"O-h! o-h! o-h!"

A long, thin, tremulous vibration, a weird, haunting note: what inspiration suggested it?

"Glo-o-ry!"

Old Aunt Mary nodded her knowing head affirmatively, as if at the fulfilment of a silent prophecy. She quietly shook the ashes out of her pipe, hunted her pocket, put it in, and rising stiffly from the root, hobbled away on her stick in the direction of her cabin.

"Glo-o-ry!"

Dead-arm Harriet stood before them, with her back to the bayou, her right arm hanging heavy at her side, her left extended, the finger pointing to the sky. A shapely arm and tapering finger; a comely, sleek, half-nude body; the moist lips, with burning red linings, barely parting to emit the sound they must have culled in uncanny practices. The heavy lids drooped over the large sleepy eyes, looking with languid passion from behind the thick black lashes.

"Glo-o-ry!" It stripped their very nerves and bared secret places of sensation! The "happy" cry of revival meetings—as if midnight were coming on, salvation and the mourners' bench before them, Judgment-day and fiery flames behind them, and "Sister Harriet" raising her voice to call them on, on, through hand-clapping, foot-stamping, shouting, groaning, screaming, out of their sins, out of their senses, to rave in religious inebriation, and fall in religious catalepsy across the floor at the preacher's feet.

With a wild rush, the hesitating emotions of the women sought the opportune outlet, their hungry blood bounding and leaping for the mid-day orgy. Obediently their bodies began the imperceptible motion right and left, and the veins in their throats to swell and stand out under their skins, while the short, fierce, intense responsive exclamations fell from their lips to relieve their own and increase the exaltation of the others.

"Sweet Christ! sweet Christ!"

"Take me, Saviour!"

"Oh, de Lamb! de Lamb!"

"I'm a-coming! I'm a-coming!"

"Hold back, Satan! we's a-catching on!"

"De blood's a-dripping! de blood's a-dripping!"

"Let me kiss dat cross! let me kiss it!"

"Sweet Master!"

"Glo-o-ry! Fre-e-dom!" It was a whisper, but it came like a crash, and transfixed them; their mouths stood open with the last words, their bodies remained bent to one side or the other, the febrile light in their eyes burning as if from their blood on fire. They could all remember the day when Dead-arm Harriet, the worst worker and most violent tongue of the gang, stood in the clearing, and raising that dead right arm over her head, cursed the overseer riding away in the distance. The wind had been blowing all day; there was a sudden loud crack above them, and a limb from a deadened tree broke, sailed, poised, and fell crashing to her shoulder, and deadening her arm forever. They looked instinctively now with a start to the oak above them, to the sky—only moss and leaves and blue and white clouds. And still Harriet's voice rose, the words faster, louder, bolder, more determined, whipping them out of their awe, driving them on again down the incline of their own passions.

"Glory! Freedom! Freedom! Glory!"

"I'm bound to see 'em! Come along!"

Heelen's wild scream rang shrill and hysterical. She jerked her breast from the sucking lips, and dropped her baby with a thud on the ground. They all followed her up the levee, pressing one after the other, slipping in the wet clay, struggling each one not to be left behind. Emmeline, the wife of little Ben, the only yellow woman on the place, was the last. Her skirt was held in a grip of iron; blinded, obtuse, she pulled forward, reaching her arms out after the others.

"You stay here!"

She turned and met the determined black face of her mother-in-law.

"You let me go!" she cried, half sobbing, half angry.

"You stay here, I tell you!" The words were muttered through clinched teeth.

"You let me go, I tell you!"

"Glory! Freedom!"

The others had already left the quarters, and were on the road. They two were alone on the bank now, except Heelen's baby, whimpering under the tree; their blazing eyes glared at each other. The singing voices grew fainter and fainter. Suddenly the yellow face grew dark with the surge of blood underneath, the brows wrinkled, and the lips protruded in a grimace of animal rage. Grasping her wet bat tightly with both hands, she turned with a furious bound, and raised it with all the force of her short muscular arms. The black woman darted to the ground; the cane-knife flashed in the air and came down pitilessly towards the soft fleshy shoulder. A wild, terrified scream burst from Emmeline's lips; the bat dropped; seizing her skirt with both hands, she pulled forward, straining her back out of reach of the knife; the homespun tore, and she fled up the bank, her yellow limbs gleaming through the rent left by the fragment in the hand of the black woman.

The prisoners were so young, so handsome, so heroic; the very incarnation of the holy spirit of patriotism in their pathetic uniform of brimless caps, ragged jackets, toeless shoes, and shrunken trousers—a veteran equipment of wretchedness out of keeping with their fresh young faces. How proud and unsubdued they walked through the hall between the file of bayonets! With what haughty, defiant eyes they returned the gaze of their insultingly resplendent conquerors! Oh, if girls' souls had been merchantable at that moment! Their hands tied behind their backs like runaway slaves! Locked up in the smoke-house! that dark, rancid, gloomy, mouldy depot of empty hogsheads, barrels, boxes, and fetid exhalations.

They were the first soldiers in gray the girls had ever seen; their own chivalrous knights, the champions of their radiant country. What was the story of their calamity? Treacherously entrapped? Overpowered by numbers? Where were their companions—staring with mute, cold, upturned faces from pools of blood? And were these to be led helplessly tethered into captivity, imprisoned; with ball and chain to gangrene and disgrace their strong young limbs, or was solitary confinement to starve their hearts and craze their minds, holding death in a thousand loathsome, creeping shapes ever threateningly over them?

The smoke-house looked sinister and inimical after its sudden promotion from keeper of food to keeper of men. The great square whitewashed logs seemed to settle more ponderously on the ground around them, the pointed roof to press down as if the air of heaven were an emissary to be dreaded; the hinges and locks were so ostentatiously massive and incorruptible. What artful, what vindictive security of carpenter and locksmith to exclude thieves or immure patriots!

The two eldest girls stood against the open armoire with their chill fingers interlaced. Beyond the wrinkled back of Uncle John's copperas-dyed coat before them lay the region of brass buttons and blue cloth and hostility; but they would not look at it; they turned their heads away; the lids of their eyes refused to lift and reveal the repugnant vision to them. If their ears had only been equally sensitive!

"And so you are the uncle of the young ladies? Brother of the father or mother?" What clear, incisive, nasal tones! Thank Heaven for the difference between them of the voice at least!

The captain's left arm was in a sling, but his hand could steadily hold the note-book in which he carefully pencilled Uncle John's answers to his minute cross-examination—a dainty, fragrant, Russia-leather note-book, with monogram and letters and numbers emblazoned on the outside in national colors. It had photographs inside, also, which he would pause and admire from time to time, reading the tender dedications aloud to his companions.

"And the lady in the kitchen called mammy? She is the mother, I guess?"

"P-p-p-peggy's a nigger, and my mistresses is white," stuttered Uncle John.

"Ah, indeed! Gentlemen in my uniform find it difficult to remember these trifling distinctions of color."

What tawdry pleasantry! What hypocritical courtesy! What exquisite ceremony and dainty manual for murderous dandies!

"Ef-ef-ef-ef I hadn't done gone and forgot dem caps!"

Uncle John stood before his young mistresses erect and determined, his old double-barrel shotgun firmly clasped in his tremulous hands, his blear, bloodshot eyes fearlessly measuring the foe. If it were to be five hundred lashes on his bare back under the trees out there (terms on which he would gladly have compromised), or, his secret fear, a running noose over one of the branches, or the murderous extravagance of powder and shot for him, he had made up his mind, despite every penalty, to fulfil his duty and stand by his word to Marse John. Ever since the time the little crawling white boy used to follow the great awkward black boy around like a shadow, John had made a cult of Marse John. He had taught him as a child to fish, hunt, trap birds, to dress skins, knit gloves, and play cards on the sly, to fight cocks on Sunday, to stutter, to cut the "pigeon wing" equal to any negro in the State—and other personal accomplishments besides. He had stood by him through all his scrapes as a youth, was valet to all his frolics as a young man, and now in his old age he gardened for him, and looked after the young ladies for him, stretching or contracting his elastic moral code as occasion required; but he had never deceived him nor falsified his word to him. He knew all about the war: Marse John had told him. He knew what Marse John meant when he left the children to him, and Marse John knew what to expect from John. He would treat them civilly as long as they were civil, but his gun was loaded, both barrels with bullets, and—

"Ef-ef-ef-ef I hadn't done gone and forgot dem caps!"

There was his powder-horn under one arm, there was his shot-flask filled with the last batch of slugs under the other; but the caps were not in his right-hand coat-pocket, they were in his cupboard, hidden for safety under a pile of garden "truck."

The busy martins twittered in and out of their little lodge under the eaves of the smoke-house. Régina and Christine were powerless to prevent furtive glances in that direction. Could the *prisoners* hear it inside? Could *they* see the sun travelling westward, crack by crack, chink by chink, in the roof? Could they feel it sinking, and with it sinking all their hopes of deliverance? Or did they hope still?

Maidens had mounted donjon towers at midnight, had eluded Argus-eyed sentinels, had drugged savage blood-hounds, had crossed lightning-flashed seas, had traversed robber-infested forests; whatever maidens had done they would do, for could ever men more piteously implore release from castle keep than these gray-clad youths from the smoke-house? And did ever maiden hearts beat more valiantly than theirs? (and did ever maiden limbs tremble more cowardly?) Many a tedious day had been lightened by their rehearsal of just such a drama as this; they had prepared roles for every imaginable sanguinary circumstance, but prevision, as usual, had overlooked the unexpected. The erstwhile feasible conduct, the erstwhile feasible weapons, of a Jeanne d'Arc or Charlotte Corday, the defiant speeches, the ringing retorts—how inappropriate, inadequate, here and now! If God would only help them! but, like the bayou, the cypresses, and the blue sky, He seemed to-day eternally above such insignificant human necessities as theirs.

Without the aid of introspection or the fear of capital punishment, Lolotte found it very difficult to maintain the prolonged state of rigidity into which her sisters had frozen themselves. All the alleviations devised during a wearisome experience of compulsory attendance on plantation funerals were exhausted in the course of this protracted, hymnless, prayerless solemnity. She stood wedged in between them and the armoire which displayed all its shelves of allurements to her. There were her bird-traps just within reach; there was the fascinating bag of nux-vomica root—crow poison; there was the little old work-box filled with ammunition, which she was forbidden to touch, and all the big gar-fish lines and harpoons and decoy-ducks. There were her own perch lines, the levy she had raised in favor of her companions; they were neatly rolled, ready to tie on the rods, only needing sinkers; and there was the old Indian basket filled with odds and ends, an unfailing treasure of resource and surprise. She was just about searching in it for sinkers when this interruption occurred.

The sky was so bright over the fields! Just the evening to go fishing, whether they caught anything or not. If the enemy would only hurry and go, there might still be time; they would leave, they said, as soon as mammy cooked them something to eat. She had seen mammy chasing a chicken through the yard. She wondered how the nice, fat little round "doodles" were getting on in their tin can under the house; she never had had such a fine box of bait; she wondered if the negro children would go all the same without her; she wondered if she could see them creeping down the road. How easy she could have got away from Uncle John! Anything almost would do for sinkers—bits of iron, nails; they had to do since her father and Uncle John made their last moulding of bullets. She thought they might have left her just one real sinker simply as a matter of distinction between herself and the little darkies. Her eyes kept returning to the Indian basket, and if she stopped twisting her fingers one over the other but a moment they would take their way to rummaging among the rusty contents.

"Glory! Freedom!"

In came the negresses, Bacchantes drunk with the fumes of their own hot blood, Dead-arm Harriet, like a triumphant sorceress, leading them, waving and gesticulating with her one "live" arm, all repeating over and over again the potent magical words, oblivious of the curious looks of the men, their own exposure, the presence of their mistresses, of everything but their own ecstasy.

"Freedom! Master! Freedom!"

Christine and Régina raised their heads and looked perplexed at the furious women in the yard, and the men gazing down to them.

What was the matter with them? What did they mean? What was it all about?

"Freedom! Freedom!"

Then light broke upon them; their fingers tightened in each other's clasp, and their cheeks flushed crimson.

"How dared they? What insolence! What—"

The opposite door stood open; they rushed across the hall and closed it between them and the humiliating scene. This, this they had not thought of, this they had never read about, this their imagination in wildest flights had not ventured upon. This was not a superficial conflict to sweep the earth with cannons and mow it with sabres; this was an earthquake which had rent it asunder, exposing the quivering organs of hidden life. What a chasm was yawning before them! There was no need to listen one to the other; the circumstances could wring from the hearts of millions but one sentiment, the tongue was left no choice of words.

"Let them go! let them be driven out! never, never to see them again!"

The anger of outraged affection, betrayed confidence, abandoned trust, traitorous denial, raged within them.

These were their servants, their possessions! From generation to generation their lives had been woven together by the shuttle of destiny. How flimsy and transparent the fabric! how grotesque and absurd the tapestry, with its vaunted traditions of mutual loyalty and devotion! What a farce, what a lying, disgusting farce it had all been! Well, it was over now; that was a comfort—all over, all ended. If the hearts had intergrown, they were torn apart now. After this there was no return, no reconciliation possible! Through the storm of their emotions a thought drifted, then another; little detached scenes flitted into memory; familiar gestures, speeches, words, one reminiscence drawing another. Thicker and thicker came little episodes of their pastoral existence together; the counter interchanges of tokens, homely presents, kind offices, loving remembrances; the mutual assistance and consolation in all the accidents of life traversed together, the sicknesses, the births, the deaths; and so many thousand trivial incidents of long, long ago—memory had not lost one—down to the fresh eggs and the pop-corn of that very morning; they were all there, falling upon their bruised hearts.

In the hearts of the women out there were only shackles and scourges. What of the long Sundays of Bible-reading and catechism, the long evenings of woodland tales; the confidences; the half-hours around the open fireplaces when supper was cooking, the potatoes under their hillocks of ashes, the thin-legged ovens of cornbread with their lids of glowing coals, the savory skillets of fried meat, the— Was it indeed all of the past, never again to be present or future? And those humble, truthful, loving eyes, which had looked up to them from the first moment of their lives: did they look with greater trust up to God Himself? It was all over, yes, all over! The color faded from their faces, the scornful resolution left their lips; they laid their faces in their hands and sobbed.

"Do you hear, Titine?" Lolotte burst into the room. "They are all going to leave, every one of them; a transport is coming to-night to take them off. They are going to bundle up their things and wait at the steamboat-landing; and they are not going to take a child, and not a single husband. The captain says the government at Washington will give them the nicest white husbands in the land; that they ought to be glad to marry them. They carried on as if they were drunk. Do you believe it, Titine? Oh, I do wish Jeff Davis would hurry up and win!"

The door opened again; it was Black Maria, still holding the cane-knife in her hand. She crossed the room with her noiseless barefooted tread, and placed herself behind them. They did not expect her to say anything; Black Maria never talked much; but they understood her, as they always did.

Her skirts were still tied up, her head-kerchief awry; they saw for the first time that the wool under it was snow-white.

Black Maria! They might have known it! They looked at her. No! She was not! She was not negro, like the others. Who was she? What was she? Where did she come from, with her white features and white nature under her ebon skin? What was the mystery that enveloped her? Why did the brain always torture itself in surmises about her? Why did she not talk as the others did, and just for a moment uncover that coffin heart of hers? Why was she, alone of all the negroes, still an alien, a foreigner, an exile among them? Was she brooding on disgrace, outrage, revenge? Was she looking at some mirage behind her—a distant equatorial country, a princely rank, barbaric state, some inherited memory transmitted by that other Black Maria, her mother? Who was the secret black father whom no one had discovered? Was it, as the negroes said, the Prince of Darkness? Who was her own secret consort, the father of Ben? What religion had she to warrant her scornful repudiation of Christianity? What code that enabled her to walk as if she were free through slavery, to assume slavery now when others hailed freedom, to be loyal in the midst of treason?

"Look!" Lolotte came into the room, and held up a rusty, irregular piece of iron. "I found this in the old Indian basket where I was looking for sinkers. Don't you see what it is? It is the old key of the smoke-house, and I am going to let those Confederates out." She spoke quietly and decidedly. There was something else in the other hand, concealed in the folds of her dress. She produced it reluctantly. It was the gun-wrench that filled so prominent a part in her active life—always coveting it, getting possession of it, being deprived of it, and accused unfailingly for its every absence and misplacement. "You see, it is so convenient; it screws so nicely on to everything," she continued, apologetically, as she demonstrated the useful qualification by screwing it on to the key. "There! it is as good as a handle. All they've got to do is to slip away in the skiff while the others are eating. And I would like to know how they can ever be caught, without another boat on the place! But oh, girls"— her black eyes twinkled maliciously—"what fools the Yankees are!"

If the Federals, as they announced, were only going to remain long enough for the lady in the kitchen to prepare them something to eat, the length of their stay clearly rested in Peggy the cook's hands, as she understood it. She walked around her kitchen with a briskness rarely permitted by her corpulent proportions, and with an intuitive faith in the common nature of man regardless of political opinion, she exerted her culinary skill to the utmost. She knew nothing of the wholesale quarrelling and fighting of a great war, but during her numerous marital experiments, not counting intermittent conjugalities for twenty-five years with Uncle John, she had seen mercy and propitiation flow more than once after a good meal from the most irate; and a healthy digestion aiding, she never despaired of even the most revengeful. The enemy, in her opinion, were simply to be treated like furious husbands, and were to be offered the best menu possible under the trying circumstances. She worked, inspired by all the wife-lore of past ages, the infiltrated wisdom that descends to women in the course of a world of empirical connubiality, that traditionary compendium to their lives by which they still hope to make companionship with men harmonious and the earth a pleasant abiding-place. With minute particularity Peggy set the table and placed the dishes. The sun was now sinking, and sending almost horizontal rays over the roof of the smoke-house, whose ugly square frame completely blocked the view of the dining-room window. Peggy carefully drew the red calico curtain across it, and after a moment's rehearsal to bring her features to the conventional womanly expression of cheerful obtuseness to existing displeasure, she opened the dining-room door.

Gina and Lolotte stood close under the window against the dwelling, looking at the locked door of the smoke-house before them, listening to the sounds falling from the dining-room above. Once in the skiff, the prisoners were safe; but the little red curtain of the window fluttering flimsily in the breeze coquetted with their hopes and the lives of three men. If the corners would but stay down a second! Titine and Black Maria were in front, busy about the skiff. Peggy's culinary success appeared, from the comments of the diners, to be complimentary to her judgment. But food alone, however, does not suffice in the critical moments of life; men are half managed when only fed. There was another menu, the ingredients of which were not limited or stinted by blockade of war. Peggy had prepared that also; and in addition to the sounds of plates, knives, forks, and glasses, came the tones of her rich voice dropping from a quick tongue the *entremets* of her piquant imagination. The attention in the room seemed tense, and at last the curtain hung straight and motionless.

"Now! now!" whispered Gina. "We must risk something."

Woman-like, they paused midway and looked back; a hand stretched from the table was carelessly drawing the curtain aside, and the window stared unhindered at the jail.

Why had they waited? Why had they not rushed forward immediately? By this time their soldiers might have been free! They could hear Peggy moving around the table; they could see her bulky form push again and again across the window.

"Mammy! Mammy!"

Could she hear them? They clasped their hands and held their faces up in imploring appeal. The sun was setting fast, almost running down the west to the woods. The dinner, if good, was not long. It all depended upon Peggy now.

"Mammy! Mammy!" They raised their little voices, then lowered them in agony of apprehension. "Mammy, do something! Help us!"

But still she passed on and about, around the table, and across the window, blind to the smoke-house, deaf to them, while her easy, familiar voice recited the comical gyrations of "old Frizzly," the half-witted hen, who had set her heart against being killed and stewed, and ran and hid, and screamed and cackled, and ducked and flew, and then, after her silly head was twisted off, "just danced, as if she were at a "Cadian' ball, all over the yard."

It would soon be too late! It was, perhaps, too late now!

Black Maria had got the skiff away from the gunnels, but they might just as well give it up; they would not have time enough now.

"Mammy!" The desperate girls made a supreme effort of voice and look. The unctuous black face, the red bead ear-rings, the bandanna head-kerchief, appeared at the window with "old Frizzly's" last dying cackle. There was one flashing wink of the left eye.

Her nurslings recognized then her *pièce de résistance oratoire*—a side-splitting prank once played upon her by another nursling, her pet, her idol, the plague of her life—Beau.

Who could have heard grating lock or squeaking hinges through the boisterous mirth that followed? Who could have seen the desperate bound of the three imprisoned soldiers for liberty through that screen of sumptuous flesh—the magnificent back of Mammy that filled to overlapping the insignificant little window?

They did not wait to hear the captain's rapturous toast to Peggy in sassafras tea, nor his voluble protestations of love to her, nor could they see him in his excitement forgetting his wounded arm, bring both clinched fists with a loud bravo to the table, and then faint dead away.

"I knew it!"

"Just like him!"

"Take him in the air—quick!"

"No, sir! You take him in there, and put him on the best bed in the house." Peggy did not move from the window, but her prompt command turned the soldiers from the door in the hall, and her finger directed them to the closed bed-chamber.

Without noticing Christine standing by the open window, they dropped their doughty burden—boots, spurs, sword, epaulets, and all—on the fresh, white little bed, the feather mattress fluffing up all around as if to submerge him.

"Oh, don't bother about that: cut the sleeve off!"

"Who has a knife?"

"There."

"That's all right now."

"He's coming round."

"There's one nice coat spoiled."

"Uncle Sam has plenty more."

"Don't let it drip on the bed."

"Save it to send to Washington—trophy—wet with rebel blood."

The captain was evidently recovering.

"You stay here while I keep 'em eating," whispered Peggy, authoritatively, to Christine.

Titine trembled as if she had an ague.

"How could they help seeing the tall form of Black Maria standing in the prow of the boat out in the very middle of the bayou? Suppose she, Titine, had not been there to close the window quick as thought? Suppose instead of passing through her room she had run through the basement, as she intended, after pushing off the skiff?"

Rollicking, careless, noisy, the soldiers went back to their interrupted meal, while the boat went cautiously down the bayou to the meeting place beyond the clearing.

"How far was Black Maria now?" Titine opened the window a tiny crack. "Heavens! how slowly she paddled! lifting the oar deliberately from side to side, looking straight ahead. How clear and distinct she was in the soft evening light! Why did she not hurry? why did she not row? She could have muffled the oars. But no, no one thought of that; that was always the way—always something overlooked and forgotten. The soldiers could finish a dozen dinners before the skiff got out of sight at this rate. Without the skiff the prisoners might just as well be locked still in the smoke-house. Did he on the bed suspect something, seeing her look out this way?" She closed the window tight.

"How dark the room was! She could hardly see the wounded man. How quiet he was! Was he sleeping, or had he fainted again? In her bed! her enemy lying in her bed! his head on her pillow, her own little pillow, the feverish confidant of so many sleepless nights! How far were they now on the bayou? She must peep out again. Why, Maria had not moved! not moved an inch! Oh, if she could only scream to her! if she were only in the skiff!

"How ghastly pale he looked on the bed! his face as white as the coverlet, his hair and beard so black; how changed without his bravado and impertinence! And he was not old, either; not older than the boys in gray. She had fancied that age and ugliness alone could go with violence and wrong. How much gold! how much glitter! Why, the sun did not rise with more splendor of equipment. Costumed as if for the conquest of worlds. If the Yankees dressed their captains this way, what was the livery of their generals? How curious the sleeveless arm looked! What a horrible mark the gash made right across the soft white skin! What a scar it would leave! What a disfigurement! And this, this is what men call love of country!"

On Saturday nights sometimes, in the quarters, when rum had been smuggled in, the negroes would get to fighting and beating their wives, and her father would be sent for in a hurry to come with his gun and separate them. Hatchets, axes, cane-knives—anything they would seize, to cut and slash one another, husbands, wives, mothers, sons, sisters, brothers; but they were negroes, ignorant, uneducated, barbarous, excited; they could not help it; they could not be expected to resist all at once the momentum of centuries of ancestral ferocity. But for white men, gentlemen, thus furiously to mar and disfigure their own mother-given bodies! All the latent maternal instinct in her was roused, all the woman in her revolted against the sacrilegious violence of mutilation. "Love of country to make her childless, or only the mother of invalids! This was only one. What of the other thousands and hundreds of thousands? Are men indeed so inexhaustible? Are the pangs of maternity so cheap? Are women's hearts of no account whatever in the settlement of disputes? O God! cannot the world get along without war? But even if men want it, even if God permits it, how can the women allow it? If the man on the bed were a negro, she could do something for his arm. Many a time, early Sunday mornings, Saturday night culprits had come to her secretly, and she had washed off the thick, gummy blood, and bandaged up their cuts and bruises; they did not show so on black skin. . . . This man had a mother somewhere among the people she called 'enemies;' a mother sitting counting day by day the continued possession of a live son, growing gray and old before that terrible next minute ever threatening to take her boy and give her a corpse. Or perhaps, like her own, his mother might be dead. They might be friends in that kingdom which the points of the compass neither unite nor divide; together they might be looking down on this quarrelling, fighting world; mothers, even though angels, looking, looking through smoke and powder and blood and hatred after their children. Their eyes might be fixed on this lonely little spot, on this room. . . ." She walked to the bed.

The blood was oozing up through the strips of plaster. She stanched and bathed and soothed the wound as she well knew how with her tender, agile fingers, and returned to the window. Maria had disappeared now; she could open the window with impunity. The trackless water was flowing innocently along, the cooling air was rising in mist, the cypress-trees checked the brilliant sky with the filigree and net-work of their bristly foliage. The birds twittered, the chickens loitered and dallied on their way to roost. The expectant dogs were lying on the levee waiting for the swampers, who, they ought to know, could not possibly return before midnight. And Molly was actually on time this evening, lowing for mammy to come and milk her; what was the war to her? How happy and peaceful it all was! What a jarring contrast to swords and bayonets! Thank God that Nature was impartial, and could not be drilled into partisanship!

If humanity were like Nature! If—if there had been no war! She paused, shocked at her first doubt; of the great Circumstance of her life it was like saying, "If there had been no God!"

As she stood at the window and thought, all the brilliant coloring of her romantic fantasies, the stories of childhood, the perversions of education, the self-delusions, they all seemed to fade with the waning light, and with the beautiful day sink slowly and quietly into the irrevocable past. "Thank God, above all, that it is a human device to uniform people into friends and enemies! The heart (her own felt so soft and loving)—the heart repudiates such attempts of blue and gray; it still clings to Nature, and belongs only to God." She thought the wound must need tending again, and returned to the bed. The patient, meanwhile, went in and out of the mazes of unconsciousness caused by weakness.

"Was that really he on this foamy bed? What a blotch his camp-battered body made down the centre of it! It was good to be on a bed once more, to look up into a mosquito-bar instead of the boughs of trees, to feel his head on a pillow. But why did they put him there? Why did they not lay him somewhere on the floor, outside on the ground, instead of soiling and crumpling this lily-white surface?"

He could observe his nurse through his half-closed lids, which fell as she approached the bed, and closed tight as she bent above him. When she stood at the window he could look full at her. "How innocent and unsuspecting she looked!" The strained rigidity had passed away from her face. Her transparent, child-like eyes were looking with all their life of expression in the direction of the bed, and then at something passing in her own mind. "Thank Heaven, the fright had all gone out of them! How horrible for a gentleman to read fear in the eyes of a woman! Her mind must be as pure and white, yes, and as impressionable, too, as her bed. Did his presence lie like a blot upon it also? How she must hate him! how she must loathe him! Would it have been different if he had come in the other uniform—if he had worn the gray? would she then have cared for him, have administered to him? How slight and frail she was! What a wan, wistful little face between him and the gloomy old bayou! He could see her more plainly now since she had opened the window and let in the cool, fragrant air. There was no joyous development of the body in her to proclaim womanhood, none of the seductive, confident beauty that follows coronation of youth; to her had only come the care and anxiety of maturity. "This—this," he exclaimed to himself, "is the way women fight a war." Was she coming this way? Yes. To the bed? Hardly. Now she was pressing against it, now bending over him, now dropping a cooling dew from heaven on his burning arm, and now—oh, why so soon?—she was going away to stand and look out of the window again.

The homely little room was filled with feminine subterfuges for ornament, feminine substitutes for comfort. How simple women are! how little they require, after all! only peace and love and quiet, only the impossible in a masculine world. What was she thinking of? If he could only have seen the expression of her eyes as she bent over him! Suppose he should open his and look straight up at her? but no, he had not the courage to frighten her again. He transplanted her in his mind to other surroundings, her proper surroundings by birthright, gave her in abundance all of which this war had deprived her, presented to her assiduous courtiers, not reckless soldiers like himself, but men whom peace had guided in the lofty sphere of intellectual pursuits. He held before her the sweet invitations of youth, the consummations of life. He made her smile, laugh.

"Ah!"—he turned his face against the pillow—"had that sad face ever laughed? Could any woman laugh during a war? Could any triumph, however glorious, atone for battles that gave men death, but left the women to live? This was only one; how many, wan and silent as she, were looking at this sunset—the sunset not of a day, but a life? When it was all over, who was to make restitution to them, the women? Was any cost too great to repurchase for them simply the privilege of hoping again? What an endless chain of accusing thoughts! What a miserable conviction tearing his heart! If he could get on his knees to her, if he could kiss her feet, if he could beg pardon in the dust—he, a man for all men, of her, a woman for all women. If he could make her his country, not to fight, but to work for, it . . ."

She came to his side again, she bent over him, she touched him.

Impulsive, thoughtless, hot-headed, he opened his eyes full, he forgot again the wounded arm. With both hands he stayed her frightened start; he saw the expression of her eyes bending over him.

"Can you forgive me? It is a heartless, cowardly trick! I am not a Yankee; I am Beau, your cousin, the guerrilla."

The door of the smoke-house opened, the escaped soldiers ran like deer between the furrows of Uncle John's vegetable garden, where the waving corn leaves could screen them; then out to the bank of the bayou—not on the levee, but close against the fence—snagging their clothes and scratching their faces and hands on the cuckleburs; Lolotte in front, with a stick in her hand, beating the bushes through habit to frighten the snakes, calling, directing, animating, in excited whispers; Régina in the rear, urging, pressing, sustaining the young soldier lagging behind, but painfully striving with stiffened limbs to keep up with the pace of his older, more vigorous companions. Ahead of them Black Maria was steadily keeping the skiff out in the current. The bayou narrowed and grew dark as it entered between the banks of serried cypress-trees, where night had already begun.

Régina looked hurriedly over her shoulder. "Had they found out yet at the house? How slowly she ran! How long it took to get to the woods! Oh, they would have time over and over again to finish their dinner and catch them. Perhaps at this very moment, as she was thinking of it, some forgotten article in the skiff was betraying them! Perhaps a gun might even now be pointing down their path! Or, now! the bullet could start and the report come too late to warn them."

She looked back again and again.

From the little cottage under the trees the curtains fluttered, but no bayonet nor smooth-bore was visible.

She met her companion's face, looking back also, but not for guns—for her. "If it had been different! If he had been a visitor, come to stay; days and evenings to be passed together!" The thought lifting the sulphurous war-clouds from her heart, primitive idyls burst into instantaneous fragrant bloom in it like spring violets. He was not only the first soldier in gray she had ever seen, but the first young man; or it seemed so to her.

Again she looked back.

"How near they were still to the house! how plainly they could yet be seen! He could be shot straight through the back, the gray jacket getting one stain, one bullet-hole, more, the country one soldier less. Would they shoot through a woman at him? Would they be able to separate them if she ran close behind him, moving this way and that way, exactly as he did? If she saw them in time she could warn him; he could lie flat down in the grass; then it would be impossible to hit him."

Increasing and narrowing the space between them at the hest of each succeeding contradictory thought, turning her head again and again to the house behind her, she lost speed. Lolotte and the two men had already entered the forest before she reached it. Coming from the fields, the swamps seemed midnight dark. Catching her companion's hand, they groped their way along, tripped by the slimy cypress knees that rose like evil gnomes to beset and entangle their feet, slipping over rolling logs, sinking in stagnant mire, noosed by the coils of heavy vines that dropped from unseen branches overhead. Invisible wings of startled birds flapped above them, the croaking of frogs ebbed and flowed around them, owls shrieked and screamed from side to side of the bayou. Lolotte had ceased her beating; swamp serpents are too sluggish to be frightened away. In the obscurity, Black Maria could be dimly seen turning the skiff to a half-submerged log, from which a turtle dropped as if ballasted with lead. A giant cypress-tree arrested them; the smooth, fluted trunk, ringed with whitish water-marks, recording floods far over their heads; where they were scrambling once swam fish and serpents. The young soldier turned and faced her, the deliverer, whose manoeuvres in the open field had not escaped him.

She had saved him from imprisonment, insult, perhaps death—the only heir of a heroic father, the only son of a widowed mother; she had restored him to a precious heritage of love and honor, replaced him in the interrupted ambitious career of patriotic duty; she had exposed her life for him—she was beautiful. She stood before him, panting, tremulous, ardent, with dumb, open red lips, and voluble, passionate eyes, and with a long scratch in her white cheek from which the blood trickled. She had much to say to him, her gray uniformed hero; but how in one moment express four years—four long years—and the last long minutes. The words were all there, had been rushing to her lips all day; her lips were parted; but the eager, overcrowded throng were jammed on the threshold; and her heart beat so in her ears! He could not talk; he could not explain. His companions were already in the boat, his enemies still in gunshot. He bent his face to hers in the dim light to learn by heart the features he must never forget—closer, closer, learning, knowing more and more, with the eager precocity of youth.

Bellona must have flown disgusted away with the wings of an owl, Columbia might have nodded her head as knowingly as old Aunt Mary could, when the callow hearts, learning and knowing, brought the faces closer and closer together, until the lips touched.

"I shall come again; I shall come again. Wait for me. Surely I shall come again."

"Yes! Yes!"

Black Maria pushed the skiff off. "Rowlock! Rowlock!" They were safe and away.

A vociferous group stood around the empty gunnels. Uncle John, with the daring of desperation, advanced, disarmed as he was, towards them.

"I-I-I-I don't keer ef you is de-de-de President o' de United States hisself, I ain't gwine to 'low no such cussin' en' swearin' in de hearin' o' de-de-de young ladies. Marse John he-he-he don't 'low it, and when Marse John ain't here I-I-I don't 'low it."

His remonstrance and heroic attitude had very little effect, for the loud talk went on, and chiefly by ejaculation, imprecation, and self-accusation published the whole statement of the case; understanding which, Uncle John added his voice also:

"Good Gord A'mighty! Wh-wh-what's dat you say? Dey—dey—dey Yankees, an' you Cornfedrits? Well, sir, an' are you Marse Beau—you wid your arm hurted? Go 'long! You can't fool me; Marse Beau done had more sense en dat. My Gord! an' dey wuz Yankees? You better cuss—cussin's about all you kin do now. Course de boat's gone. You'll never ketch up wid 'em in Gord's world now. Don't come along arter me about it? 'Tain't my fault. How wuz I to know? You wuz Yankees enough for me. I declar', Marse Beau, you ought to be ashamed o' yourself! You wanted to l'arn dem a lesson! I reckon dey l'arnt you one! You didn't mean 'em no harm! Humph! dey've cut dey eye-teeth, dey have! Lord! Marse Beau, I thought you done knowed us better. Did you really think we wuz a-gwine to let a passel o' Yankees take us away off our own plantation? You must done forgot us. We jes cleaned out de house for 'em, we did—clo'es, food, tobacco, rum. De young ladies 'ain't lef' a mossel for Marse John. An'—an'—an' 'fore de good Gord, my gun! Done tuck my gun away wid 'em! Wh-wh-wh-what you mean by such doin's? L-l-look here, Marse Beau, I don't like dat, nohow! Wh-wh-what! you tuck my gun and gin it to de Yankees? Dat's my gun! I done had dat gun twenty-five year an' more! Dog-gone! Yes, sir, I'll cuss—I'll cuss ef I wants to! I 'ain't got no use for gorillas, nohow! Lem me 'lone, I tell you! lem me 'lone! Marse John he'll get de law o' dat! Who's 'sponsible? Dat's all I want to know—who's 'sponsible? Ef-ef-ef-ef—No, sir; dar ain't nary boat on de place, nor hereabouts. Yes, sir; you kin cross de swamp ef you kin find de way. No, sir—no, sir; dar ain't no one to show you. I ain't gwine to leave de young ladies twell Marse John he comes back. Yes, I reckon you kin git to de cut-off by to-morrow mornin', ef you ain't shot on de way for Yankees, en' ef your company is fool enough to wait for you. No, sir, I don't know nothin' 'bout nothin'; you better wait an' arsk Marse John. . . . My Gord! I'm obleeged to laugh; I can't help it. Dem fool nigger wimen a-sittin' on de brink o' de byer, dey clo'es tied up in de bedquilts, an' de shotes an' de pullits all kilt, a-waitin' for freedom! I lay dey'll git freedom enough to-night when de boys come home. Dey git white gentlemen to marry 'em! Dey'll git five hundred apiece. Marse Beau, Gord'll punish you for dis—He surely will. I done tole Marse John long time ago he oughter sell dat brazen nigger Dead-arm Harriet, en' git shet o' her. Lord! Lord! Lord! Now you done gone to cussin' an' swearin' agin. Don't go tearin' off your jackets an' flingin' 'em at me. We don't want 'em; we buys our clo'es—what we don't make. Yes, Marse John'll be comin' along pretty soon now. What's your hurry, Marse Beau? Well, so long, ef you won't stay. He ain't got much use for gorillas neither, Marse John hain't."

The young officer wrote a few hasty words on a leaf torn from the pretty Russia-leather note-book, and handed it to the old darky. "For your Marse John."

"For Marse John—yes, sir; I'll gin hit to him soon 's he comes in."

They had dejectedly commenced their weary tramp up the bayou; he called him back, and lowered his voice confidentially: "Marse Beau, when you captured dat transport and stole all dem fixin's an' finery, you didn't see no good chawin' tobacco layin' round loose, did you? Thanky! thanky, child! Now I looks good at you, you ain't so much changed sence de times Marse John used to wallop you for your tricks. Well, good-bye, Marse Beau."

On the leaf were scrawled the words:

"All's up! Lee has surrendered.—BEAU."

The Eve of the Fourth
1894

HAROLD FREDERIC

Harold Frederic (1856–1898) spent his boyhood in Utica, New York, where he could only read about the battles of the Civil War in newspapers or hear of them from returning veterans. Although he later gained celebrity as the author of The Damnation of Theron Ware *(1896) and other novels, Frederic wrote numerous stories of the Civil War, gathered in two collections,* The Copperhead and Other Stories *(1894) and* Marsena and Other Stories *(1894). One of these, "The Eve of the Fourth," from the former collection, treats of a woman's trauma on hearing of her lover being killed at the front.*

*I*t was well on toward evening before this Third of July all at once made itself gloriously different from other days in my mind.

There was a very long afternoon, I remember, hot and overcast, with continual threats of rain which never came to anything. The other boys were too excited about the morrow to care for present play. They sat instead along the edge of the broad platform-stoop in front of Delos Ingersoll's grocery-store, their brown feet swinging at varying heights above the sidewalk, and bragged about the manner in which they contemplated celebrating the anniversary of their Independence. Most of the elder lads were very independent indeed; they were already secure in the parental permission to stay up all night, so that the Fourth might be ushered in with its full quota of ceremonial. The smaller urchins pretended that they also had this permission, or were sure of getting it. Little Denny Cregan attracted admiring attention by vowing that he should remain out, even if his father chased him with a policeman all around the ward, and he had to go and live in a cave in the gulf until he was grown up.

My inferiority to these companions of mine depressed me. They were allowed to go without shoes and stockings; they wore loose and comfortable old clothes, and were under no responsibility to keep them dry or clean or whole; they had their pockets literally bulging now with all sorts of portentous engines of noise and racket—huge brown "double-enders," bound with waxed cord; long, slim, vicious-looking "nigger-chasers"; big "Union torpedoes," covered with clay, which made a report like a horse pistol, and were invaluable for frightening farmers' horses;—and so on through an extended catalogue of recondite and sinister explosives upon which I looked with awe, as their owners from time to time exhibited them with the proud simplicity of those accustomed to greatness. Several of these boys also possessed toy cannons, which would be brought forth at twilight. They spoke firmly of ramming them to the muzzle with grass, to produce a greater noise—even if it burst them and killed everybody.

By comparison, my lot was one of abasement. I was a solitary child, and a victim to conventions. A blue necktie was daily pinned under my Byron collar, and there were gilt buttons on my zouave jacket. When we were away in the pasture playground near the gulf, and I ventured to take off my foot-gear, every dry old thistlepoint in the whole territory seemed to arrange itself to be stepped upon by my whitened and tender soles. I could not swim, so, while my lithe bold comrades dived out of sight under the deep water, and darted about chasing one another far beyond their depth, I paddled ignobly around the "baby-hole" close to the bank, in the warm and muddy shallows.

Especially apparent was my state of humiliation on this July afternoon. I had no "double-enders," nor might hope for any. The mere thought of a private cannon seemed monstrous and unnatural to me. By some unknown process of reasoning my mother had years before reached the theory that a good boy ought to have two ten-cent packs of small fire-crackers on the Fourth of July. Four or five succeeding anniversaries had hardened this theory into an orthodox tenet of faith, with all its observances rigidly fixed. The fire-crackers were bought for me overnight, and placed on the hall table. Beside them lay a long rod of punk. When I hastened down and out in the morning, with these ceremonial implements in my hands, the hired-girl would give me, in an old kettle, some embers from the wood-fire in the summer kitchen. Thus furnished, I went into the front yard, and in solemn solitude fired off these crackers one by one. Those which, by reason of having lost their tails, were only fit for "fizzes,"

I saved till after breakfast. With the exhaustion of these, I fell reluctantly back upon the public for entertainment. I could see the soldiers, hear the band and the oration, and in the evening, if it didn't rain, enjoy the fireworks; but my own contribution to the patriotic noise was always over before the breakfast-dishes had been washed.

My mother scorned the little paper torpedoes as flippant and wasteful things. You merely threw one of them, and it went off, she said, and there you were. I don't know that I ever grasped this objection in its entirety, but it impressed my whole childhood with its unanswerableness. Years and years afterward, when my own children asked for torpedoes, I found myself unconsciously advising against them on quite the maternal lines. Nor was it easy to budge the good lady from her position on the great two-packs issue. I seem to recall having successfully undermined it once or twice, but two was the rule. When I called her attention to the fact that our neighbour, Tom Hemingway, thought nothing of exploding a whole pack at a time inside their wash-boiler, she was not dazzled, but only replied: "Wilful waste makes woeful want."

Of course the idea of the Hemingways ever knowing what want meant was absurd. They lived a dozen doors or so from us, in a big white house with stately white columns rising from verandah to gable across the whole front, and a large garden, flowers and shrubs in front, fruit trees and vegetables behind. Squire Hemingway was the most important man in our part of the town. I know now that he was never anything more than United States Commissioner of Deeds, but in those days, when he walked down the street with his gold-headed cane, his blanket-shawl folded over his arm, and his severe, dignified, close-shaven face held well up in the air, I seemed to behold a companion of Presidents.

This great man had two sons. The elder of them, De Witt Hemingway, was a man grown, and was at the front. I had seen him march away, over a year before, with a bright drawn sword, at the side of his company. The other son, Tom, was my senior by only a twelvemonth. He was by nature proud, but often consented to consort with me when the selection of other available associates was at low ebb.

It was to this Tom that I listened with most envious eagerness, in front of the grocery-store, on the afternoon of which I speak. He did not sit on the stoop with the others—no one expected quite that degree of condescension—but leaned nonchalantly against a post, whittling out a new ramrod for his cannon. He said that this year he was not going to have any ordinary fire-crackers at all; they, he added with a meaning glance at me, were only fit for girls. He might do a little in "double-enders," but his real point would be in "ringers"—an incredible giant variety of cracker, Turkey-red like the other, but in size almost a rolling-pin. Some of them he would fire off singly—between volleys from his cannon. But a good many he intended to explode, in bunches say of six, inside the tin wash-boiler, brought out into the middle of the road for that purpose. It would doubtless blow the old thing sky-high, but that didn't matter. They could get a new one.

Even as he spoke, the big bell in the tower of the town-hall burst forth in a loud clangour of swift-repeated strokes. It was half a mile away, but the moist air brought the urgent, clamorous sounds to our ears as if the belfry had stood close above us. We sprang off the stoop and stood poised, waiting to hear the number of the ward struck, and ready to scamper off on the instant if the fire was anywhere in our part of the town. But the excited peal went on and on, without a pause. It became obvious that this meant something beside a fire. Perhaps some of us wondered vaguely what that something might be, but as a body our interest had lapsed. Billy Norris, who was the son of poor parents, but could whip even Tom Hemingway, said he had been told that the German boys on the other side of the gulf were coming over to "rush" us on the following day, and that we ought all to collect nails to fire at them from our cannon. This we pledged ourselves to do—the bell keeping up its throbbing tumult ceaselessly.

Suddenly we saw the familiar figure of Johnson running up the street toward us. What his first name was I never knew. To every one, little or big, he was just Johnson. He and his family had moved into our town after the War began; I fancy they moved away again before it ended. I do not even know what he did for a living. But he seemed always drunk, always turbulently good-natured, and always shouting out the news at the top of his lungs. I cannot pretend to guess how he found out everything as he did, or why, having found it out, he straightway rushed homeward, scattering the intelligence as he ran. Most probably Johnson was moulded by Nature for a town-crier, but was born by accident some generations after the race of bellmen had disappeared. Our neighbourhood did not like him; our mothers did not know Mrs. Johnson, and we boys behaved with snobbish roughness to his children. He seemed not to mind this at all, but came up unwearyingly to shout out the tidings of the day for our benefit.

"Vicksburg's fell! Vicksburg fell!" was what we heard him yelling, as he approached.

Delos Ingersoll and his hired-boy ran out of the grocery. Doors opened along the street and heads were thrust inquiringly out.

"Vicksburg's fell!" he kept hoarsely proclaiming, his arms waving in the air, as he staggered along at a dogtrot past us, and went into the saloon next to the grocery.

I cannot say how definite an idea these tidings conveyed to our boyish minds. I have a notion that at the time I assumed that Vicksburg had something to do with Gettysburg, where I knew from the talk of my elders that an awful fight had been proceeding since the middle of the week. Doubtless this confusion was aided by the fact that an hour or so later on that same wonderful day, the wire brought us word that this terrible battle on Pennsylvanian soil had at last taken the form of a Union victory. It is difficult now to see how we could have known both these things on the Third of July—that is to say, before the people actually concerned seem to have been sure of them. Perhaps it was only inspired guesswork, but I know that my town went wild over the news, and that the clouds overhead cleared away as if by magic.

The sun did well to spread that summer-sky at eventide with all the pageantry of colour the spectrum knows. It would have been preposterous that such a day should slink off in dull, quaker drabs. Men were shouting in the streets now. The old cannon left over from the Mexican war had been dragged out onto the ricketty covered river-bridge, and was frightening the fishes, and shaking the dry, worm-eaten rafters, as fast as the swab and rammer could work. Our town bandsmen were playing as they had never played before, down in the square in front of the post-office. The management of the Universe could not hurl enough wild fireworks into the exultant sunset to fit our mood.

The very air was filled with the scent of triumph—the spirit of conquest. It seemed only natural that I should march off to my mother and quite collectedly tell her that I desired to stay out all night with the other boys. I had never dreamed of daring to prefer such a request in other years. Now I was scarcely conscious of surprise when she gave her permission, adding with a smile that I would be glad enough to come in and go to bed before half the night was over.

I steeled my heart after supper with the proud resolve that if the night turned out to be as protracted as one of those Lapland winter nights we read about in the geography, I still would not surrender.

The boys outside were not so excited over the tidings of my unlooked-for victory as I had expected them to be. They received the news, in fact, with a rather mortifying stoicism. Tom Hemingway, however, took enough interest in the affair to suggest that, instead of spending my twenty cents in paltry fire-crackers, I might go down-town and buy another can of powder for his cannon. By doing so, he pointed out, I would be a part-proprietor, as it were, of the night's performance, and would be entitled to occasionally touch the cannon off. This generosity affected me, and I hastened down the long hill-street to show myself worthy of it, repeating the instruction of "Kentucky Bear-Hunter-coarse-grain" over and over again to myself as I went.

Half-way on my journey I overtook a person whom, even in the gathering twilight, I recognized as Miss Stratford, the school-teacher. She also was walking down the hill, and rapidly. It did not need the sight of a letter in her hand to tell me that she was going to the post-office. In those cruel war-days everybody went to the post-office. I myself went regularly to get our mail, and to exchange shin-plasters for one-cent stamps with which to buy yeast and other commodities that called for minute fractional currency.

Although I was very fond of Miss Stratford—I still recall her gentle eyes, and pretty, rounded, dark face, in its frame of long, black curls, with tender liking—I now coldly resolved to hurry past, pretending not to know her. It was a mean thing to do; Miss Stratford had always been good to me, shining in that respect in brilliant contrast to my other teachers, whom I hated bitterly. Still, the "Kentucky Bear-Hunter-coarse-grain" was too important a matter to wait upon any mere female friendships, and I quickened my pace into a trot, hoping to scurry by unrecognised.

"O Andrew! is that you?" I heard her call out as I ran past. For the instant I thought of rushing on, quite as if I had not heard. Then I stopped, and walked beside her.

"I am going to stay up all night; mother says I may; and I am going to fire off Tom Hemingway's big cannon every fourth time, straight through till breakfast-time," I announced to her, loftily.

"Dear me! I ought to be proud to be seen walking with such an important citizen," she answered, with kindly playfulness. She added more gravely, after a moment's pause: "Then Tom is out, playing with the other boys, is he?"

"Why, of course!" I responded. "He always lets us stand round when he fires off his cannon. He's got some 'ringers' this year, too."

I heard Miss Stratford murmur an impulsive "Thank God!" under her breath.

Full as the day had been of surprises, I could not help wondering that the fact of Tom's ringers should stir up such profound emotions in the teacher's breast. Since the subject so interested her, I went on with a long catalogue of Tom's other pyrotechnic possessions, and from that to an account of his almost supernatural collection of postage stamps. In a few minutes more I am sure I should have revealed to her the great secret of my life, which was my determination, in case I came to assume the victorious rôle and rank of Napoleon, to immediately make Tom a Marshal of the Empire.

But we had reached the post-office square. I had never before seen it so full of people.

Even to my boyish eyes the tragic line of division which cleft this crowd in twain was apparent. On one side, over by the Seminary, the youngsters had lighted a bonfire, and were running about it—some of the bolder ones jumping through it in frolicsome recklessness. Close by stood the band, now valiantly thumping out "John Brown's Body" upon the noisy night air. It was quite dark by this time, but the musicians knew the tune by heart. So did the throng about them, and sang it with lusty fervour. The doors of the saloon toward the corner of the square were flung wide open. Two black streams of men kept in motion under the radiance of the big reflector-lamp over these doors—one going in, one coming out. They slapped one another on the back as they passed, with exultant screams and shouts. Every once in a while, when movement was for the instant blocked, some voice lifted above the others would begin "Hip-hip-hip-hip—" and then would come a roar that fairly drowned the music.

On the post-office side of the square there was no bonfire. No one raised a cheer. A densely packed mass of men and women stood in front of the big square stone-building, with its closed doors, and curtained windows upon which, from time to time, the shadow of some passing clerk, bare-headed and hurried, would be momentarily thrown. They waited in silence for the night-mail to be sorted. If they spoke to one another, it was in whispers—as if they had been standing with uncovered heads at a funeral service in a graveyard. The dim light reflected over from the bonfire, or down from the shaded windows of the post-office, showed solemn, hard-lined, anxious faces. Their lips scarcely moved when they muttered little low-toned remarks to their neighbours. They spoke from the side of the mouth, and only on one subject.

"He went all through Fredericksburg without a scratch—"

"He looks so much like me—General Palmer told my brother he'd have known his hide in a tan-yard—"

"He's been gone—let's see—it was a year some time last April—"

"He was counting on a furlough the first of this month—I suppose nobody got one as things turned out—"

"He said, 'No; it ain't my style. I'll fight as much as you like, but I won't be nigger-waiter for no man, captain or no captain'—"

Thus I heard the scattered murmurs among the grown-up heads above me, as we pushed into the outskirts of the throng, and stood there, waiting with the rest. There was no sentence without a "he" in it. A stranger might have fancied that they were all talking of one man. I knew better. They were the fathers and mothers, the sisters, brothers, wives of the men whose regiments had been in that horrible three days' fight at Gettysburg. Each was thinking and speaking of his own, and took it for granted the others would understand. For that matter, they all did understand. The town knew the name and family of every one of the twelve-score sons she had in this battle.

It is not very clear to me now why people all went to the post-office to wait for the evening papers that came in from the nearest big city. Nowadays they would be brought in bulk and sold on the street before the mail-bags had reached the post-office. Apparently, that had not yet been thought of in our slow old town.

The band across the square had started up afresh with "Annie Lisle"— the sweet old refrain of "Wave willows, murmur waters" comes back to me now after a quarter-century of forgetfulness,—when all at once there was a sharp forward movement of the crowd. The doors had been thrown open, and the hallway was on the instant filled with a swarming multitude. The band had stopped as suddenly as it began, and no more cheering was heard. We could see whole troops of dark forms scudding toward us from the other side of the square.

"Run in for me—that's a good boy—ask for Dr. Stratford's mail," the teacher whispered, bending over me.

It seemed an age before I finally got back to her, with the paper in its postmarked wrapper buttoned up inside my jacket. I had never been in so fierce and determined a crowd before, and I emerged from it at last, confused in wits and panting for breath. I was still looking about through the gloom in a foolish way for Miss Stratford, when I felt her hand laid sharply on my shoulder.

"Well—where is it?—did nothing come?" she asked, her voice trembling with eagerness, and the eyes which I had thought so soft and dove-like flashing down upon me as if she were Miss Pritchard, and I had been caught chewing gum in school.

I drew the paper out from under my roundabout, and gave it to her. She grasped it, and thrust a finger under the cover to tear it off. Then she hesitated for a moment, and looked about her. "Come where there is some light," she said, and started up the street. Although she seemed to have spoken more to herself than to me, I followed her in silence, close to her side.

For a long way the sidewalk in front of every lighted store-window was thronged with a group of people clustered tight about some one who had a paper, and was reading from it aloud. Beside broken snatches of this monologue, we caught, now groans of sorrow and horror, now exclamations of proud approval, and even the beginnings of cheers, broken in upon by a general "'Sh-h!" as we hurried past outside the kerb.

It was under a lamp in the little park nearly half-way up the hill that Miss Stratford stopped, and spread the paper open. I see her still, white-faced, under the flickering gaslight, her black curls making a strange dark bar between the pale-straw hat and the white of her shoulder-shawl and muslin dress, her hands trembling as they held up the extended sheet. She scanned the columns swiftly, skimmingly for a time, as I could see by the way she moved her round chin up and down. Then she came to a part which called for closer reading. The paper shook perceptibly now, as she bent her eyes upon it. Then all at once it fell from her hands, and without a sound she walked away.

I picked the paper up, and followed her along the gravelled path. It was like pursuing a ghost, so weirdly white did her summer attire now look to my frightened eyes, with such a swift and deathly silence did she move. The path upon which we were, described a circle touching the four sides of the square. She did not quit it when the intersection with our street was reached, but followed straight round again toward the point where we had entered the park. This, too, in turn she passed, gliding noiselessly forward under the black arches of the overhanging elms. The suggestion that she did not know she was going round and round in a ring startled my brain. I would have run up to her now if I had dared.

Suddenly she turned, and saw that I was behind her. She sank slowly into one of the garden-seats, by the path, and held out for a moment a hesitating hand toward me. I went up at this and looked into her face. Shadowed as it was, the change I saw there chilled my blood. It was like the face of some one I had never seen before, with fixed, wide-open, staring eyes which seemed to look beyond me through the darkness, upon some terrible sight no other could see.

"Go—run and tell—Tom—to go home! His brother—his brother has been killed," she said to me, choking over the words as if they hurt her throat, and still with the same strange dry-eyed, far-away gaze covering yet not seeing me.

I held out the paper for her to take, but she made no sign, and I gingerly laid it on the seat beside her. I hung about for a minute or two longer, imagining that she might have something else to say—but no word came. Then, with a feebly inopportune "Well, good-bye," I started off alone up the hill.

It was a distinct relief to find that my companions were congregated at the lower end of the common, instead of their accustomed haunt further up near my home, for the walk had been a lonely one, and I was deeply depressed by what had happened. Tom, it seems, had been called away some quarter of an hour before. All the boys knew of the calamity which had befallen the Hemingways. We talked about it from time to time, as we loaded and fired the cannon which Tom had obligingly turned over to my friends. It had been out of deference to the feelings of the stricken household that they had betaken themselves and their racket off to the remote corner of the common. The solemnity of the occasion silenced criticism upon my conduct in forgetting to buy the powder. "There would be enough as long as it lasted," Billy Norris said, with philosophic decision.

We speculated upon the likelihood of De Witt Hemingway being given a military funeral. These mournful pageants had by this time become such familiar things to us that the prospect of one more had no element of excitement in it, save as it involved a gloomy sort of distinction for Tom. He would ride in the first mourning-carriage with his parents, and this would associate us, as we walked along ahead of the band, with the most intimate aspects of the demonstration. We regretted now that the soldier-company which we had so long projected remained still unorganised. Had it been otherwise we would probably have been awarded the right of the line in the procession. Some one suggested that it was not too late—and we promptly bound ourselves to meet after breakfast next day to organise and begin drilling. If we worked at this night and day, and our parents instantaneously provided us with uniforms and guns, we should be in time. It was also arranged that we should be called the De Witt C. Hemingway Fire Zouaves, and that Billy Norris should be side-captain. The chief command would, of course, be reserved for Tom. We would specially salute him as he rode past in the closed carriage and then fall in behind, forming his honorary escort.

None of us had known the dead officer closely, owing to his advanced

age. He was seven or eight years older than even Tom. But the more elderly among our group had seen him play baseball in the academy nine, and
our neighbourhood was still alive with legends of his early audacity and
skill in collecting barrels and dry-goods boxes at night for election bonfires.
It was remembered that once he carried away a whole front-stoop from
the house of a little German tailor on one of the back streets. As we stood
around the heated cannon, in the great black solitude of the common, our
fancies pictured this redoubtable young man once more among us—not in
his blue uniform, with crimson sash and sword laid by his side, and the
gauntlets drawn over his lifeless hands, but as a taller and glorified Tom, in
a roundabout jacket and copper-toed boots, giving the law on this his playground. The very cannon at our feet had once been his. The night air
became peopled with ghosts of his contemporaries—handsome boys who
had grown up before us, and had gone away to lay down their lives in far-
off Virginia or Tennessee.

These heroic shades brought drowsiness in their train. We lapsed into
long silences, punctuated by yawns, when it was not our turn to ram and
touch off the cannon. Finally some of us stretched ourselves out on the
grass, in the warm darkness, to wait comfortably for this turn to come.

What did come instead was daybreak—finding Billy Norris and myself
alone constant to our all-night vow. We sat up and shivered as we rubbed
our eyes. The morning air had a chilling freshness that went to my bones—
and these, moreover, were filled with those novel aches and stiffnesses
which beds were invented to prevent. We stood up, stretching out our
arms, and gaping at the pearl-and-rose beginnings of the sunrise in the
eastern sky. The other boys had all gone home, and taken the cannon with
them. Only scraps of torn paper and tiny patches of burnt grass marked
the site of our celebration.

My first weak impulse was to march home without delay, and get into
bed as quickly as might be. But Billy Norris looked so finely resolute and
resourceful that I hesitated to suggest this, and said nothing, leaving the
initiative to him. One could see, by the most casual glance, that he was
superior to mere considerations of unseasonableness in hours. I remembered now that he was one of that remarkable body of boys, the paper-
carriers, who rose when all others were asleep in their warm nests, and
trudged about long before breakfast distributing the *Clarion* among the
well-to-do households. This fact had given him his position in our neighbourhood as quite the next in leadership to Tom Hemingway.

He presently outlined his plans to me, after having tried the centre of light on the horizon, where soon the sun would be, by an old brass compass he had in his pocket—a process which enabled him, he said, to tell pretty well what time it was. The paper wouldn't be out for nearly two hours yet—and if it were not for the fact of a great battle there would have been no paper at all on this glorious anniversary—but he thought we would go down-town and see what was going on around about the newspaper office. Forthwith we started. He cheered my faint spirits by assuring me that I would soon cease to be sleepy, and would, in fact, feel better than usual. I dragged my feet along at his side, waiting for this revival to come, and meantime furtively yawning against my sleeve.

Billy seemed to have dreamed a good deal, during our nap on the common, about the De Witt C. Hemingway Fire Zouaves. At least he had now in his head a marvellously elaborated system of organisation, which he unfolded as we went along. I felt that I had never before realised his greatness, his born genius for command. His scheme halted no where. He allotted offices with discriminating firmness; he treated the question of uniforms and guns as a trivial detail which would settle itself; he spoke with calm confidence of our offering our services to the Republic in the autumn; his clear vision saw even the materials for a fife-and-drum corps among the German boys in the back streets. It was true that I appeared personally to play a meagre part in these great projects: the most that was said about me was that I might make a fair third-corporal. But Fate had thrown in my way such a wonderful chance of becoming intimate with Billy, that I made sure I should swiftly advance in rank—the more so as I discerned in the background of his thoughts, as it were, a grim determination to make short work of Tom Hemingway's aristocratic pretensions, once the funeral was over.

We were forced to make a detour of the park on our way down, because Billy observed some half-dozen Irish boys at play with a cannon inside, whom we knew to be hostile. If there had been only four, he said, he would have gone in and routed them. He could whip any two of them, he added, with one hand tied behind his back. I listened with admiration. Billy was not tall, but he possessed great thickness of chest and length of arm. His skin was so dark that we canvassed the theory from time to time of his having Indian blood. He did not discourage this, and he admitted himself that he was double-jointed.

The streets of the business-part of the town into which we now made our way, were quite deserted. We went around into the yard behind the printing-office, where the carrier-boys were wont to wait for the press to get to work; and Billy displayed some impatience at discovering that here too there was no one. It was now broad daylight, but through the windows of the composing-room we could see some of the printers, still setting type by kerosene lamps.

We seated ourselves at the end of the yard on a big, flat, smooth-faced stone, and Billy produced from his pocket a number of "m" quads, he called them, with which the carriers had learned from the printers' boys to play a very beautiful game. You shook the pieces of metal in your hands, and threw them on the stone; your score depended upon the number of nicked sides that were turned uppermost. We played this game in the interest of good-fellowship for a little. Then Billy told me that the carriers always played it for pennies—and that it was unmanly for us to do otherwise. He had no pennies at that precise moment, but would pay at the end of the week what he had lost; in the meantime there was my twenty cents to go on with. After this Billy threw so many nicks uppermost that my courage gave way, and I made an attempt to stop the game; but a single remark from him as to the military destiny which he was reserving for me if I only displayed true soldierly nerve and grit, sufficed to quiet me once more, and the play went on. I had now only five cents left.

Suddenly a shadow interposed itself between the sunlight and the stone. I looked up, to behold a small boy with bare arms and a blackened apron standing over me, watching our game. There was a great deal of ink on his face and hands, and a hardened, not to say rakish, expression in his eye.

"Why don't you 'jeff' with somebody of your own size?" he demanded of Billy, after having looked me over critically.

He was not nearly so big as Billy, and I expected to see the latter instantly rise and crush him, but Billy only laughed and said we were playing for fun; he was going to give me all my money back. I was rejoiced to hear this, but still felt surprised at the propitiatory manner Billy adopted toward this diminutive inky boy. It was not the demeanour befitting a side-captain—and what made it worse was that the strange boy loftily declined to be cajoled by it. He sniffed when Billy told him about the military company we were forming; he coldly shook his head, with a curt "nixie!" when invited to join it; and he laughed aloud at hearing the name our organisation was to bear.

"He ain't dead at all—that De Witt Hemingway," he said, with jeering contempt.

"Hain't he though!" exclaimed Billy. "The news come last night. Tom had to go home—his mother sent for him—on account of it!"

"I'll bet you a quarter he ain't dead," responded the practical inky boy. "Money up, though!"

"I've only got fifteen cents. I'll bet you that, though," rejoined Billy, producing my torn and dishevelled shin-plasters.

"All right! wait here!" said the boy, running off to the building and disappearing through the door. There was barely time for me to learn from my companion that this printer's-apprentice was called "the devil," and could not only whistle between his teeth and crack his fingers but chew tobacco, when he reappeared, with a long narrow strip of paper in his hand. This he held out for us to see, indicating with an ebon forefinger the special paragraph we were to read. Billy looked at it sharply, for several moments, in silence. Then he said to me: "What does it say there? I must 'a' got some powder in my eyes last night."

I read this paragraph aloud, not without an unworthy feeling that the inky boy would now respect me deeply:

"CORRECTION. Lieutenant De Witt C. Hemingway, of Company A, —th New York, reported in earlier despatches among the killed, is uninjured. The officer killed is Lieutenant Carl Heinninge, Company F, same regiment."

Billy's face visibly lengthened as I read this out, and he felt us both looking at him. He made a pretence of examining the slip of paper again, but in a half-hearted way. Then he ruefully handed over the fifteen cents, and, rising from the stone, shook himself.

"Them Dutchmen never was no good!" was what he said.

The inky boy had put the money in the pocket under his apron, and grinned now with as much enjoyment as dignity would permit him to show. He did not seem to mind any longer the original source of his winnings, and it was apparent that I could not with decency recall it to him. Some odd impulse prompted me, however, to ask him if I might have the paper he had in his hand. He was magnanimous enough to present me with the proofsheet on the spot. Then with another grin he turned and left us.

Billy stood sullenly kicking with his bare toes into a sand-heap by the stone. He would not answer me when I spoke to him. It flashed across my perceptive faculties that he was not such a great man, after all, as I had imagined. In another instant or two it had become quite clear to me that I had no admiration for him whatever. Without a word, I turned on my heel and walked determinedly out of the yard and into the street, homeward bent.

All at once I quickened my pace; something had occurred to me. The purpose thus conceived grew so swiftly that soon I found myself running. Up the hill I sped, and straight through the park. If the Irish boys shouted after me I knew it not, but dashed on heedless of all else save the one idea. I only halted, breathless and panting, when I stood on Dr. Stratford's doorstep, and heard the night-bell inside jangling shrilly in response to my excited pull.

As I waited, I pictured to myself the old doctor as he would presently come down, half-dressed and pulling on his coat as he advanced. He would ask eagerly, "Who is sick? Where am I to go?" and I would calmly reply that he unduly alarmed himself, and that I had a message for his daughter. He would, of course, ask me what it was, and I, politely but firmly, would decline to explain to any one but the lady in person. Just what might ensue was not clear—but I beheld myself throughout commanding the situation, at once benevolent, polished, and inexorable.

The door opened with unlooked-for promptness, while my self-complacent vision still hung in mid-air. Instead of the bald and spectacled old doctor, there confronted me a white-faced, solemn-eyed lady in a black dress, whom I did not seem to know. I stared at her, tongue-tied, till she said, in a low, grave voice: "Well, Andrew, what is it?"

Then of course I saw that it was Miss Stratford, my teacher, the person whom I had come to see. Some vague sense of what the sleepless night had meant in this house came to me as I gazed confusedly at her mourning, and heard the echo of her sad tones in her ears.

"Is some one ill?" she asked again.

"No; some one—some one is very well!" I managed to reply, lifting my eyes again to her wan face. The spectacle of its drawn lines and pallor all at once assailed my wearied and overtaxed nerves with crushing weight. I felt myself beginning to whimper, and rushing tears scalded my eyes. Something inside my breast seemed to be dragging me down through the stoop.

I have now only the recollection of Miss Stratford's kneeling by my side, with a supporting arm around me, and of her thus unrolling and reading the proof-paper I had in my hand. We were in the hall now, instead of on the stoop, and there was a long silence. Then she put her head on my shoulder and wept. I could hear and feel her sobs as if they were my own.

"I—I didn't think you'd cry—that you'd be so sorry," I heard myself saying, at last, in despondent self-defence.

Miss Strattord lifted her head, and, still kneeling as she was, put a finger under my chin to make me look her in her face. Lo! the eyes were laughing through their tears; the whole countenance was radiant once more with the light of happy youth, and with that other glory which youth knows only once.

"Why, Andrew, boy," she said, trembling, smiling, sobbing, beaming all at once, "didn't you know that people cry for very joy sometimes?"

And as I shook my head she bent down and kissed me.

Part IV

Aftermath

An Independent Ku-Klux
1872

JOHN WILLIAM DE FOREST

John William De Forest (1826–1906) spent much of his youth in Connecticut but found himself, with his wife and son, in Charleston at the outbreak of the Civil War. He described the siege of Charleston in an article, "The First Time Under Fire," published in Harper's *(September 1864). On January 1, 1862, he joined the Connecticut Volunteers, serving until the end of 1864. His account of his military service was published posthumously as* A Volunteer's Adventures *(1946). Although a Northerner, De Forest developed considerable sympathy for the South, especially during his service in South Carolina in the Freedman's Bureau. His novel,* Miss Ravenel's Conversion from Secession to Loyalty *(1867), focusing on a love triangle with the war as a backdrop, has been called one of the finest Civil War novels ever written. De Forest also wrote several stories about the war and its aftermath, many of them laced with racism. "An Independent Ku-Klux," published in the* Galaxy *of April 1872, is a tour de force of sorts in being a* comic *story about the Ku Klux Klan.*

ay," observed Selnarten Bowen to his wife, Nan Bowen, "these niggers is gone in for stealin' worse 'n ever. Hev we lost anythin'?" Nan Bowen drew herself up to the full height of her five feet nine inches, grappled her mighty hips with her large sinewy hands as if she were about to throw herself at somebody's head, ground her quid of tobacco with a cowlike opening of the mouth and twisting of the lower jaw, and hit a sapling ten feet away with nicotine enough to poison a rattlesnake.

Having thus got her mind in trim and cleared her upper decks for action, she proceeded to fire the following contemptuous queries at her "old man," meanwhile not once turning her clear gray eyes upon his diminutive figure, but staring fixedly and with a curiously blank expression at the rotten roof of her log cabin.

"What hev we got to lose?" said Nan Bowen, in a slow, hard, scornful monotone, and with long pauses between her sentences. "What did we ever own? What did you ever own? What is there in our house? Anythin' that niggers would steal? Not as I knows on."

"I've arned as much as you hev," retorted Selnarten, meanwhile sidling away from his partner, who was the better man of the two.

"Who said you didn't?" answered Nan, still speaking with icy delibera-tion, and still eying her rack-o'-bones dwelling.

"An' I've done some shootin'," continued Selnarten.

"Yes, shot rich folkses' hogs, jest like these niggers," commented Nan.

"Wild hogs," put in Selnarten. "I allays allowed them hogs was wild. An' who said anythin' agin it? Did you? You et yer part, I reckon."

It must be explained that Selnarten was very suspicious of wildness in hogs. He hardly ever saw a porker anywhere or under any conditions, not even when shut up in a pen, but what he was ready to impute wildness to him, and wanted to shoot or otherwise slay him; and not only slay him, but tote him home, and not only tote him home, but eat him. If he had encountered a pig in the shape of spareribs and slices of bacon and strings of sausages, he would have been disposed to pronounce them wild spareribs and wild slices of bacon and wild sausages, and to lay expropri-ating hands upon them accordingly. It is hardly too much to assert that, had a pig come to him in a black dress coat and white neckchoker, and exhorted him to attend a camp-meeting, he would still have been inclined to fall upon him for a wild pig, and proceed to butcher. One wonders, by the way, what would have become of Selnarten had swine been thus inim-ical to wildness in men, and felt it to be their mission to put an end to it. There would surely have been a drove after him intent upon civilizing him by picking his bones.

"Nobody ever complained," continued Selnarten. "Nobody ever said hogs to *me*. Now, as for these yere niggers, they're complained of. Folks want to put 'em down. An' I go for it."

"*I* don't keer what you do to niggers," responded Nan, still speaking with an air and tone of uttermost scorn, as if there were nothing in cre-ation that she did not despise, beginning with negroes and ending with her husband. "You can go for 'em ef you like. Only ef you get yourself in a muss don't come howlin' around me. I won't hev it."

"They're settin' up for white folks," resumed Selnarten in a grunting undertone, as if in his much chasing of wild hogs he had caught the swine pronunciation. "Folks gen'rally is gwine in for to put 'em down. Square Anderson an' Rarry Saxton, an' a lot more, has jined the Ku-Klux. I'm gwine to try to git to jine."

"Jine away!" answered Nan, with her habitual air of sarcastic and bitter indifference.

"I'll start for Saxonburg now," decided Selnarten, turning on his heels and striking out without further good-bye.

"Take care yerself," said Nan, which was her usual adieu when she did not say "Go to the devil!"

In the next breath she turned toward her husband and called sharply, "Say! When you comin' back?"

"Some time before sun-up," responded Selnarten, rather wondering that she should care.

"Fetch home somethin'," added Nan. "Thar ain't much in the barl."

"If I see ary wild hog," promised Selnarten, and pushed on with a rapid, slouching lope, not even looking over his shoulder.

We positively cannot attend further to Selnarten's adventures without first pausing to consider his extraordinary name. Bowen is well enough; there have been other people in the world entitled Bowen; we can accept Bowen without an effort. But Selnarten is a puzzler, and one might almost say, in the phrase of Mr. Boffin, a "scarer." The man himself could give no sort of information upon the subject, as indeed he never thought of giving any or asking any. Why he was christened thus, or whether he was christened at all, he could no more tell than he could tell the origin of the word christened, or of any other word connected with the Christian religion, or with any other religion. All he knew about it was that ever since he could remember anything, people had addressed him as Selnarten, and he had answered, "Yere," or to that effect. As the mind refuses to concede that any native American of Anglo-Saxon stock could really lay claim to such a nomenclature, we have spent more thought on this philological riddle than it deserves, and have ended by guessing that the word Selnarten began life as Elnathan, and got warped into its present shape by some hostile influence, perhaps fever and ague.

Selnarten's person, like his cognomen, had a made-over look. In build and features and expression he was not so much a natural human being as a sort of shabby work of art, like a totem or a fetish. That Rembrandt of the spirits of the air, that grotesque and malicious sculptor and painter, Malaria, had taken him in hand from the days of his doughy infancy, and had moulded and colored him in accordance with its wayward taste. He could not show a limb nor a muscle which had not been scraped down and withered and distorted by this indefatigable and pitiless carver. Malaria had hollowed his abdomen and gouged out his cheeks and sunk his eyes and pinched his temples. Then, laying aside the chisel, it had gone at him with the brush; staining him from within outwards, as if he were a meerschaum pipe; cramming him to reeking with all the monotonous tints of dumb ague; taking a fresh dab at him every time it got him around to a new swamp; using up on him the richness of acres of decaying trees and of creeks full of oozing vegetable mud; running the pencil along every sur-face vein and into the whites of his eyes and the roots of his hair; spotting him here and stippling him there, and streaking him in other places; in short, giving him the finish of a masterpiece.

Even the long, thin, and dry locks (seemingly dry enough to rustle) that hung short over his narrow forehead and long behind his grimy ears, were of a dead-and-alive yellow, which could only have come from the palette of Malaria. When he combed them, which happened perhaps once a quarter, or when he took off his hat, which he generally did on going to bed, he must have dispensed fever-and-ague spores through the atmosphere. If he had been a side of leather, and had passed his regulation seven years in a vat, he could not have been tanned more thoroughly than he was. It seemed also as if Malaria had not stopped with his person, but had gone over his very gar-ments and taken extra pains with them. His broad-brimmed wool hat was as ragged as though it had shaken itself to pieces in "cold fits"; and its var-nished, spotted, bistred drab complexion appeared very much like a contin-uation of Selnarten's countenance; much as if his head had spread out at the top, after the fashion of a toadstool. Same tint in his short-waisted, short-sleeved, buttonless frock coat, inadequate vest, wizened trousers, and gap-ing shoes. Butternut and gray and black had all alike become foxy. His entire wardrobe looked as if it needed a course of quinine.

Thus haggard, and warped, and stained, and threadbare, he favored the scarecrow species rather than the human; and a scarecrow, for that matter, who had fallen from his first estate—a scarecrow badly impoverished, out at elbows, and faded—a scarecrow broken down by the "agur." A specta-tor with a bold imagination and a keen eye for color might also have been reminded by him of one of those barkless logs which may be seen floating on the mud or sticking in the edging reeds of a southern creek, dark yellow with wet rot and light yellow with dry rot, whimsically carved by peckings of birds and gnawings of the atmosphere, unwholesome and ugly and dismally picturesque. A white man he sometimes proudly called himself; but an unprejudiced observer would sooner have classed him as a Malay; and philology, bending its mind to the subject, might ask, Why not a Malay when so malarious?

Through the wintry sloughs of one of those roads whose mission it is to render travelling difficult, Selnarten Bowen tramped out the five lonesome miles which lay between his cabin and the straggling, rusty village of Saxonburg.

The first person whom he addressed was Squire John Calhoun Rawson. Squire Jack, as he was commonly styled, had been useful in other days to Selnarten, having brought him clear of a charge of hog-stealing, the defence being wildness in the hog. He was a man of not more than thirty-five, but already so corpulent that it seemed as if it would be a comfort to him to disembowel him, and a still greater comfort to hang him up by the heels in a breeze, with perhaps a cob in his mouth. Even the unimaginative Selnarten could hardly look at his legal friend without thinking of an enticing porker. His face was large and flattened and pasty, reminding one of a batch of dough set away to rise. His eyes were slightly yellowish, for Malaria had given him a touch or two; but, for all that, they were not disagreeable eyes to meet; there was both kindness and drollery in them. His expression, too, was good-humored, and he was almost always smiling quietly, as if his mind ran upon jokes for casters.

It was dull times with Squire Jack Rawson. Since the war everybody in and around Saxonburg had gone more or less bankrupt, and "lawing" had fallen into disrepute, with other luxuries. Squire Jack did little but stand in his office door, like Giant Pope in the mouth of his cave, and survey the passers-by; only, instead of biting his nails at them, he smiled upon them and cheered them with puns and illuminated them with views on politics. At intervals, finding the winter dampness too shrewish, he retreated into his sanctum, threw a small green stick on a sulky fire which smoked and spit against the sooty back of a cracked Franklin stove, drew himself up to the same in a willow-bottomed arm-chair, clapped his puffy feet patronizingly on the stove's shoulders, read anew the local items of the Saxonburg "Banner," found them stupid and yawned in their faces. Then out he would sally again, like a restless dog out of his kennel, to lean against the door-post with hands in pockets, to talk if there was a talker at hand, and if not, to smile vaguely.

"Evenin', Squire," was the salutation of Selnarten. In Saxonburg, by the way, it was morning until twelve o'clock, and after that it was evening.

"How are you, Mr. Bowen?" nodded the lawyer, with that civility which a Southerner habitually accords to a white fellow citizen, no matter how poor and ignorant. "Anything stirring your way?"

"Nary," replied Mr. Bowen, who could not remember that he had seen a hog loose. After pondering a moment, he sidled up to Squire Jack, taking a circuitous course, so as to get a little behind him, and muttered in his ear, "Want to see ye."

"Well, what is it, Mr. Bowen? Another wild hog case?"

"Nary," whispered Selnarten. "But how about jinin' the Ku-Klux?"

Squire Jack meditated; then his dreamy smile brightened; then a merry twinkle lighted up his moist eyes. This stupid, unlettered vagabond wanted to join the Ku-Klux, undoubtedly with a view to robbing nigger pig-pens with impunity. It was a good joke, and it might be worked up into something capital; and Squire Jack reflected no further. He was not himself a Ku-Klux, and in fact he called himself since the war a Union man, though meanwhile he abominated a carpet-bagger. A good-hearted creature, with honorable instincts, he abhorred the extremists of both parties who were disgracing and ruining South Carolina. It seemed to him equally dreadful that the carpet-bag adventurers should plunder the State treasury, and that the reactionist desperadoes who opposed them should bushwhack and maltreat the poor "niggers." Still, he was not a deeply reflective man, and it was not in his nature to take things violently to heart, and he never could resist the temptation of a joke. Without a thought of the consequences, he determined to have some sport out of Selnarten.

"What am I to understand, Mr. Bowen?" he asked. "Do you wish to join the Ku-Klux?"

"Yes," mumbled Selnarten, while a tremor of anxiety shook his ill-covered skeleton, as if his life-long master, the "agur," had come for him.

"Walk to my office, Mr. Bowen," continued Squire Jack. "Walk in and sit. I'll get together some of the leading members of the order. We'll have you on the gridiron directly. By the way, how about whiskey? Could you raise a quart?"

"I hain't got no whiskey, and I hain't got no money," confessed Selnarten.

"Oh well, never mind," answered Squire Jack, looking, however, a little disappointed, as if the joke were drier than he had hoped. "It isn't absolutely necessary, though it's always best to have it."

He turned Selnarten into his office and locked the door on him to keep out intruders. Then he trundled his broad face and a load of abdomen into two or three neighboring sanctums of brother lawyers, and soon brought together half a dozen gentlemen as out of work and as in for fun as himself. Whether any one of the six were a Ku-Klux Squire Jack did not and could not know, and light-mindedly did not care. But as head-centres and high joint commissioners and grand sojourners of the famous order, he ceremoniously introduced them to Selnarten.

"Gentlemen, take seats," bowed Squire Jack, forcing his obese thumbs into the pockets of his over-crowded waistcoat, and slowly turning his jolly smile, like a lantern, from face to face of the company. "This chapter will now come to order," he proceeded, assuming an elocutionary manner, "for the purpose of receiving into the bosom of Ku-Kluxery and all other luxery a most acceptable candidate, Mr. Selnarten Bowen. Gentlemen, we all know this candidate; he was born and brought up in our very midst; we know him as Norval knew the Grampian Hills. We know who his mother was; we have reason to believe that we know who his grandmother was; and, gentlemen, if we had lived long enough ago, I venture to say that we might have known who his great-grandmother was; and, gentlemen, it would not surprise me in the least to learn that that great-grandmother was a continental dam."

Here Squire Jack looked blandly and steadily into the saffron eyes of Selnarten, who, being in a state of extreme intimidation and confusion, responded meekly, "That's so!" much to the delight of the counterfeit Ku-Klux.

But we have not space to report Squire Jack's oratory. For ten minutes he ran a stream of extravagances; it was a grotesque imitation of the so-called spread-eagle style of eloquence; it was a farrago of hifalutin which would have charmed an Arkansas jury. He ended by demanding in a voice of thunder that whoever objected to the reception of *this* candidate into the holy alliance and brotherhood of Ku-Kluxery should now set forth cause for his opposition, or else forever thereafter hold his peace.

"We all seem to assent to the nomination," observed Colonel Gallop of the ex-Confederate army. "Let the neophyte be inducted into the mysteries."

"Stand up, neophyte," ordained Squire Jack.

"Me?" inquired Selnarten.

"Yes," said Squire Jack.

Selnarten rose to his feet.

"Now stand on your head."

The poor ignoramus tried to obey, and naturally fell in a heap. Next he was mounted on a table, then made to crawl under it on his hands and knees, and so on through a variety of ridiculous gymnastics, the ceremony ending with seating him cross-legged on the Franklin stove, which fortunately was in a lukewarm condition, as it generally was. At last the jokers were tired of their poor fun, and put an end to it.

"Mr. Bowen, you are now a Ku-Klux," said Squire Jack. "You are now a free and accepted member of our great order. All that remains is to instruct you in your new responsibilities and duties, which consist in being at peace and amity with all men, and in bearing enmity and hate toward wild hogs. In the words of our classic founder, *Quousque tandem, Catilina, abutere patientia nostra?*—that is to say, how long shall these wild hogs abuse our patience? Go, Brother Ku-Klux; go, Brother Selnarten Bowen— take care of yourself. And if, in the performance of what shall come to pass, you get into trouble, come to me."

Out of the presence of these jesters went Selnarten, much in the dark as to what a Ku- Klux was bound or permitted to do, but not in the least doubting that he was a Ku-Klux.

How should he doubt it? All his life he had looked up to "high-tone gentlemen" for instruction and direction. He was simple, he was profoundly ignorant, and he was the child of simplicity and ignorance from untold generations, inheriting simplicity and ignorance as he inherited the name of Bowen. He could not read; his father before him could not read; he was sprung from a race of illiterate low-downers; they, probably, from illiterate convicts deported to the Virginias; they, probably, from illiterate tramps or hinds in Old England. All the way back to the days of the Heptarchy, it may be; all the way back to the pirate keels of Hengist and Horsa; all the way through the Germanic forests and the Scythian steppes; all the way back across the Indo-European cradle in Aryana; there is no certainty that a Bowen of this stock ever did read—no certainty that a Bowen of this stock was ever anything but illiterate and stupid. With the inherited, accumulated, and concentrated ignorance of so many generations in his brain and his very marrow, how should Selnarten fail to be the bubble of every high-toned gentleman who chose to puff him out with a breath of nonsense, and shake him loose for folly or mischief?

"What did they tell me I oughter do?" queried this American freeman and elector, as he trudged homeward through clinging mire and gathering darkness. "Said suthin' about peace with all men. That means white men, reckon. Of course don't mean niggers; can't mean niggers. Anyhow, said I mought go for hogs, wild hogs. Reckon I will. Reckon I will *now.* Nan tole me to fetch home suthin'."

On the road, or rather a quarter of a mile off the road, lived a fellow-citizen and elector who was as simple and ignorant as Selnarten himself, but who in the matter of wealth had considerably the advantage of him, being the owner of a pig. Ham Irvine was a one-legged negro, pretty well advanced in middle life, but otherwise a stout and hearty "chunk of a man." Being unfitted for field work through his infirmity, he had picked up the art of cobbling, and gained a meagre living by mending brogans for his colored brethren, and putting new vitality into old harnesses, etc., for white farmers. He was often seen in the village, stumping grimly about in search of jobs or dues, his solid figure draped to the heels in the greasy azure of a cast-off military overcoat, underneath which were other garments vastly in need of a washtub.

Notwithstanding his fifty years and his deficiency in members, Ham was a fervent seeker after the gentle sex, and much in the habit of matrimony. He had had nobody knows how many wives; in fact, there never was a more marrying man in a monogamous country; and this saint's perseverence was needed to keep him spliced, for his better halves were addicted to absconding. Ham, you see, believed in loving and chastening; if a woman was what he called foolish, he used to "lam" her; and if a hickory wouldn't answer, he laid on with his wooden leg. The result was that his hymeneal bliss was subject to frequent interruptions, and that he spent about as much time in hunting wives, old or new, as in looking up jobs of cobbling.

The last prize which he had drawn at the altar was a fat, lazy, ragged, fatherless and motherless young offscouring of the earth, known to Saxonburg by the unsupported name of Phillis. This offscouring had married Ham, as whiter ladies have married more numerously-legged men, for the sake of getting a home. Her opinion of said home may be inferred from the fact that at the end of a week she decided to dispense with the rest of the honeymoon, took an early start for parts unknown, and ran clean away from her old man, who of course had not a high turn of speed. Ham, who never gave up a spouse willingly, stumped after her as far as the village, left messages of mercy or of threatening for her with all her acquaintance, and in short did his dull best to get her back. While engaged in pegging to and fro on this labor of love, he had been observed by his brother elector, the candidate for Ku-Klux. Selnarten at once conceived the suspicion that Ham's pig had gone wild, and resolved to look into the animal's moral status on his way home.

"Wonder if he's back," mused the cracker, as he came to a turn in the miry road, whence diverged a still mirier path leading to the cobbler's cabin. "Reckon not yet. Wooden legs can't travel much. Reckon I'll see after his shoat."

He had his gun with him—a gun that had been dropped on more than one battle-field—a gun that had seen service, and showed it, yet not quite a cripple. With his rusty Enfield under his arm, its lock shielded from the dripping of dank branches by his ragged coat, Selnarten struck through a slip of swampy wood (with Malaria painting away at him) and came out upon a bare, sandy old field, the passepartout of Ham's cabin. No dog barking, he guessed that the negro was still absent, and boldly approached the lonely dwelling. The shoat, he knew, pastured by day at his own sweet will, but at night was always housed with his master for safety, and probably now would not be far distant. Selnarten hunted and Selnarten grunted; but piggy neither appeared nor answered.

"Dog gone the critter!" muttered our Ku-Klux. "He's run wild, sure pop; an' I'll cut his durned throat. Reckon he's inside. That's it. Ham shet him up afore he put out."

It was not difficult to enter the cabin. The only lock was a wooden latch pulled by a string which hung outside. After a little fumbling and listening, Selnarten crossed the teetering threshold, closed the door after him, and began a game of blind man's buff among Ham's benches, barrels, and other rude furniture, his object of course being to find the shoat. He was quite easy about it; in other days he had hunted pork with an evil conscience, but now he had not the least idea that he was committing a crime. Holding himself to be a true member of the Ku-Klux society, and supposing that every Ku-Klux had a right to "go for niggers" in any way that pleased him, he had no more scruples of conscience about his person than if he had been a sheriff duly provided with a search-warrant.

The shoat, too, was there. He could hear him snuffling and grunting and capering in a most appetizing manner, fairly making a cracker's mouth water. But catch him he could not; the animal had a surprising aptitude for blind man's buff; he was like the famous pig who was too spry to be counted. After falling down several times, Selnarten decided to have a light; he turned over the smouldering back-log, threw on some bits of pitch pine, and roused a blaze. Now he had a clear view of the cobbler's interior; and we also cannot do better than take a look at it. A sketch of Ham's cabin will be doubly useful, as it will give us a tolerably exact idea of Selnarten's cabin, and of the cabin of many another negro and low-downer.

It was a log house, and not a very fine one of the kind, and not ending its career so fine as it had begun it. The logs had gone into the job in such a hurry that they had not taken time to get themselves seasoned or squared, or even to pull off their jackets; and the consequence was that they were now in a lamentably shrunken, warped, deformed, knock-kneed, bow-legged condition; leaning apart as if they were mutually afraid of catching the dry rot of each other; their remnants of bark peeling up in worm-eaten tatters; neither clothed nor in their right minds. Originally they had been chinked in with clay; but this filling had been soaked out by rains or nibbled out by winds or poked out by rampaging outsiders; and now the gaps had either nothing at all in them, or only some crumbling edgings of common earth. Thus the walls had become a sort of open-work, or trellis, more fitted for vines to clamber upon than useful as a protection against the weather. If the man in the moon, surveying the house with his best telescope, had taken it for a hencoop, or a squirrel cage with the wheel off, he would not thereby have incurred a just charge of lunacy. Counting from top to bottom and all around the four sides, there must have been something like two or three hundred drafts in this residence. The roof was of a piece with the rest; the unpainted boards of which it was constructed had been blown apart so much and put together again so little that they were all at sixes and sevens; and there were any number of openings to let the glory of the heavens through. Standing aside, you could see any constellation you liked; and standing in any constellation you liked, you could see inside.

The floor was much the same with the roof. Every board in it had its own mind as to the way it wanted to lie, and also as to whether it wanted to lie down or get up. Some of them had both extremities aloft, as if they were sticking up their heads to see whether their toes were covered. Some were fastened at one end and some at the other, and some in the middle, each according to his luck. You could not walk across this floor without producing a succession of slams and clatters, and other ligneous grumblings, as if it were complaining of your awkwardness and wanting to know when you would get off it. It was a dreadful floor for a stranger to venture upon in the dark, being always ready to make a sly grab at his toes and a vicious spring at his nose, as Selnarten Bowen by this time well knew. In one spot there were no boards at all, but a man trap or quadruped trap in the shape of a large hole, the result of a short and easy method of manufacturing kindlings. This hole did not precipitate you into a cellar, but into something in the way of open country between the cabin and the earth, where the wind and Ham's shoat were accustomed to root among straws, feathers, bones, and other refuse, and where Ham's successive pickaninnies had disported themselves until they were carried away by their absquatulating mammies.

Selnarten took no note of all these picturesque details. Neither did he pause to examine the rough furniture of the cabin, the home-made cobbler's bench, the one low stool, the two limping chairs, the pot and frying pan. His mind, the whole of it, what little there was of it, was bent upon the pig. At last he discovered his game. The cunning little beast (a forty-pounder or thereabouts) had sought refuge behind Ham's bed. This bed was not on a bedstead, but on the floor in one corner. It was a rabble of old straw mattress, ragged empty sacks, tatters of carpeting and greasy coverlets, all lying in tangled confusion, as if they had got drunk, gone to fighting, and fallen in a heap. In the rear of this rampart appeared the shoat, his spine bristling, his snout twitching, and his eyes twinkling.

Selnarten stood his gun in one corner, drew and opened his large jack-knife, and made a rush. There was a wonderful chase; the shoat dodged, galloped, grunted, and squealed; the rheumatic boards of the floor jumped about in an agony; the cracker ran and stumbled and rolled and rose and ran again. A complete account of the ups and downs of that hunt, of all its adventures, horizontal and perpendicular, would make too long a story. We must cut the matter short by stating, with brutal brevity, that Selnarten killed the pig.

And now came new excitement. Just as the suffering innocent gave forth his last gurgle the door of the cabin flew open with a bang, and its owner stumped in. Ham Irvine, returning wifeless from the village, had discovered a light in his domicile, and, suspecting danger to his shoat, had hurried to the rescue. Mr. Bowen was disagreeably surprised, but he was unnaturally intelligent in whatever related to pig-stealing, and he showed himself equal to the emergency. Snatching a piece of carpeting from Ham's miscellany of a bed, he flung it upon the blazing light-wood and produced darkness.

"Who's yere?" demanded Ham.

"The Ku-Klux," responded Mr. Bowen, suddenly recollecting that he belonged to that noble society, and claiming its lawful privileges.

"Somebody's been worryin' my shoat," continued Ham, either not hearing the awful name, or not caring for it.

"You better clar!" advised Mr. Bowen, who by this time had got hold of his gun.

"You clar yourself," retorted Ham. "Whoever you is, you no business inside my do', when I ain't yere."

Then came a fight in the dark. Ham, who was very muscular, and much more lively on his badly-matched supporters than one might imagine, got a grip of Selnarten's baggy clothing, floored him at the first jerk, and fell across him. For a minute there was an amazing clatter, the loose boards floundering and bouncing as if they were determined to get out from under, and the wooden leg joining in the uproar with extraordinary emphasis, rapping and tapping as if it were carrying on a scuffle of its own. At last the combatants separated in three divisions, one being the cracker, another the negro, and another the negro's spare limb. This last was a weapon which Ham well knew how to use. He caught it up, gave it a vicious swing in the direction of his antagonist, and laid him prostrate.

And now the gun came into play. Under ordinary circumstances Selnarten would not have ventured to carry out a job of mere pig-stealing by shooting a human being, even though that human being were no more than a "nigger." But this evening he believed he was a Ku-Klux, and that as such he had a right to kill whosoever resisted him. He seized his Enfield, aimed it at a dark something which he knew must be Ham, aimed it with intent to take life, and fired. When he left the cabin, with the defunct shoat upon his shoulder, he was not only a pig-stealer and a burglar, but a murderer.

Weeks later, when martial law was declared in his district, when troopers in blue jackets arrived to trample out a silly and savage reign of terror, when high-toned and low-toned members of the famous order were confessing their atrocities and surrendering themselves for trial, this almost incredibly ignorant creature came into military headquarters and gave himself up as a Ku-Klux, revealing for the first time who it was that had killed Ham Irvine.

A Wizard from Gettysburg
1892

KATE CHOPIN

Kate Chopin (1850–1904) was born Catherine O'Flaherty in St. Louis, but moved with her husband, Oscar Chopin, to New Orleans in 1870. The Civil War had hit her close to home when her half-brother George O'Flaherty, with whom she was very close, was captured by the Federals; he was released from prison in 1862 and died shortly thereafter. Chopin has gained greatest celebrity for her novel, The Awakening *(1899), but she wrote many short stories for adults and for children. Among the latter is "A Wizard from Gettysburg," first published in* Youth's Companion *on July 7, 1892, and included in her volume,* Bayou Folk *(1894). Although somewhat contrived, it is a touching story of the surprising return of a long-lost Civil War veteran.*

It was one afternoon in April, not long ago, only the other day, and the shadows had already begun to lengthen.

Bertrand Delmandé, a fine, bright-looking boy of fourteen years,—fifteen, perhaps,—was mounted, and riding along a pleasant country road, upon a little Creole pony, such as boys in Louisiana usually ride when they have nothing better at hand. He had hunted, and carried his gun before him.

It is unpleasant to state that Bertrand was not so depressed as he should have been, in view of recent events that had come about. Within the past week he had been recalled from the college of Grand Coteau to his home, the Bon-Accueil plantation.

He had found his father and his grand-mother depressed over money matters, awaiting certain legal developments that might result in his permanent withdrawal from school. That very day, directly after the early dinner, the two had driven to town, on this very business, to be absent till the late afternoon. Bertrand, then, had saddled Picayune and gone for a long jaunt, such as his heart delighted in.

He was returning now, and had approached the beginning of the great tangled Cherokee hedge that marked the boundary line of Bon-Accueil, and that twinkled with multiple white roses.

The pony started suddenly and violently at something there in the turn of the road, and just under the hedge. It looked like a bundle of rags at first. But it was a tramp, seated upon a broad, flat stone.

Bertrand had no maudlin consideration for tramps as a species; he had only that morning driven from the place one who was making himself unpleasant at the kitchen window.

But this tramp was old and feeble. His beard was long, and as white as new-ginned cotton, and when Bertrand saw him he was engaged in stanching a wound in his bare heel with a fistful of matted grass.

"What's wrong, old man?" asked the boy, kindly.

The tramp looked up at him with a bewildered glance, but did not answer.

"Well," thought Bertrand, "since it's decided that I'm to be a physician some day, I can't begin to practice too early."

He dismounted, and examined the injured foot. It had an ugly gash. Bertrand acted mostly from impulse. Fortunately his impulses were not bad ones. So, nimbly, and as quickly as he could manage it, he had the old man astride Picayune, whilst he himself was leading the pony down the narrow lane.

The dark green hedge towered like a high and solid wall on one side. On the other was a broad, open field, where here and there appeared the flash and gleam of uplifted, polished hoes, that negroes were plying between the even rows of cotton and tender corn.

"This is the State of Louisiana," uttered the tramp, quaveringly.

"Yes, this is Louisiana," returned Bertrand cheerily.

"Yes, I know it is. I've been in all of them since Gettysburg. Sometimes it was too hot, and sometimes it was too cold; and with that bullet in my head—you don't remember? No, you don't remember Gettysburg."

"Well, no, not vividly," laughed Bertrand.

"Is it a hospital? It isn't a factory, is it?" the man questioned.

"Where we're going? Why, no, it's the Delmandé plantation—Bon-Accueil. Here we are. Wait, I'll open the gate."

This singular group entered the yard from the rear, and not far from the house. A big black woman, who sat just without a cabin door, picking a pile of rusty-looking moss, called out at sight of them:—

"W'at's dat you's bringin' in dis yard, boy? top dat hoss?"

She received no reply. Bertrand, indeed, took no notice of her inquiry.

"Fu' a boy w'at goes to school like you does—whar's yo' sense?" she went on, with a fine show of indignation; then, muttering to herself, "Ma'ame Bertrand an' Marse St. Ange ain't gwine stan' dat, I knows dey ain't. Dah! ef he ain't done sot 'im on de gall'ry, plumb down in his pa's rockin'-cheer!"

Which the boy had done; seated the tramp in a pleasant corner of the veranda, while he went in search of bandages for his wound.

The servants showed high disapproval, the housemaid following Bertrand into his grandmother's room, whither he had carried his investigations.

"W'at you tearin' yo' gra'ma's closit to pieces dat away, boy?" she complained in her high soprano.

"I'm looking for bandages."

"Den w'y you don't ax fu' ban'ges, an' lef yo' gra'ma's closit 'lone? You want to listen to me; you gwine git shed o' dat tramp settin' dah naxt to de dinin'-room! W'en de silva be missin', 'tain' you w'at gwine git blame, it's me."

"The silver? Nonsense, 'Cindy; the man's wounded, and can't you see he's out of his head?"

"No mo' outen his head 'an I is. 'Tain' me w'at want to tres' 'im wid de sto'-room key, ef he is outen his head," she concluded with a disdainful shrug.

But Bertrand's protégé proved so unapproachable in his long-worn rags, that the boy concluded to leave him unmolested till his father's return, and then ask permission to turn the forlorn creature into the bathhouse, and array him afterward in clean, fresh garments.

So there the old tramp sat in the veranda corner, stolidly content, when St. Ange Delmandé and his mother returned from town.

St. Ange was a dark, slender man of middle age, with a sensitive face, and a plentiful sprinkle of gray in his thick black hair; his mother, a portly woman, and an active one for her sixty-five years.

They were evidently in a despondent mood. Perhaps it was for the cheer of her sweet presence that they had brought with them from town a little girl, the child of Madame Delmandé's only daughter, who was married, and lived there.

Madame Delmandé and her son were astonished to find so uninviting an intruder in possession. But a few earnest words from Bertrand reassured them, and partly reconciled them to the man's presence; and it was with wholly indifferent though not unkindly glances that they passed him by when they entered. On any large plantation there are always nooks and corners where, for a night or more, even such a man as this tramp may be tolerated and given shelter.

When Bertrand went to bed that night, he lay long awake thinking of the man, and of what he had heard from his lips in the hushed starlight. The boy had heard of the awfulness of Gettysburg, till it was like something he could feel and quiver at.

On that field of battle this man had received a new and tragic birth. For all his existence that went before was a blank to him. There, in the black desolation of war, he was born again, without friends or kindred; without even a name he could know was his own. Then he had gone forth a wanderer; living more than half the time in hospitals; toiling when he could, starving when he had to.

Strangely enough, he had addressed Bertrand as "St. Ange," not once, but every time he had spoken to him. The boy wondered at this. Was it because he had heard Madame Delmandé address her son by that name, and fancied it?

So this nameless wanderer had drifted far down to the plantation of Bon-Accueil, and at last had found a human hand stretched out to him in kindness.

When the family assembled at breakfast on the following morning, the tramp was already settled in the chair, and in the corner which Bertrand's indulgence had made familiar to him.

If he had turned partly around, he would have faced the flower garden, with its graveled walks and trim parterres, where a tangle of color and perfume were holding high revelry this April morning; but he liked better to gaze into the back yard, where there was always movement: men and women coming and going, bearing implements of work; little negroes in scanty garments, darting here and there, and kicking up the dust in their exuberance.

Madame Delmandé could just catch a glimpse of him through the long window that opened to the floor, and near which he sat.

Mr. Delmandé had spoken to the man pleasantly; but he and his mother were wholly absorbed by their trouble, and talked constantly of that, while Bertrand went back and forth ministering to the old man's wants. The boy knew that the servants would have done the office with ill grace, and he chose to be cup-bearer himself to the unfortunate creature for whose presence he alone was responsible.

Once, when Bertrand went out to him with a second cup of coffee, steaming and fragrant, the old man whispered:—

"What are they saying in there?" pointing over his shoulder to the dining-room.

"Oh, money troubles that will force us to economize for a while," answered the boy. "What father and *mé-mère* feel worst about is that I shall have to leave college now."

"No, no! St. Ange must go to school. The war's over, the war's over! St. Ange and Florentine must go to school."

"But if there's no money," the boy insisted, smiling like one who humors the vagaries of a child.

"Money! money!" murmured the tramp. "The war's over—money! money!"

His sleepy gaze had swept across the yard into the thick of the orchard beyond, and rested there.

Suddenly he pushed aside the light table that had been set before him, and rose, clutching Bertrand's arm.

"St. Ange, you must go to school!" he whispered. "The war's over," looking furtively around. "Come. Don't let them hear you. Don't let the negroes see us. Get a spade—the little spade that Buck Williams was digging his cistern with."

Still clutching the boy, he dragged him down the steps as he said this, and traversed the yard with long, limping strides, himself leading the way.

From under a shed where such things were to be found, Bertrand selected a spade, since the tramp's whim demanded that he should, and together they entered the orchard.

The grass was thick and tufted here, and wet with the morning dew. In long lines, forming pleasant avenues between, were peach-trees growing, and pear and apple and plum. Close against the fence was the pomegranate hedge, with its waxen blossoms, brick-red. Far down in the centre of the orchard stood a huge pecan-tree, twice the size of any other that was there, seeming to rule like an old-time king.

Here Bertrand and his guide stopped. The tramp had not once hesitated in his movements since grasping the arm of his young companion on the veranda. Now he went and leaned his back against the pecan-tree, where there was a deep knot, and looking steadily before him he took ten paces forward. Turning sharply to the right, he made five additional paces. Then pointing his finger downward, and looking at Bertrand, he commanded:—

"There, dig. I would do it myself, but for my wounded foot. For I've turned many a spade of earth since Gettysburg. Dig, St. Ange, dig! The war's over; you must go to school."

Is there a boy of fifteen under the sun who would not have dug, even knowing he was following the insane dictates of a demented man? Bertrand entered with all the zest of his years and his spirit into the curious adventure; and he dug and dug, throwing great spadefuls of the rich, fragrant earth from side to side.

The tramp, with body bent, and fingers like claws clasping his bony knees, stood watching with eager eyes, that never unfastened their steady gaze from the boy's rhythmic motions.

"That's it!" he muttered at intervals. "Dig, dig! The war's over. You must go to school, St. Ange."

Deep down in the earth, too deep for any ordinary turning of the soil with spade or plow to have reached it, was a box. It was of tin, apparently, something larger than a cigar box, and bound round and round with twine, rotted now and eaten away in places.

The tramp showed no surprise at seeing it there; he simply knelt upon the ground and lifted it from its long resting place.

Bertrand had let the spade fall from his hands, and was quivering with the awe of the thing he saw. Who could this wizard be that had come to him in the guise of a tramp, that walked in cabalistic paces upon his own father's ground, and pointed his finger like a divining-rod to the spot where boxes—may be treasures—lay? It was like a page from a wonder-book.

And walking behind this white-haired old man, who was again leading the way, something of childish superstition crept back into Bertrand's heart. It was the same feeling with which he had often sat, long ago, in the weird firelight of some negro's cabin, listening to tales of witches who came in the night to work uncanny spells at their will.

Madame Delmandé had never abandoned the custom of washing her own silver and dainty china. She sat, when the breakfast was over, with a pail of warm suds before her that 'Cindy had brought to her, with an abundance of soft linen cloths. Her little granddaughter stood beside her playing, as babies will, with the bright spoons and forks, and ranging them in rows on the polished mahogany. St. Ange was at the window making entries in a note-book, and frowning gloomily as he did so.

The group in the dining-room were so employed when the old tramp came staggering in, Bertrand close behind him.

He went and stood at the foot of the table, opposite to where Madame Delmandé sat, and let fall the box upon it.

The thing in falling shattered, and from its bursting sides gold came, clicking, spinning, gliding, some of it like oil; rolling along the table and off it to the floor, but heaped up, the bulk of it, before the tramp.

"Here's money!" he called out, plunging his old hand in the thick of it. "Who says St. Ange shall not go to school? The war's over—here's money! St. Ange, my boy," turning to Bertrand and speaking with quick authority, "tell Buck Williams to hitch Black Bess to the buggy, and go bring Judge Parkerson here."

Judge Parkerson, indeed, who had been dead for twenty years and more!

"Tell him that—that"—and the hand that was not in the gold went up to the withered forehead, "that—Bertrand Delmandé needs him!"

Madame Delmandé, at sight of the man with his box and his gold, had given a sharp cry, such as might follow the plunge of a knife. She lay now in her son's arms, panting hoarsely.

"Your father, St. Ange,—come back from the dead—your father!"

"Be calm, mother!" the man implored. "You had such sure proof of his death in that terrible battle, this *may* not be he."

"I know him! I know your father, my son!" and disengaging herself from the arms that held her, she dragged herself as a wounded serpent might to where the old man stood.

His hand was still in the gold, and on his face was yet the flush which had come there when he shouted out the name Bertrand Delmandé.

"Husband," she gasped, "do you know me—your wife?"

The little girl was playing gleefully with the yellow coin.

Bertrand stood, pulseless almost, like a young Actaeon cut in marble.

When the old man had looked long into the woman's imploring face, he made a courtly bow.

"Madame," he said, "an old soldier, wounded on the field of Gettysburg, craves for himself and his two little children your kind hospitality."

The Gray Jacket of "No. 4"
1892

THOMAS NELSON PAGE

Thomas Nelson Page (1853–1922) grew up in Hanover County, Virginia, where his family owned sixty slaves. Although too young to have participated directly in the Civil War, Page must have heard reports of the numerous battles that took place in his vicinity. Page developed a powerful nostalgia for the Southern past, and many of his novels deal poignantly with the Old South. Red Rock (1898), a novel about Reconstruction, is his most substantial contribution to the literature of the war. Several of Page's short stories also deal with the conflict, among them "The Grey Jacket of 'No. 4,'" first published in Century Magazine *in May 1892 and collected in* The Burial of the Guns *(1894). Although slightly marred by sentimentality, it is a touching account of the physical and moral decline of a Southern veteran.*

My meeting with him was accidental. I came across him passing through "the square." I had seen him once or twice on the street, each time lurching along so drunk that he could scarcely stagger, so that I was surprised to hear what he said about the war. He was talking to someone who evidently had been in the army himself, but on the other side—a gentleman with the loyal-legion button in his coat, and with a beautiful star, a saber-cut across his face. He was telling of a charge in some battle or skirmish in which, he declared, his company, not himself—for I remember he said he was "No. 4," and was generally told off to hold the horses; and that that day he had had the ill luck to lose his horse and get a little scratch himself, so he was not in the charge—did the finest work he ever saw, and really (so he claimed) saved the day. It was this self-abnegation that first arrested my attention, for I had been accustomed all my life to hear the war talked of; it was one of the inspiring influences in my humdrum existence. But the speakers, although they generally boasted of their commands, never of themselves individually, usually admitted that they themselves had been in the active force, and thus tacitly shared in the credit. "No. 4," however, expressly disclaimed that he was entitled to any of the praise, declaring that he was safe behind the crest of the hill (which he said he "hugged mighty close"), and claimed the glory for the rest of the command.

"It happened just as I have told you here," he said, in closing. "Old Joe saw the point as soon as the battery went to work, and sent Binford Terrell to the colonel to ask him to let him go over there and take it; and when Joe gave the word the boys went. They didn't go at a walk either, I tell you; it wasn't any promenade: they went clipping. At first the guns shot over 'em; didn't catch 'em till the third fire; then they played the devil with 'em: but the boys were up there right in 'em before they could do much. They turned the guns on 'em as they went down the hill (oh, our boys could handle the tubes then as well as the artillery themselves), and in a little while the rest of the line came up, and we formed a line of battle right there on that crest, and held it till nearly night. That's when I got jabbed. I picked up another horse, and with my foolishness went over there. That evening, you know, you all charged us—we were dismounted then. We lost more men then than we had done all day; there were forty-seven out of seventy-two killed or wounded. They walked all over us; two of 'em got hold of me (you see, I went to get our old flag some of you had got hold of), but I was too worthless to die. There were lots of 'em did go through, I tell you; old Joe in the lead. Yes, sir; the old company won that day, and old Joe led 'em. There ain't but a few of us left; but when you want us, Colonel, you can get us. We'll stand by you."

He paused in deep reflection; his mind evidently back with his old company and its gallant commander "old Joe," whoever he might be, who was remembered so long after he passed away in the wind and smoke of that unnamed evening battle. I took a good look at him—at "No. 4," as he called himself. He was tall, but stooped a little; his features were good, at least his nose and brow were; his mouth and chin were weak. His mouth was too stained with the tobacco which he chewed to tell much about it—and his chin was like so many American chins, not strong. His eyes looked weak. His clothes were very much worn, but they had once been good; they formerly had been black, and well made; the buttons were all on. His shirt was clean. I took note of this, for he had a dissipated look, and a rumpled shirt would have been natural. A man's linen tells on him before his other clothes. His listener had evidently been impressed by him also, for he arose, and said, abruptly, "Let's go and take a drink." To my surprise "No. 4" declined. "No, I thank you," he said, with promptness. I instinctively looked at him again to see if I had not misjudged him; but I concluded not, that I was right, and that he was simply "not drinking." I was flattered at my discrimination when I heard him say that he had "sworn off." His friend said no more, but remained standing while "No. 4" expatiated on the difference between a man who is drinking and one who is not. I never heard a more striking exposition of it. He said he wondered that any man could be such a fool as to drink liquor; that he had determined never to touch another drop. He presently relapsed into silence, and the other reached out his hand to say good-by. Suddenly rising, he said: "Well, suppose we go and have just one for old times' sake. Just one now, mind you; for I have not touched a drop in—" He turned away, and I did not catch the length of the time mentioned. But I have reason to believe that "No. 4" overstated it.

The next time I saw him was in the police court. I happened to be there when he walked out of the pen among as miscellaneous a lot of chronic drunkards, thieves, and miscreants of both sexes and several colors as were ever gathered together. He still had on his old black suit, buttoned up; but his linen was rumpled and soiled like himself, and he was manifestly just getting over a debauch, the effects of which were still visible on him in every line of his perspiring face and thin figure. He walked with that exaggerated erectness which told his self-deluded state as plainly as if he had pronounced it in words. He had evidently been there before, and more than once. The justice nodded to him familiarly:

"Here again?" he asked, in a tone part pleasantry, part regret.

"Yes, your honor. Met an old soldier last night, and took a drop for good fellowship, and before I knew it—" A shrug of the shoulders completed the sentence, and the shoulders did not straighten any more.

The tall officer who had picked him up said something to the justice in a tone too low for me to catch; but "No. 4" heard it—it was evidently a statement against him—for he started to speak in a deprecating way. The judge interrupted him:

"I thought you told me last time that if I let you go you would not take another drink for a year."

"I forgot," said "No. 4," in a low voice.

"This officer says you resisted him?"

The officer looked stolidly at the prisoner as if it were a matter of not the slightest interest to him personally. "Cursed me and abused me," he said, dropping the words slowly as if he were checking off a schedule.

"I did not, your honor; indeed, I did not," said "No. 4," quickly. "I swear I did not; he is mistaken. Your honor does not believe I would tell you a lie! Surely I have not got so low as that."

The justice turned his pencil in his hand doubtfully, and looked away. "No. 4" took in his position. He began again.

"I fell in with an old soldier, and we got to talking about the war—about old times." His voice was very soft. "I will promise your honor that I won't take another drink for a year. Here, I'll take an oath to it. Swear me." He seized the greasy little Bible on the desk before him, and handed it to the justice. The magistrate took it doubtfully. He looked down at the prisoner half kindly, half humorously.

"You'll just break it." He started to lay the book down.

"No; I want to take the pledge," said "No. 4," eagerly. "Did I ever break a pledge I made to your honor?"

"Didn't you promise me not to come back here?"

"I have not been here for nine months. Besides, I did not come of my own free will," said "No. 4," with a faint flicker of humor on his perspiring face.

"You were here two months ago, and you promised not to take another drink."

"I forgot that. I did not mean to break it; indeed, I did not. I fell in with—"

The justice looked away, considered a moment, and ordered him back into the pen with, "Ten days, to cool off."

"No. 4" stood quite still till the officer motioned him to the gate, behind which the prisoners sat in stolid rows. Then he walked dejectedly back into the pen, and sat down by another drunkard. His look touched me, and I went around and talked to the magistrate privately. But he was inexorable; he said he knew more of him than I did, and that ten days in jail would "dry him out and be good for him." I told him the story of the battle. He knew it already, and said he knew more than that about him; that he had been one of the bravest soldiers in the whole army; did not know what fear was; had once ridden into the enemy and torn a captured standard from its captors' hands, receiving two desperate bayonet-wounds in doing it; and had done other acts of conspicuous gallantry on many occasions. I pleaded this, but he was obdurate; hard, I thought at the time, and told him so; told him he had been a soldier himself, and ought to be easier. He looked troubled, not offended; for we were friends, and I think he liked to see me, who had been a boy during the war, take up for an old soldier on that ground. But he stood firm. I must do him the justice to say that I now think it would not have made any difference if he had done otherwise. He had tried the other course many times.

"No. 4" must have heard me trying to help him, for one day, about a month after that, he walked in on me quite sober, and looking somewhat as he did the first day I saw him, thanked me for what I had done for him; delivered one of the most impressive discourses on intemperance that I ever heard; and asked me to try to help him get work. He was willing to do anything, he said; that is, anything he could do. I got him a place with a friend of mine which he kept a week, then got drunk. We got hold of him, however, and sobered him up, and he escaped the police and the justice's court. Being out of work, and very firm in his resolution never to drink again, we lent him some money—a very little—with which to keep along a few days, on which he got drunk immediately, and did fall into the hands of the police, and was sent to jail as before. This, in fact, was his regular round: into jail, out of jail; a little spell of sobriety, "an accidental fall," which occurred as soon as he could get a drop of liquor, and into jail again for thirty or sixty days, according to the degree of resistance he gave the police—who always, by their own account, simply tried to get him to go home, and, by his, insulted him—and to the violence of the language he applied to them. In this he excelled; for although as quiet as possible when he was sober, when he was drunk he was a terror, so the police said, and his resources of vituperation were cyclopedic. He possessed in this particular department an eloquence which was incredible. His blasphemy was vast, illimitable, infinite. He told me once that he could not explain it; that when he was sober he abhorred profanity, and never uttered an oath; when he was in liquor his brain took this turn, and distilled blasphemy in volumes. He said that all of his energies were quickened and concentrated in this direction, and then he took not only pleasure, but pride in it.

He told me a good deal of his life. He had got very low at this time, much lower than he had been when I first knew him. He recognized this himself, and used to analyze and discuss himself in quite an impersonal way. This was when he had come out of jail, and after having the liquor "dried out" of him. In such a state he always referred to his condition in the past as being something that never would or could occur; while on the other hand, if he were just over a drunk, he frankly admitted his absolute slavery to his habit. When he was getting drunk he shamelessly maintained, and was ready to swear on all the Bibles in creation, that he had not touched a drop, and never expected to do so again—indeed, could not be induced to do it—when in fact he would at the very time be reeking with the fumes of liquor, and perhaps had his pocket then bulging with a bottle which he had just emptied, and would willingly have bartered his soul to refill.

I never saw such absolute dominion as the love of liquor had over him. He was like a man in chains. He confessed it frankly and calmly. He said he had a disease, and gave me a history of it. It came on him, he said, in spells; that when he was over one he abhorred it, but when the fit seized him it came suddenly, and he was in absolute slavery to it. He said his father was a gentleman of convivial habits (I have heard that he was very dissipated, though not openly so, and "No. 4" never admitted it). He was killed at the battle of Bull Run. His mother—he always spoke of her with unvarying tenderness and reverence—had suffered enough, he said, to canonize her if she were not a saint already; she had brought him up to have a great horror of liquor, and he had never touched it till he went into the army. In the army he was in a convivial crowd, and they had hard marching and poor rations, often none. Liquor was scarce and was regarded as a luxury; so although he was very much afraid of it, yet for good fellowship's sake, and because it was considered mannish, he used to drink it. Then he got to like it; and then got to feel the need of it, and took it to stimulate him when he was run down. This want brought with it a great depression when he did not have the means to satisfy it. He never liked the actual taste of it; he said few drunkards did. It was the effect that he was always after. This increased on him, he said, until finally it was no longer a desire, but a passion, a necessity; he was obliged to have it. He felt then that he would commit murder for it. "Why, I dream about it," he said. "I will tell you what I have done. I have made the most solemn vows, and have gone to bed and gone to sleep, and waked up and dressed and walked miles through the rain and snow to get it. I believe I would have done it if I had known I was going next moment to hell." He said it had ruined him; said so quite calmly; did not appear to have any special remorse about it; at least, never professed any; said it used to trouble him, but he had got over it now. He had had a plantation—that is, his mother had had—and he had been quite successful for a while; but he said, "A man can't drink liquor and run a farm," and the farm had gone.

I asked him how?

"I sold it," he said calmly; "that is, persuaded my mother to sell it. The stock that belonged to me had nearly all gone before. A man who is drinking will sell anything," he said. "I have sold everything in the world I had, or could lay my hands on. I have never got quite so low as to sell my old gray jacket that I used to wear when I rode behind old Joe. I mean to be buried in that—if I can keep it."

He had been engaged to a nice girl; the wedding-day had been fixed; but she had broken off the engagement. She married another man. "She was a mighty nice girl," he said, quietly. "Her people did not like my drinking so much. I passed her not long ago on the street. She did not know me." He glanced down at himself quietly. "She looks older than she did." He said that he had had a place for some time, did not drink a drop for nearly a year, and then got with some of the old fellows, and they persuaded him to take a little. "I cannot touch it. I have either got to drink or let it alone—one thing or the other," he said. "But I am all right now," he declared triumphantly, a little of the old fire lighting up in his face. "I never expect to touch a drop again."

He spoke so firmly that I was persuaded to make him a little loan, taking his due-bill for it, which he always insisted on giving. That evening I saw him being dragged along by three policemen, and he was cursing like a demon.

In the course of time he got so low that he spent much more than half his time in jail. He became a perfect vagabond, and with his clothes ragged and dirty might be seen reeling about or standing around the street corners near disreputable bars, waiting for a chance drink, or sitting asleep in doorways of untenanted buildings. His companions would be one or two chronic drunkards like himself, with red noses, bloated faces, dry hair, and filthy clothes. Sometimes I would see him hurrying along with one of these as if they had a piece of the most important business in the world. An idea had struck their addled brains that by some means they could manage to secure a drink. Yet in some way he still held himself above these creatures, and once or twice I heard of him being under arrest for resenting what he deemed an impertinence from them.

Once he came very near being drowned. There was a flood in the river, and a large crowd was watching it from the bridge. Suddenly a little girl's dog fell in. It was pushed in by a ruffian. The child cried out, and there was a commotion. When it subsided a man was seen swimming for life after the little white head going down the stream. It was "No. 4." He had slapped the fellow in the face, and then had sprung in after the dog. He caught it, and got out himself, though in too exhausted a state to stand up. When he was praised for it, he said, "A member of old Joe's company who would not have done that could not have ridden behind old Joe." I had this story from eye-witnesses, and it was used shortly after with good effect; for he was arrested for burglary, breaking into a man's house one night. It looked at first like a serious case, for some money had been taken out of a drawer; but when the case was investigated it turned out that the house was a bar-room over which the man lived,—he was the same man who had pitched the dog into the water,—and that "No. 4," after being given whisky enough to make him a madman, had been put out of the place, had broken into the bar during the night to get more, and was found fast asleep in a chair with an empty bottle beside him. I think the jury became satisfied that if any money had been taken the barkeeper, to make out a case against "No. 4," had taken it himself. But there was a technical breaking, and it had to be got around; so his counsel appealed to the jury, telling them what he knew of "No. 4," together with the story of the child's dog, and "No. 4's" reply. There were one or two old soldiers on the jury, and they acquitted him, on which he somehow managed to get whisky enough to land him back in jail in twenty-four hours.

In May, 1890, there was a monument unveiled in Richmond. It was a great occasion, and not only all Virginia, but the whole South, participated in it with great fervor, much enthusiasm, and many tears. It was an occasion for sacred memories. The newspapers talked about it for a good while beforehand; preparations were made for it as for the celebration of a great and general ceremony in which the whole South was interested. It was interested, because it was not only the unveiling of a monument for the old commander, the greatest and loftiest Southerner, and, as the South holds, man, of his time; it was an occasion consecrated to the whole South; it was the embalming in precious memories, and laying away in the tomb of the Southern Confederacy: the apotheosis of the Southern people. As such all were interested in it, and all prepared for it. It was known that all that remained of the Southern armies would be there: of the armies that fought at Shiloh, and Bull Run, and Fort Republic; at Seven Pines, Gaines's Mill, and Cold Harbor; at Antietam, Fredericksburg, Chancellorsville, and Gettysburg; at Franklin, Atlanta, Murfreesboro, and Chickamauga, Spottsylvania, the Wilderness, and Petersburg; and the whole South, Union as it is now and ready to fight the nation's battles, gathered to glorify Lee, the old commander, and to see and glorify the survivors of those and other bloody fields in which the volunteer soldiers of the South had held the world at bay, and added to the glorious history of their race. Men came all the way from Oregon and California to be present. Old one-legged soldiers stumped it from West Virginia. Even "No. 4," though in the gutter, caught the contagion, and shaped up and became sober. He got a good suit of clothes somewhere—not new—and appeared quite respectable. He even got something to do, and, in token of what he had been, was put on one of the many committees having a hand in the entertainment arrangements. I never saw a greater change in anyone. It looked as if there was hope for him yet. He stopped me on the street a day or two before the unveiling and told me he had a piece of good news: the remnant of his old company was to be here; he had got hold of the last one—there were nine of them left—and he had his old jacket that he had worn in the war, and he was going to wear it on the march. "It's worn, of course," be said, "but my mother put some patches over the holes, and except for the stain on it it's in good order. I believe I am the only one of the boys that has his jacket still; my mother kept this for me; I have never got so hard up as to part with it. I'm all right now. I mean to be buried in it."

I had never remarked before what a refined face he had; his enthusiasm made him look younger than I had ever seen him.

I saw him on the day before the eve of the unveiling; he was as busy as a bee, and looked almost handsome. "The boys are coming in by every train," he said. "Look here." He pulled me aside, and unbuttoned his vest. A piece of faded gray cloth was disclosed. He had the old gray jacket on under his other coat. "I know the boys will like to see it," he said. "I'm going down to the train now to meet one—Binford Terrell. I don't know whether I shall know him. Binford and I used to be much of a size. We did not use to speak at one time; had a falling-out about which one should hold the horses; I made him do it, but I reckon he won't remember it now. I don't. I have not touched a drop. Good-by." He went off.

The next night about bedtime I got a message that a man wanted to see me at the jail immediately. It was urgent. Would I come down there at once? I had a foreboding, and I went down. It was as I suspected. "No. 4" was there behind the bars. "Drunk again," said the turnkey, laconically, as he let me in. He let me see him. He wanted me to see the judge and get him out. He besought me. He wept. "It was all an accident;" he had "found some of the old boys, and they had got to talking over old times, and just for old times' sake," etc. He was too drunk to stand up; but the terror of being locked up next day had sobered him, and his mind was perfectly clear. He implored me to see the judge and to get him to let him out. "Tell him I will come back here and stay a year if he will let me out to-morrow," he said, brokenly. He showed me the gray jacket under his vest, and was speechless. Even then he did not ask release on the ground that he was a veteran. I never knew him to urge this reason. Even the officials who must have seen him there fifty times were sympathetic; and they told me to see the justice, and they believed he would let him out for next day. I applied to him as they suggested. He said, "Come down to court to-morrow morning." I did so. "No. 4" was present, pale and trembling. As he stood there he made a better defence than any one else could have made for him. He admitted his guilt, and said he had nothing to say in extenuation except that it was the "old story," he "had not intended it; he deserved it all, but would like to get off that day; had a special reason for it, and would, if necessary, go back to jail that evening and stay there a year, or all his life." As he stood awaiting sentence, he looked like a damned soul. His coat was unbuttoned, and his old, faded gray jacket showed under it. The justice, to his honor, let him off: let all offenders off that day. "No. 4" shook hands with him, unable to speak, and turned away. Then he had a strange turn. We had hard work to get him to go into the procession. He positively refused; said he was not fit to go, or to live; began to cry, and took off his jacket. He would go back to jail, he said. We finally got him straight; accepted from him a solemn promise not to touch a drop till the celebration was over, so help him God, and sent him off to join his old command at the tobacco-warehouse on the slip where the cavalry rendezvoused. I had some apprehension that he would not turn up in the procession; but I was mistaken. He was there with the old cavalry veterans, as sober as a judge, and looking every inch a soldier.

It was a strange scene, and an impressive one even to those whose hearts were not in sympathy with it in any respect. Many who had been the hardest fighters against the South were in sympathy with much of it, if not with all. But to those who were of the South, it was sublime. It passed beyond mere enthusiasm, however exalted, and rested in the profoundest and most sacred deeps of their being. There were many cheers, but more tears; not tears of regret or mortification, but tears of sympathy and hallowed memory. The gaily decorated streets, in all the bravery of fluttering ensigns and bunting; the martial music of many bands; the constant tramp of marching troops; the thronged sidewalks, verandas, and roofs; the gleam of polished arms and glittering uniforms; the flutter of gay garments, and the smiles of beautiful women sweet with sympathy; the long line of old soldiers, faded and broken and gray, yet each self-sustained, and inspired by the life of the South that flowed in their veins, marching under the old Confederate battle-flags that they had borne so often in victory and in defeat—all contributed to make the outward pageant a scene never to be forgotten. But this was merely the outward image; the real fact was the spirit. It was the South. It was the spirit of the South; not of the new South, not yet merely of the old South, but the spirit of the great South. When the young troops from every Southern State marched by in their fresh uniforms, with well-drilled battalions, there were huzzas, much applause and enthusiasm; when the old soldiers came there was a tempest: wild cheers choking with sobs and tears, the well-known, once-heard-never-forgotten cry of the battling South, known in history as "the rebel yell." Men and women and children joined in it. It began at the first sight of the regular column, swelled up the crowded streets, rose to the thronged housetops, ran along them for squares like a conflagration, and then came rolling back in volume only to rise and swell again greater than before. Men wept; children shrilled; women sobbed aloud. What was it! Only a thousand or two of old or aging men riding or tramping along through the dust of the street, under some old flags, dirty and ragged and stained. But they represented the spirit of the South; they represented the spirit which when honor was in question never counted the cost; the spirit that had stood up for the South against overwhelming odds for four years, and until the South had crumbled and perished under the forces of war; the spirit that is the strongest guaranty to us to-day that the Union is and is to be; the spirit that, glorious in victory, had displayed a fortitude yet greater in defeat. They saw in every stain on those tattered standards the blood of their noblest, bravest, and best; in every rent a proof of their glorious courage and sacrifice. They saw in those gray and careworn faces, in those old clothes interspersed now and then with a faded gray uniform, the men who in the ardor of their youth had, for the South, faced death undaunted on a hundred fields, and had never even thought it great; men who had looked immortality in the eyes, yet had been thrown down and trampled underfoot, and who were greater in their overthrow than when glory poured her light upon their upturned faces. Not one of them all but was self-sustaining, sustained by the South, or had ever even for a moment thought in his direst extremity that he would have what was, undone.

The crowd was immense; the people on the fashionable street up which the procession passed were fortunate; they had the advantage of their yards and porticos, and they threw them open to the public. Still the throng on the sidewalks was tremendous, and just before the old veterans came along the crush increased. As it resettled itself I became conscious that a little old woman in a rusty black dress whom I had seen patiently standing alone in the front line on the street corner for an hour had lost her position, and had been pushed back against the railing, and had an anxious, disappointed look on her face. She had a little, faded knot of

Confederate colors fastened in her old dress, and, almost hidden by the crowd, she was looking up and down in some distress to see if she could not again get a place from which she could see. Finally she seemed to give it up, and stood quite still, tiptoeing now and then to try to catch a glimpse. I saw someone about to help her when, from a gay and crowded portico above her, a young and beautiful girl in a white dress, whom I had been observing for some time as the life of a gay party, as she sat in her loveliness, a queen on her throne with her courtiers around her, suddenly arose and ran down into the street. There was a short colloquy. The young beauty was offering something which the old lady was declining; but it ended in the young girl leading the older woman gently up onto her veranda and giving her the chair of state. She was hardly seated when the old soldiers began to pass.

As the last mounted veterans came by, I remembered that I had not seen "No. 4;" but as I looked up, he was just coming along. In his hand, with staff resting on his toe, he carried an old standard so torn and tattered and stained that it was scarcely recognizable as a flag. I did not for a moment take in that it was he, for he was not in the gray jacket which I had expected to see. He was busy looking down at the throng on the sidewalk, apparently searching for some one whom he expected to find there. He was in some perplexity, and pulled in his horse, which began to rear. Suddenly the applause from the portico above arrested his attention, and he looked toward it and bowed. As he did so his eye caught that of the old lady seated there. His face lighted up, and, wheeling his prancing horse half around, he dipped the tattered standard, and gave the royal salute as though saluting a queen. The old lady pressed her wrinkled hand over the knot of faded ribbon on her breast, and made a gesture to him, and he rode on. He had suddenly grown handsome. I looked at her again; her eyes were closed, her hands were clasped, and her lips were moving. I saw the likeness; she was his mother. As he passed me I caught his eye. He saw my perplexity about the jacket, glanced up at the torn colors, and pointed to a figure just beyond him dressed in a short, faded jacket. "No. 4" had been selected, as the highest honor, to carry the old colors which he had once saved; and not to bear off all the honors from his friend, he had with true comradeship made Binford Terrell wear his cherished jacket. He made a brave figure as he rode away, and my cheer died on my lips as I thought of the sad, old mother in her faded knot, and of the dashing young soldier who had saved the colors in that unnamed fight.

After that we got him a place, and he did well for several months. He seemed to be cured. New life and strength appeared to come back to him. But his mother died, and one night shortly afterward he disappeared, and remained lost for several days. When we found him he had been brought to jail, and I was sent for to see about him. He was worse than I had ever known him. He was half-naked and little better than a madman. I went to a doctor about him, an old army surgeon, who saw him, and shook his head. "*Mania a potu*. Very bad; only a question of time," he said. This was true. "No. 4" was beyond hope. Body and brain were both gone. It got to be only a question of days, if not of hours. Some of his other friends and I determined that he should not die in jail; so we took him out and carried him to a cool, pleasant room looking out on an old garden with trees in it. There in the dreadful terror of raving delirium he passed that night. I with several others sat up with him. I could not have stood many more like it. All night long he raved and tore. His oaths were blood-curdling. He covered every past portion of his life. His army life was mainly in his mind. He fought the whole war over. Sometimes he prayed fervently; prayed against his infirmity; prayed that his chains might be broken. Then he would grow calm for a while. One thing recurred constantly: he had sold his honor, betrayed his cause. This was the order again and again, and each time the paroxysm of frightful fury came on, and it took all of us to hold him. He was covered with snakes: they were chains on his wrists and around his body. He tried to pull them from around him. At last, toward morning, came one of those fearful spells, worse than any that had gone before. It passed, and he suddenly seemed to collapse. He sank, and the stimulant administered failed to revive him.

"He is going," said the doctor, quietly, across the bed. Whether his dull ear caught the word or not, I cannot say; but he suddenly roused up, tossed one arm, and said:

"Binford, take the horses. I'm going to old Joe," and sank back.

"He's gone," said the doctor, opening his shirt and placing his ear over his heart. As he rose up I saw two curious scars on "No. 4's" emaciated breast. They looked almost like small crosses, about the size of the decorations the European veterans wear. The old doctor bent over and examined them.

"Hello! Bayonet-wounds," he said briefly.

A little later I went out to get a breath of fresh morning air to quiet my nerves, which were somewhat unstrung. As I passed by a little second-hand clothing-store of the meanest kind, in a poor back street, I saw hanging up outside an old gray jacket. I stopped to examine it. It was stained behind with mud, and in front with a darker color. An old patch hid a part of the front; but a close examination showed two holes over the breast. It was "No. 4's" lost jacket. I asked the shopman about it. He had bought it, he said, of a pawnbroker, who had got it from some drunkard, who had probably stolen it last year from some old soldier. He readily sold it, and I took it back with me; and the others being gone, an old woman and I cut the patch off it and put "No. 4's" stiffening arms into the sleeves. Word was sent to us during the day to say that the city would bury him in the poor-house grounds. But we told them that arrangements had been made; that he would have a soldier's burial. And he had it.

A War Debt
1895

SARAH ORNE JEWETT

Sarah Orne Jewett (1849–1909) was born in Maine, spending the Civil War years at the Berwick Academy. She published her first short story in 1868, and from then on she wrote prolifically. Her most celebrated collection is The Country of the Pointed Firs *(1896), a poignant series of sketches of an isolated community in Maine. But Jewett also developed a sympathy for the South, writing several tales with a Southern setting. One of them is "A War Debt," included in her collection* The Life of Nancy *(1895), which speaks tenderly of a Northerner who makes peace with his former foe in the South.*

I

There was a tinge of autumn color on even the English elms as Tom Burton walked slowly up Beacon Street. He was wondering all the way what he had better do with himself; it was far too early to settle down in Boston for the winter, but his grandmother kept to her old date for moving up to town, and here they were. As yet nobody thought of braving the country weather long after October came in, and most country houses were poorly equipped with fireplaces, or even furnaces: this was some years ago, and not the very last autumn that ever was.

There was likely to be a long stretch of good weather, a month at least, if one took the trouble to go a little way to the southward. Tom Burton quickened his steps a little, and began to think definitely of his guns, while a sudden resolve took shape in his mind. Just then he reached the doorsteps of his grandmother's fine old-fashioned house, being himself

the fourth Thomas Burton that the shining brass door-plate had represented. His old grandmother was the only near relative he had in the
world; she was growing older and more dependent upon him every day.
That summer he had returned from a long wandering absence of three
years, and the vigorous elderly woman whom he had left, busy and self-
reliant, had sadly changed in the mean time; age had begun to strike telling
blows at her strength and spirits. Tom had no idea of leaving her again for
the long journeys which had become the delightful habit of his life; but
there was no reason why he should not take a fortnight's holiday now and
then, particularly now.

"Has Mrs. Burton come down yet, Dennis? Is there any one with her?"
asked Tom, as he entered.

"There is not, sir. Mrs. Burton is in the drawing-room," answered
Dennis precisely. "The tea is just going up; I think she was waiting for
you." And Tom ran upstairs like a schoolboy, and then walked discreetly
into the drawing-room. His grandmother gave no sign of having expected
him, but she always liked company at that hour of the day: there had come
to be too many ghosts in the empty chairs.

"Can I have two cups?" demanded the grandson, cheerfully. "I don't
know when I have had such a walk!" and they began a gay gossiping hour
together, and parted for a short season afterward, only to meet again at
dinner, with a warm sense of pleasure in each other's company. The young
man always insisted that his grandmother was the most charming woman
in the world, and it can be imagined what the grandmother thought of
Tom. She was only severe with him because he had given no signs of wishing to marry, but she was tolerant of all delay, so long as she could now and
then keep the subject fresh in his mind. It was not a moment to speak again
of the great question that afternoon, and she had sat and listened to his
talk of people and things, a little plaintive and pale, but very handsome,
behind the tea-table.

II

At dinner, after Dennis had given Tom his cup of coffee and cigars, and
disappeared with an accustomed air of thoughtfully leaving the family
alone for a private interview, Mrs. Burton, who sometimes lingered if she
felt like talking, and sometimes went away to the drawing-room to take a
brief nap before she began her evening book, and before Tom joined her
for a few minutes to say good-night if he were going out,—Mrs. Burton
left her chair more hurriedly than usual. Tom meant to be at home that

evening, and was all ready to speak of his plan for some Southern shooting, and he felt a sudden sense of disappointment.

"Don't go away," he said, looking up as she passed. "Is this a bad cigar?"

"No, no, my dear," said the old lady, hurrying across the room in an excited, unusual sort of way. "I wish to show you something while we are by ourselves." And she stooped to unlock a little cupboard in the great sideboard, and fumbled in the depths there, upsetting and clanking among some pieces of silver. Tom joined her with a pair of candles, but it was some moments before she could find what she wanted. Mrs. Burton appeared to be in a hurry, which almost never happened, and in trying to help her Tom dropped much wax unheeded at her side.

"Here it is at last," she said, and went back to her seat at the table. "I ought to tell you the stories of some old silver that I keep in that cupboard; if I were to die, nobody would know anything about them."

"Do you mean the old French spoons, and the prince's porringer, and those things?" asked Tom, showing the most lively interest. But his grandmother was busy unfastening the strings of a little bag, and shook her head absently in answer to his question. She took out and handed to him a quaint old silver cup with two handles, that he could not remember ever to have seen.

"What a charming old bit!" said he, turning it about. "Where in the world did it come from? English, of course; and it looks like a loving-cup. A copy of some old Oxford thing, perhaps; only they didn't copy much then. I should think it had been made for a child." Tom turned it round and round and drew the candles toward him. "Here's an inscription, too, but very much worn."

"Put it down a minute," said Mrs. Burton impatiently. "Every time I have thought of it I have been more and more ashamed to have it in the house. People weren't so shocked by such things at first; they would only be sentimental about the ruined homes, and say that, 'after all, it was the fortune of war.' That cup was stolen."

"But who stole it?" inquired Tom, with deep interest.

"Your father brought it here," said Mrs. Burton, with great spirit, and even a tone of reproach. "My son, Tom Burton, your father, brought it home from the war. I think his plan was to keep it safe to send back to the owners. But he left it with your mother when he was ordered suddenly to the front; he was only at home four days, and the day after he got back to camp was the day he was killed, poor boy"—

"I remember something about it now," Tom hastened to say. "I remember my mother's talking about the breaking up of Southern homes, and all that; she never believed it until she saw the cup, and I thought it was awfully silly. I was at the age when I could have blown our own house to pieces just for the sake of the racket."

"And that terrible year your grandfather's and your mother's death followed, and I was left alone with you—two of us out of the five that had made my home"—

"I should say one and a half," insisted Tom, with some effort. "What a boy I was for a grandson! Thank Heaven, there comes a time when we are all the same age! We are jolly together now, aren't we? Come, dear old lady, don't let's think too much of what's gone by;" and he went round the table and gave her a kiss, and stood there where she need not look him in the face, holding her dear thin hand as long as ever she liked.

"I want you to take that silver cup back, Tom," she said presently, in her usual tone. "Go back and finish your coffee." She had seldom broken down like this. Mrs. Burton had been self-possessed, even to apparent coldness, in earlier life.

"How in the world am I going to take it back?" asked Tom, most businesslike and calm. "Do you really know just where it came from? And then it was several years ago."

"Your grandfather knew; they were Virginia people, of course, and happened to be old friends; one of the younger men was his own classmate. He knew the crest and motto at once, but there were two or three branches of the family, none of them, so far as he knew, living anywhere near where your father was in camp. Poor Tom said that there was a beautiful old house sacked and burnt, and everything scattered that was saved. He happened to hear a soldier from another regiment talking about it, and saw him tossing this cup about, and bought it from him with all the money he happened to have in his pockets."

"Then he didn't really steal it himself!" exclaimed Tom, laughing a little, and with a sense of relief.

"No, no, Tom!" said Mrs. Burton impatiently. "Only you see that it really is a stolen thing, and I have had it all this time under my roof. For a long time it was packed away with your father's war relics, those things that I couldn't bear to see. And then I would think of it only at night after I had once seen it, and forget to ask any one else while you were away, or wait for you to come. Oh, I have no excuse. I have been very careless, but here it has been all the time. I wish you would find out about the people; there must be some one belonging to them—some friend, perhaps, to whom we could give it. This is one of the things that I wish to have done, and to forget. Just take it back, or write some letters first: you will know what to do. I should like to have the people understand."

"I'll see about it at once," said Tom, with great zest. "I believe you couldn't have spoken at a better time. I have been thinking of going down to Virginia this very week. I hear that they are in a hurry with fitting out that new scientific expedition in Washington that I declined to join, and they want me to come on and talk over things before they are off. One of the men is a Virginian, an awfully good fellow; and then there's Clendennin, my old chum, who's in Washington, too, just now; they'll give me my directions; they know all Virginia between them. I'll take the cup along, and run down from Washington for a few days, and perhaps get some shooting."

Tom's face was shining with interest and satisfaction; he took the cup and again held it under the candle-light. "How pretty this old chasing is round the edge, and the set of the little handles! Oh, here's the motto! What a dear old thing, and enormously old! See here, under the crest," and he held it toward Mrs. Burton:—

"*Je vous en prie*
    Bel-ami."

Mrs. Burton glanced at it with indifference. "Yes, it is charming, as you say. But I only wish to return it to its owners, Tom."

"*Je vous en prie*
    Bel-ami."

Tom repeated the words under his breath, and looked at the crest carefully.

"I remember that your grandfather said it belonged to the Bellamys," said his grandmother. "Of course: how could I forget that? I have never looked at it properly since the day I first saw it. It is a charming motto—they were very charming and distinguished people. I suppose this is a pretty way of saying that they could not live without their friends. I beg of you, Bel-ami;—it is a quaint fancy; one might turn it in two or three pretty ways."

"Or they may have meant that they only looked to themselves for what they wanted, *Je vous en prie Bellamy!*" said Tom gallantly. "All right; I think that I shall start to-morrow or next day. If you have no special plans," he added.

"Do go, my dear; you may get some shooting, as you say," said Mrs. Burton, a little wistfully, but kindly personifying Tom's inclination.

"You've started me off on a fine romantic adventure," said the young man, smiling. "Come; my cigar's gone out, and it never was good for much; let's go in and try the cards, and talk about things; perhaps you'll think of something more about the Bellamys. You said that my grandfather had a classmate"—

Mrs. Burton stopped to put the cup into its chamois bag again, and handed it solemnly to Tom, then she took his arm, and dismissing all unpleasant thoughts, they sat down to the peaceful game of cribbage to while away the time. The grandson lent himself gayly to pleasure-making, and they were just changing the cards for their books, when one of the elder friends of the house appeared, one of the two or three left who called Mrs. Burton Margaret, and was greeted affectionately as Henry in return. This guest always made the dear lady feel young; he himself was always to the front of things, and had much to say. It was quite forgotten that a last charge had been given to Tom, or that the past had been wept over. Presently, the late evening hours being always her best, she forgot in eager talk that she had any grandson at all, and Tom slipped away with his book to his own sitting-room and his pipe. He took the little cup out of its bag again, and set it before him, and began to lay plans for a Southern journey.

III

The Virginia country was full of golden autumn sunshine and blue haze. The long hours spent on a slow-moving train were full of shocks and surprises to a young traveler who knew almost every civilized country better than his own. The lonely look of the fields, the trees shattered by war, which had not yet had time enough to muffle their broken tops with green; the negroes, who crowded on board the train, lawless, and unequal to holding their liberty with steady hands, looked poor and less respectable than in the old plantation days—it was as if the long discipline of their former state had counted for nothing. Tom Burton felt himself for the first time to have something of a statesman's thoughts and schemes as he moralized along the way. Presently he noticed with deep sympathy a lady who came down the crowded car, and took the seat just in front of him. She carried a magazine under her arm—a copy of "Blackwood," which was presently proved to bear the date of 1851, and to be open at an article on the death of Wordsworth. She was the first lady he had seen that day— there was little money left for journeying and pleasure among the white

Virginians; but two or three stations beyond this a group of young English men and women stood with the gay negroes on the platform, and came into the train with cheerful greetings to their friends. It seemed as if England had begun to settle Virginia all over again, and their clear, lively voices had no foreign sound. There were going to be races at some court-house town in the neighborhood. Burton was a great lover of horses himself, and the new scenes grew more and more interesting. In one of the gay groups was a different figure from any of the fresh-cheeked young wives of the English planters—a slender girl, pale and spirited, with a look of care beyond her years. She was the queen of her little company. It was to her that every one looked for approval and sympathy as the laugh went to and fro. There was something so high-bred and elegant in her bearing, something so exquisitely sure and stately, that her companions were made clumsy and rustic in their looks by contrast. The eager talk of the coming races, of the untried thoroughbreds, the winners and losers of the year before, made more distinct this young Virginia lady's own look of high-breeding, and emphasized her advantage of race. She was the newer and finer Norman among Saxons. She alone seemed to have that inheritance of swiftness of mind, of sureness of training. It was the highest type of English civilization refined still further by long growth in favoring soil. Tom Burton read her unconscious face as if it were a romance; he believed that one of the great Virginia houses must still exist, and that she was its young mistress. The house's fortune was no doubt gone; the long-worn and carefully mended black silk gown that followed the lines of her lovely figure told plainly enough that worldly prosperity was a thing of the past. But what nature could give of its best, and only age and death could take away, were hers. He watched her more and more; at one moment she glanced up suddenly and held his eyes with hers for one revealing moment. There was no surprise in the look, but a confession of pathos, a recognition of sympathy, which made even a stranger feel that he had the inmost secret of her heart.

IV

The next day our hero, having hired a capital saddle-horse, a little the worse for age, was finding his way eastward along the sandy roads. The country was full of color; the sassafras and gum trees and oaks were all ablaze with red and yellow. Now and then he caught a glimpse of a sail on one of the wide reaches of the river which lay to the northward; now and then he passed a broken gateway or the ruins of a cabin. He carried a light gun before him across the saddle, and a game-bag hung slack and empty at his shoulder except for a single plump partridge in one corner, which had whirred up at the right moment out of a vine-covered thicket. Something small and heavy in his coat pocket seemed to correspond to the bird, and once or twice he unconsciously lifted it in the hollow of his hand. The day itself, and a sense of being on the road to fulfill his mission, a sense of unending leisure and satisfaction under that lovely hazy sky, seemed to leave no place for impatience or thought of other things. He rode slowly along, with his eye on the roadside coverts, letting the horse take his own gait, except when a ragged negro boy, on an unwilling, heavy-footed mule, slyly approached and struck the dallying steed from behind. It was past the middle of the October afternoon.

"'Mos' thar now, Cun'l," said the boy at last, eagerly. "See them busted trees pas' thar, an' chimblies? You tu'n down nax' turn; ride smart piece yet, an' you come right front of ol' Mars Bell'my's house. See, he comin' 'long de road now. Yas, 'tis Mars Bell'my shore, an' 's gun."

Tom had been looking across the neglected fields with compassion, and wondering if such a plantation could ever be brought back to its days of prosperity. As the boy spoke he saw the tall chimneys in the distance, and then, a little way before him in the shadow of some trees, a stately figure that slowly approached. He hurriedly dismounted, leading his horse until he met the tall old man, who answered his salutation with much dignity. There was something royal and remote from ordinary men in his silence after the first words of courteous speech.

"Yas, sir; that's Mars Bell'my, sir," whispered the boy on the mule, reassuringly, and the moment of hesitation was happily ended.

"I was on my way to call upon you, Colonel Bellamy; my name is Burton," said the younger man.

"Will you come with me to the house?" said the old gentleman, putting out his hand cordially a second time; and though he had frowned slightly at first at the unmistakable Northern accent, the light came quickly to his eyes. Tom gave his horse's bridle to the boy, who promptly transferred himself to the better saddle, and began to lead the mule instead.

"I have been charged with an errand of friendship," said Tom. "I believe that you and my grandfather were at Harvard together." Tom looked boyish and eager and responsive to hospitality at this moment. He was straight and trim, like a Frenchman. Colonel Bellamy was much the taller of the two, even with his bent shoulders and relaxed figure.

"I see the resemblance to your grandfather, sir. I bid you welcome to Fairford," said the Colonel. "Your visit is a great kindness."

They walked on together, speaking ceremoniously of the season and of the shooting and Tom's journey, until they left the woods and overgrown avenue at the edge of what had once been a fine lawn, with clusters of huge oaks; but these were shattered by war and more or less ruined. The lopped trunks still showed the marks of fire and shot; some had put out a fresh bough or two, but most of the ancient trees stood for their own monuments, rain-bleached and gaunt. At the other side of the wide lawn, against young woodland and a glimpse of the river, were the four great chimneys which had been seen from the highroad. There was no dwelling in sight at the moment, and Tom stole an apprehensive look at the grave face of his companion. It appeared as if he were being led to the habitation of ghosts, as if he were purposely to be confronted with the desolation left in the track of Northern troops. It was not so long since the great war that these things could be forgotten.

The Colonel, however, without noticing the ruins in any way, turned toward the right as he neared them, and passing a high fragment of brick wall topped by a marble ball or two—which had been shot at for marks— and passing, just beyond, some huge clumps of box, they came to a square brick building with a rude wooden addition at one side, and saw some tumble-down sheds a short distance beyond this, with a negro cabin.

They came to the open door. "This was formerly the billiard-room. Your grandfather would have kept many memories of it," said the host simply. "Will you go in, Mr. Burton?" And Tom climbed two or three perilous wooden steps and entered, to find himself in a most homelike and charming place. There was a huge fireplace opposite the door, with a thin whiff of blue smoke going up, a few old books on the high chimney-piece, a pair of fine portraits with damaged frames, some old tables and chairs of different patterns, with a couch by the square window covered with a piece of the tapestry folded together and still showing its beauty, however raveled and worn. By the opposite window, curtained only by vines, sat a lady with her head muffled in lace, who greeted the guest pleasantly, and begged pardon for not rising from her chair. Her face wore an unmistakable look of pain and sorrow. As Tom Burton stood at her side, he could find nothing to say in answer to her apologies. He was not wont to be abashed, and a real court could not affect him like this ideal one. The poor surroundings could only be seen through the glamour of their owner's presence—it seemed a most elegant interior.

"I am sorry to have the inconvenience of deafness," said Madam Bellamy, looking up with an anxious little smile. "Will you tell me again the name of our guest?"

"He is my old classmate Burton's grandson, of Boston," said the Colonel, who now stood close at her side; he looked apprehensive as he spoke, and the same shadow flitted over his face as when Tom had announced himself by the oak at the roadside.

"I remember Mr. Burton, your grandfather, very well," said Madam Bellamy at last, giving Tom her hand for the second time, as her husband had done. "He was your guest here the autumn before we were married, my dear; a fine rider, I remember, and a charming gentleman. He was much entertained by one of our hunts. I saw that you also carried a gun. My dear," and she turned to her husband anxiously, "did you bring home any birds?"

Colonel Bellamy's face lengthened. "I had scarcely time, or perhaps I had not my usual good fortune," said he. "The birds have followed the grain-fields away from Virginia, we sometimes think."

"I can offer you a partridge," said Tom eagerly. "I shot one as I rode along. I am afraid that I stopped Colonel Bellamy just as he was going out."

"I thank you very much," said Madam Bellamy. "And you will take supper with us, certainly. You will give us the pleasure of a visit? I regret very much my granddaughter's absence, but it permits me to offer you her room, which happens to be vacant." But Tom attempted to make excuse. "No, no," said Madam Bellamy, answering her own thoughts rather than his words. "You must certainly stay the night with us; we shall make you most welcome. It will give my husband great pleasure; he will have many questions to ask you."

Tom went out to search for his attendant, who presently clattered away on the mule at an excellent homeward pace. An old negro man servant led away the horse, and Colonel Bellamy disappeared also, leaving the young guest to entertain himself and his hostess for an hour, that flew by like light. A woman who is charming in youth is still more charming in age to a man of Tom Burton's imagination, and he was touched to find how quickly the first sense of receiving an antagonist had given way before a desire to show their feeling of kindly hospitality toward a guest. The links of ancient friendship still held strong, and as Tom sat with his hostess by the window they had much pleasant talk of Northern families known to them both, of whom, or of whose children and grandchildren, he could give much news. It seemed as if he should have known Madam Bellamy all his life. It is impossible to say how she illumined her poor habitation, with what dignity and sweetness she avoided, as far as possible, any reference to the war or its effects. One could hardly remember that she was poor, or ill, or had suffered such piteous loss of friends and fortune.

Later, when Tom was walking toward the river through the woods and overgrown fields of the plantation, he came upon the ruins of the old cabins of what must have been a great family of slaves. The crumbling heaps of the chimneys stood in long lines on either side of a weed-grown lane; not far beyond he found the sinking mounds of some breastworks on a knoll which commanded the river channel. The very trees and grass looked harrowed and distressed by war; the silence of the sunset was only broken by the cry of a little owl that was begging mercy of its fears far down the lonely shore.

V

At supper that night Burton came from his room to find Colonel Bellamy bringing his wife in his arms to the table, while the old bent-backed and gray-headed man servant followed to place her chair. The mistress of Fairford was entirely lame and helpless, but she sat at the head of her table like a queen. There was a bunch of damask-roses at her plate. The Colonel himself was in evening dress, antique in cut, and sadly worn, and Tom heartily thanked his patron saint that the boy had brought his portmanteau in good season. There was a glorious light in the room from the fire, and the table was served with exquisite care, and even more luxurious delay, the excellent fish which the Colonel himself must have caught in his unexplained absence, and Tom's own partridge, which was carved as if it had been the first wild turkey of the season, were followed by a few peaches touched with splendid color as they lay on a handful of leaves in a bent and dented pewter plate. There seemed to be no use for the stray glasses, until old Milton produced a single small bottle of beer, and uncorked and poured it for his master and his master's guest with a grand air. The Colonel lifted his eyebrows slightly, but accepted its appearance at the proper moment.

They sat long at table. It was impossible to let one's thought dwell upon any of the meagre furnishings of the feast. The host and hostess talked of the days when they went often to France and England, and of Tom's grandfather when he was young. At last Madam Bellamy left the table, and Tom stood waiting while she was carried to her own room. He had kissed her hand like a courtier as he said good-night. On the Colonel's return the old butler ostentatiously placed the solitary bottle between them and went away. The Colonel offered some excellent tobacco, and Tom begged leave to fetch his pipe. When he returned he brought with it the chamois-skin bag that held the silver cup, and laid it before him on the table. It was like the dread of going into battle, but the moment had arrived. He laid his hand on the cup for a moment as if to hide it, then he waited until his pipe was fairly going.

"This is something which I have come to restore to you, sir," said Tom presently, taking the piece of silver from its wrappings. "I believe that it is your property."

The old Colonel's face wore a strange, alarmed look; his thin cheeks grew crimson. He reached eagerly for the cup, and held it before his eyes. At last he bent his head and kissed it. Tom Burton saw that his tears began to fall, that he half rose, turning toward the door of the next room, where his wife was; then he sank back again, and looked at his guest appealingly.

"I ask no questions," he faltered; "it was the fortune of war. This cup was my grandfather's, my father's, and mine; all my own children drank from it in turn; they are all gone before me. We always called it our lucky cup. I fear that it has come back too late"— The old man's voice broke, but he still held the shining piece of silver before him, and turned it about in the candle-light.

"Je vous en prie Bel-ami."

he whispered under his breath, and put the cup before him on the scarred mahogany.

VI

"Shall we move our chairs before the fire, Mr. Burton? My dear wife is but frail," said the old man, after a long silence, and with touching pathos. "She sees me companioned for the evening, and is glad to seek her room early; if you were not here she would insist upon our game of cards. I do not allow myself to dwell upon the past, and I have no wish for gay company;" he added, in a lower voice, "My daily dread in life is to be separated from her."

As the evening wore on, the autumn air grew chilly, and again and again the host replenished his draughty fireplace, and pushed the box of delicious tobacco toward his guest, and Burton in his turn ventured to remember a flask in his portmanteau, and begged the Colonel to taste it, because it had been filled from an old cask in his grandfather's cellar. The butler's eyes shone with satisfaction when he was unexpectedly called upon to brew a little punch after the old Fairford fashion, and the later talk ranged along the youthful escapades of Thomas Burton the elder to the beauties and the style of Addison; from the latest improvement in shot-guns to the statesmanship of Thomas Jefferson, while the Colonel spoke tolerantly, in passing, of some slight misapprehensions of Virginia life made by a delightful young writer, too early lost—Mr. Thackeray.

Tom Burton had never enjoyed an evening more; the romance, the pathos of it, as he found himself more and more taking his grandfather's place in the mind of this hereditary friend, waked all his sympathy. The charming talk that never dwelt too long or was hurried too fast, the exquisite faded beauty of Madam Bellamy, the noble dignity and manliness of the old planter and soldier, the perfect absence of reproach for others or whining pity for themselves, made the knowledge of their regret and loss doubly poignant. Their four sons had all laid down their lives in what they believed from their hearts to be their country's service; their daughters had died early, one from sorrow at her husband's death, and one from exposure in a forced flight across country; their beloved ancestral home lay in ruins; their beloved cause had been put to shame and defeat—yet they could bow their heads to every blast of misfortune, and could make a man welcome at their table whose every instinct and tradition of loyalty made him their enemy. The owls might shriek from the chimneys of Fairford, and the timid wild hares course up and down the weed-grown avenues on an autumn night like this, but a welcome from the Bellamys was a welcome still. It seemed to the young imaginative guest that the old motto of the house was never so full of significance as when he fancied it exchanged between the Colonel and himself, Southerner and Northerner, elder and younger man, conquered and conqueror in an unhappy war. The two old portraits, with their warped frames and bullet-holes, faded and gleamed again in the firelight; the portrait of an elderly man was like the Colonel himself, but the woman, who was younger, and who seemed to meet Tom's eye gayly enough, bore a resemblance which he could only half recall. It was very late when the two men said good-night. They were each conscious of the great delight of having found a friend. The candles had flickered out long before, but the fire still burned, and struck a ray of light from the cup on the table.

VII

The next morning Burton waked early in his tiny sleeping-room. The fragrance of ripe grapes and the autumn air blew in at the window, and he hastened to dress, especially as he could hear the footstep and imperious voice of Colonel Bellamy, who seemed to begin his new day with zest and courage in the outer room. Milton, the old gray-headed negro, was there too, and was alternately upbraided and spoken with most intimately and with friendly approval. It sounded for a time as if some great excitement and project were on foot; but Milton presently appeared, eager for morning offices, and when Tom went out to join the Colonel he was no longer there. There were no signs of breakfast. The birds were singing in the trees outside, and the sun shone in through the wide-opened door. It was a poor place in the morning light. As he crossed the room he saw an old-fashioned gift-book lying on the couch, as if some one had just laid it there face downward. He carried it with him to the door; a dull collection enough, from forgotten writers of forgotten prose and verse, but the Colonel had left it open at some lines which, with all their faults, could not be read without sympathy. He was always thinking of his wife; he had marked the four verses because they spoke of her.

Tom put the old book down just as Colonel Bellamy passed outside, and hastened to join him. They met with pleasure, and stood together talking. The elder man presently quoted a line or two of poetry about the beauty of the autumn morning, and his companion stood listening with respectful attention, but he observed by contrast the hard, warriorlike lines of the Colonel's face. He could well believe that, until sorrow had softened him, a fiery impatient temper had ruled this Southern heart. There was a sudden chatter and noise of voices, and they both turned to see a group of negroes, small and great, coming across the lawn with bags and baskets, and after a few muttered words the old master set forth hurriedly to meet them, Tom following.

"Be still, all of you!" said the Colonel sternly. "Your mistress is still asleep. Go round to Milton, and he will attend to you. I'll come presently."

They were almost all old people, many of them were already infirm, and it was hard to still their requests and complaints. One of the smaller children clasped Colonel Bellamy about the knees. There was something patriarchal in the scene, and one could not help being sure that some reason for the present poverty of Fairford was the necessity for protecting these poor souls. The merry, well-fed colored people, who were indulging their late-won liberty of travel on the trains, had evidently shirked any responsibilities for such stray remnants of humanity. Slavery was its own provider for old age. There had once been no necessity for the slaves themselves to make provision for winter, as even a squirrel must. They were worse than children now, and far more appealing in their helplessness.

The group slowly departed, and Colonel Bellamy led the way in the opposite direction, toward the ruins of the great house. They crossed the old garden, where some ancient espaliers still clung to the broken brick-work of the walls, and a little fruit still clung to the knotted branches, while great hedges of box, ragged and uncared for, traced the old order of the walks. The heavy dew and warm morning sun brought out that antique fragrance,—the faint pungent odor which wakes the utmost mem-ories of the past. Tom Burton thought with a sudden thrill that the girl with the sweet eyes yesterday had worn a bit of box in her dress. Here and there, under the straying boughs of the shrubbery, bloomed a late scarlet poppy from some scattered seed of which such old soil might well be full. It was a barren, neglected garden enough, but still full of charm and delight, being a garden. There was a fine fragrance of grapes through the undergrowth, but the whole place was completely ruined; a little snake slid from the broken base of a sun-dial; the tall chimneys of the house were already beginning to crumble, and birds and squirrels lived in their crevices and flitted about their lofty tops. At some distance an old negro was singing,—it must have been Milton himself, still unbesought by his dependents,—and the song was full of strange, monotonous wails and plaintive cadences, like a lament for war itself, and all the misery that fol-lows in its train.

Colonel Bellamy had not spoken for some moments, but when they reached the terrace which had been before the house there were two flights of stone steps that led to empty air, and these were still adorned by some graceful railings and balusters, bent and rusty and broken.

"You will observe this iron-work, sir," said the Colonel, stopping to regard with pride almost the only relic of the former beauty and state of Fairford. "My grandfather had the pattern carefully planned in Charleston, where such work was formerly well done by Frenchmen." He stopped to point out certain charming features of the design with his walking-stick, and then went on without a glance at the decaying chimneys or the weed-grown cellars and heaps of stones beneath.

The lovely October morning was more than half gone when Milton brought the horse round to the door, and the moment came to say farewell. The Colonel had shown sincere eagerness that the visit should be prolonged for at least another day, but a reason for hurry which the young man hardly confessed to himself was urging him back along the way he had come. He was ready to forget his plans for shooting and wandering eastward on the river shore. He had paid a parting visit to Madam Bellamy in her own room, where she lay on a couch in the sunshine, and had seen the silver cup—a lucky cup he devoutly hoped it might indeed be—on a light stand by her side. It held a few small flowers, as if it had so been brought in to her in the early morning. Her eyes were dim with weeping. She had not thought of its age and history, neither did the sight of such pathetic loot wake bitter feelings against her foes. It was only the cup that her little children had used, one after another, in their babyhood; the last and dearest had kept it longest, and even he was dead—fallen in battle, like the rest.

She wore a hood and wrapping of black lace, which brought out the delicacy of her features like some quaint setting. Her hand trembled as she bade her young guest farewell. As he looked back from the doorway she was like some exiled queen in a peasant's lodging, such dignity and sweet patience were in her look. "I think you bring good fortune," she said. "Nothing can make me so happy as to have my husband find a little pleasure."

As the young man crossed the outer room the familiar eyes of the old portrait caught his own with wistful insistency. He suddenly suspected the double reason: he had been dreaming of other eyes, and knew that his fellow-traveler had kept him company. "Madam Bellamy," he said, turning back, and blushing as he bent to speak to her in a lower voice,—"the portrait; is it like any one? is it like your granddaughter? Could I have seen her on my way here?"

Madam Bellamy looked up at his eager face with a light of unwonted pleasure in her eyes. "Yes," said she, "my granddaughter would have been on her way to Whitfields. She has always been thought extremely like the picture: it is her great-grandmother. Good-by; pray let us see you at Fairford again;" and they said farewell once more, while Tom Burton promised something, half to himself, about the Christmas hunt.

"*Je vous en prie Belle amie,*"

he whispered, and a most lovely hope was in his heart.

"You have been most welcome," said the Colonel at parting. "I beg that you will be so kind as to repeat this visit. I shall hope that we may have some shooting together."

"I shall hope so too," answered Tom Burton warmly. Then, acting from sudden impulse, he quickly unslung his gun, and begged his old friend to keep it—to use it, at any rate, until he came again.

The old Virginian did not reply for a moment. "Your grandfather would have done this, sir. I loved him, and I take it from you both. My own gun is too poor a thing to offer in return." His voice shook; it was the only approach to a lament, to a complaint, that he had made.

Tom Burton rode slowly away, and presently the fireless chimneys of Fairford were lost to sight behind the clustering trees. The noonday light was shining on the distant river; the road was untraveled and untenanted for miles together, except by the Northern rider and his Southern steed.

This was the way that, many years ago, a Northerner found his love, a poor but noble lady in the South, and Fortune smiled again upon the ruined house of Fairford.

The Little Faded Flag
1908

EDWARD LUCAS WHITE

Edward Lucas White (1866–1934) was not born until after the conclusion of the Civil War, but he must have heard first-hand accounts of the conflict during his boyhood in Baltimore. Best known for such historical novels of the ancient world as The Unwilling Vestal *(1918) and* Andivius Hedulio *(1921), as well as the tales of fantasy and the supernatural gathered in* The Song of the Sirens *(1919) and* Lukundoo *(1927), White also wrote several other tales of human drama that remain uncollected. One of these, "The Little Faded Flag" (first published in the* Atlantic Monthly *of May 1908), echoes Sarah Orne Jewett's "A War Debt" in speaking hopefully of an ultimate reconciliation between North and South.*

Any objection to graveyards?" the American inquired.

"I should object to taking up my permanent abode in one unnecessarily soon," the Frenchman replied, his black eyes twinkling, his thin lips smiling between his jetty mustache and his pointed sable beard.

"Monseer Daypurtwee," said his host, "I'm not joking, you understand. I've showed you most of this neighborhood, and I rather like to drive through our cemetery, myself. I'm trying to find out how the idea strikes you."

"I should be charmed, I am sure," Des Pertuis answered in his unexceptionable English.

"Some people don't like to go to a graveyard," Wade resumed, "any oftener or any sooner than they have to. Sure you're not just being polite?"

"Quite sure," René replied, smiling again.

"Honor bright, no reservations?" Wade queried anxiously, half turning, and glancing into his guest's eyes.

"None whatever," René answered him smilingly.

"Then we'll drive through the cemetery," Wade informed him, settling back comfortably, not a muscle showing effort, except his outstretched arms, tense against the taut reins.

"I shall be charmed, I am sure," René repeated.

"You may think it queer," Wade remarked, "my taking you to the cemetery, but I'll explain afterwards, you understand, or perhaps you'll find out for yourself before we leave it, why I took you there. I want to try an experiment, want to see whether something is going to strike you the way it strikes me, you understand."

"You are very kind, I am sure," said Des Pertuis. "I shall be interested to learn the result of your experiment."

"Ferris wrote me," Wade went on, "that what you wanted was real American atmosphere, and he thought I could let you into some at Middleville. I believe you've found some, haven't you?"

"Yes," the Frenchman agreed, "I have been in what I am sure is a genuinely American atmosphere."

"I've watched you absorbing it, you understand," Wade chuckled. "You've had to take in quite an amount of hot air with your American atmosphere."

Des Pertuis smiled deprecatingly.

"Oh yes," his host continued. "You've been polite about it. I could appreciate that, you understand. You've smiled and looked interested while Uncle George talked bushels-to-the-acre and all that, while Tupper talked tons of tomatoes and the rest of it, while Bowe talked reapers and thrashers and iron fences and cutlery, while Parks talked tonnage-per-mile and tonnage-per-landing; you've taken it all in: farm-brag, trade-brag, railroad-brag, and steamboat-brag; you've appeared charmed, but you've got everlastingly tired of the brag all the same."

"I have not heard you brag, Mr. Wade," René reminded him quietly, his twinkling black eyes fixed on his host's plump, smooth-shaven visage.

"Perhaps I'm going to brag," Wade replied. "Brag is part of what you came after, part of the American atmosphere, you understand, and I brag myself, but not about the same things, nor in just the same way. I love the Eastern Shore, I like to hear it called 'God's Footstool,' or 'The Garden Spot of the World.' But I've quit using those terms myself,—to foreigners, anyhow. I never run down my home state or my home country, you understand, but when I meet a man like you, who has seen Holland and Belgium and Luxembourg and Saxony and Provence and Lombardy, let alone other

places I haven't seen, I let others do the bragging about density of population and fertility and productivity and all that. I don't call them down, I sit
and smoke and look on. But I'm not saying much, you understand."

"I quite comprehend," René assured him. "Enthusiasm for one's own is
not by any means unpleasant."

"Not unless you get too much of it," his host commented, "or unless the
enthusiasm is for the wrong things, you understand. Enthusiasm for the
wrong thing makes me mad. We Americans have plenty to brag of; things
really worth boasting of. But it makes me hot to hear these half-baked
countrymen blat about the area of the United States, which is an accident;
or our coal and iron and copper and petroleum and what not, which are
quite as accidental; or our population, which is the result of the other accidents; or the volume of immigration, which is a menace. I want them to
distinguish what we really ought to be proud of from what we have no call
to boast of. And I bet you feel that way, too. I've been watching you, you
understand."

"Boasting about one's own country is an amiable foible," René
remarked. "I do not object to such chauvinism, as we call it."

"But you are a trifle uneasy," Wade put in, "when they begin to draw
comparisons,—especially if they are undeserved, you understand,—and to
run down France and French things. Is that what you mean?"

"Precisely," Des Pertuis replied. "You have penetrated my meaning; and
I may remind you that you yourself have done nothing of the kind, nor
Madame Wade."

"It's good of you to notice it," his host said. "Naturally she wouldn't any
more than I. We've been in France, you understand. But perhaps I'm going
to do that, too, as well as brag. No offense, you understand. But I'm commercial. I take a commercial view of things. I fail to see through a great
many things other people seem to comprehend, you understand, and one
thing they told me in France surprised me. I thought I heard Mary asking
you about it last night. But I wasn't sure, what with Humphreys and all the
other fellows talking at once, you understand. Anyhow, I want to ask you
about it."

"What is it?" his guest queried civilly.

"What was the name of that part of France, over toward England,
where there was no end of a civil war during your revolution?"

"You mean La Vendée?" René asked.

"That's it," his host replied. "I never can remember that sort of a name.
I'm commercial, you understand. Well, somebody told us while we were

in Paris (I think it was the Rogerses, who live there, but I'm not sure), that the descendants of the people who fought on opposite sides in that war won't sit down to table together this minute, nor be under the same roof. Is that true?"

"Not wholly," René responded; "two might be in the same theatre or in the same public building, and neither think it necessary to leave after recognizing the other. But certainly it is true of not dining together. No one would invite a Charette to meet a Hoche; neither would remain in any house a moment after learning the presence of the other. Still less would a Cathelineau or Rochejaquelein consent to spend an instant in a drawing-room with a Turreau or a Carrier; no, nor in a restaurant or hotel."

"Don't you think that is carrying personal hostility pretty far?" Wade asked.

Des Pertuis stroked his short spike of a beard.

"You do not comprehend," he said, "how fierce, how implacable, how ferocious was the fighting in that war. You have never heard of the devastations and counter-devastations, of the massacres and retaliatory massacres, of the savageries, the tortures, the insults, the ingenious horrors inflicted on the vanquished by the victors on both sides; of the brutal ruthlessness and refined cruelties."

"Perhaps not," Wade rejoined. "But when did all that happen?"

"From sometime in 1793," René replied, "to sometime in 1796."

"All over a hundred and ten years ago," his host commented. "No offense, you understand, but speaking as between friends, don't you think that is a long time to hold a grudge?"

"The families concerned," Des Pertuis made answer, "do not take that view of it. They still smart under the reciprocal wrongs inflicted, they still recall the gloating fiendishness of their foes, and apart from any recollections of outrage, they rather make a point of honor of their inflexibility. Why, not only the families involved on one side or the other of the war in La Vendée, but the old legitimist nobility generally and the descendants of the revolutionists at large, stand upon the same punctilio. No son of a noble house which never bowed to Bonapartism or to the Orleanist ascendancy, or to the party of the Citizen King, no member of any such noble family would ever meet socially any descendant of a Bonapartist, still less of a regicide, were he Montagnard, Jacobin, or Girondist. No La Rochefoucauld or Château-Reynaud would unbend to any Murat or Carnot."

"Don't you think yourself,—no offense, you understand," Wade suggested, "that that is rather a peevish and childish way to behave?"

René again stroked his beard, even more slowly.

"They do not so look upon it," he said; "they take pride in their tenacity."

"What's that national motto of yours on your coins," Wade asked argumentatively. "What does it mean in English?"

"Liberty, Equality, and Fraternity is the translation of that motto," Des Pertuis answered, a trifle stiffly.

"Do you call that fraternity?" Wade queried triumphantly.

"You do not comprehend," the Frenchman began ardently.

"I allow that," his host cut in. "I'm commercial, you know, and miss the fine points. No offense, Daypurtwee, go on."

"Indeed, you do not comprehend," René declared. "Our national motto is for us as the—what do you call it?—Golden Rule for all Christians; the ideal which is aimed at rather than an injunction which all live up to. The Golden Rule has not made all Christians always treat others as they wish themselves to be treated. We strive for fraternity. But a motto cannot make human nature otherwise than it is."

"Human nature," Wade remarked, "varies with the race and country, you understand. Some kinds don't need to be made over."

"I see," said his guest shortly.

"No offense, I hope, Daypurtwee," his host spoke anxiously. "No offense meant, you understand."

"Yes, I understand," René replied, smiling again.

"Here's the cemetery," Wade proclaimed. "We've driven miles around. I wanted to talk before we reached it."

He pointed with his whip to one gravestone after another, telling of the families, their characteristics, and their relationships to one another and to his own. The horse walked slowly. René, his hat in his hand, listened affably.

Wade halted his team under four big wide-spreading maples.

"That's my father's grave," he said, pointing.

René bowed in silence.

"And that's my uncle's," Wade went on, "my mother's brother. Colonel William Spence."

"He was a soldier in the Federal armies during your late war," René remarked.

"What makes you think that?" Wade remarked.

"I have visited many of your cemeteries," René answered, "at Boston, New York, Philadelphia, Baltimore, and other cities. I have learned your customs in respect to the graves of all such soldiers."

"So you think he fought for the Union?" Wade queried.

"I am sure of it," René replied confidently.

"Well," said his host, "you never were more mistaken in your life. My father's brothers both fought for the Union, but my mother's kin were all fire-eating rebels. Colonel William Spence fought under Lee."

"What!" the Frenchman cried, "the Union flag on a Confederate soldier's grave!"

"You'll find," Wade told him, "that this is not the only part of the country where they put the Stars and Stripes on the graves of ex-Confederates."

The Frenchman said nothing. They sat silent, side by side, the stout, blond, jolly-faced, red-cheeked, smooth-shaven American, his gray felt hat on the back of his head, looking sideways with quizzical blue eyes at his guest; the compact, black-haired, black-bearded Frenchman gazing steadily down at the white headstone, the narrow grass-mound, the month-old withered flowers, the draggled, mud-streaked, rain-bleached muslin flag, no bigger than a handkerchief. One of the geldings tossed his head and champed at his bit, and the reins tinkled and clanked softly.

"Who put it there?" René queried at last.

"The veterans," Wade answered lightly.

"When?" René inquired.

"The thirtieth of last May," his host replied.

"Why," Des Pertuis exclaimed, "that is your national Decoration Day. I was told that the Confederates had a different decoration day of their own; in June, I think."

"Yes," Wade responded. "They observe it all over the South, you understand. But here and in many of the border districts, in small towns, where there are not many veterans, they all walk out here, blue and gray together, and put Old Glory on every grave indifferently."

"I had been led to think," René ruminated, "that there was much rancor after your civil war; but I fancy from what you tell me that there was less animosity than I had conceived."

"There was much rancor," his host declared. "The animosity at the time of the war cannot be exaggerated, could not be conveyed to you by any description, you understand. There is rancor yet, mostly among the Southern women, particularly those born since the war, or those whose families really suffered least or whose men did not fight at all,—a sort of artificial cult of rancor. But the families who lost everything, whose estates were trampled by the armies, whose homes were burned, whose best men died in battle, who were left beggars when it was all over,—well, they and theirs talk now as they acted then, like the thoroughbreds they are. Not a complaint then, not a recrimination now. And the Northern families who gave most lives on the field are as mute on their side. As for the men who did the fighting, their animosity has all faded away. They forgive and forget."

"If the bitterness of feeling has so soon effaced itself," the Frenchman argued, "the war must have been waged without any exasperating atrocities on either side."

"If you mean by atrocities," Wade replied, "such massacres of prisoners by the regular authorities as you spoke of a while ago, or such butchery of surrendered adversaries as goes on in the South American revolutions, nothing of the kind occurred. But the bushwhackers and jayhawkers who hung about the armies and infested the border were often worse than Apache Indians. The Confederate raiders burned some buildings, the devastation of the Shenandoah Valley caused much suffering and venom. But that is about the list of what you might call atrocities. Yet without any unnecessary ferocity, the mere inevitable horrors of fair, honorable, open warfare roused enough exasperation and bitterness and animosity and rancor, you understand. The hatred on both sides was at white heat while it lasted."

"I can scarcely credit," René said, "that what has cooled so soon could have been so fierce."

"You are comparing our forty years," Wade conjectured, "with your hundred and ten after the war in what's-its-name?"

"Just so," his guest replied. "It seems the hatred can scarcely have been so intense as you claim, nor the provocations so frightful."

"You ought to have heard the veterans last Decoration Day," Wade told him. "They had a sort of reunion of both sides here. Several of them stayed at my house and they made my porch their headquarters. You ought to have heard the stories they told."

"For instance," the Frenchman suggested.

"Oh, I can't begin to tell them," Wade disclaimed. "I'm commercial, you understand. I never can remember the names of the battles and generals and colonels, nor the number of the regiments, nor the dates either, for that matter; any more than I can remember the names of all those high-and-mighty families you were telling me about, you understand. But I took in the gist of their talk, you bet. I just sat there and smoked and listened, and when they ran dry I'd take 'em out in the pantry for a little ammunition. One evening in particular, I think it was the 29th of May, they got going.

"There were two of them staying with me, my uncle, General Tom

Wade of Milwaukee, and Colonel Melrose of Boston, an uncle of my wife's. They were both born in Middleville, you understand, but one went west and one went north, and they live there yet. They were back in Middleville for a visit. Then there was Captain Tupper, cousin of the farmer you met, and Captain Bowe, uncle of the storekeeper. They both live here, came back after they made their pile, but they were out west when the war broke out. They were Union men too, you understand.

"We had five Confeds. Captain John Spence, my mother's youngest brother, Colonel Parks, father of the Parks you met, and old General Humphreys, Dick Humphreys's father. They live here, and with them were Colonel Janney, Henry Tupper's father-in-law, and Colonel Rhett, my sister-in-law's uncle.

"They were all right there on my porch, where you and I were sitting this morning. It was a beautiful night, hot for May and still. They had had a snifter or two all around and had rather limbered up to each other and warmed up to their talk. They talked war, of course, talked it good-naturedly. They had all been in it, had all lost near relatives in battle: Colonel Rhett had lost most,—never heard of such a connection as the Rhetts. But Colonel Janney had lost nearly as many. The five Confeds had all come out of the war beggars, lost every cent they ever had. Yet they all talked good-naturedly, you understand. They got to talking about a cornfield; not the cornfield at Gettysburg, but one famous in some small battle, early in the war, soon after Bull Run, I think. Anyhow they called it Rumbold's cornfield. I can't remember the name of the battle or of the locality, but they remembered it all right, you understand. They talked about the first charge and the second charge, and the second day's fighting, and the third charge across that same cornfield.

"Colonel Melrose said nothing.

"Uncle Wade asked, 'Weren't you there, Melrose?'

"Melrose tugged at his curly gray beard.

"'Yes, I was there,' he said. 'The most fearful moment of my life was in Rumbold's cornfield.'

"We expected him to tell a story, but he said no more.

"General Humphreys launched into an account of the difficulties the Confederates labored under, their shortness of supplies, and all that. He told how they got five field-guns in position to cover that cornfield, and he made a good story of it too. You could just feel what an exploit it was merely to plant those guns after all they had to overcome. Then, when they were in position, they found they had just three shells. Only three shells, you understand. And before they could get more the first charge across the cornfield began.

"You ought to have heard Humphreys describe just how they felt, how they could not see the men charging, but could see the movement in the corn, how they made each one of those shells tell, and at short range too. How the shells failed to stop the charge, how the rifle-fire failed to stop the charge, how they barely saved their guns, how they lost one and recaptured it next day. He made you feel the fierceness, the hurry, the sweat of it all, you understand. He had sighted one of the guns himself for the second shot.

"When he stopped every cigar was out. They all started to light up. After they settled down again, Colonel Melrose began:—

"'So you sighted the gun that fired that second shell, Humphreys! I was a private then. It was my third fight. When we scrambled over the rail-fence Nathan Adams was next me. We were on one end of the line. I was a strong runner then and must have drawn ahead of him farther than I thought as we forced ourselves through the tall corn. The second shell burst midway of the company a little toward the rear. The force of the explosion knocked me flat on my face, though I was not hit. When I scrambled to my feet I glanced behind me, could not see Nathan, and ran back to look for him. I had heard of the horrors of war, but then I first realized them.

"'A fragment of shell had torn him open from hip to hip. His heart could scarcely have ceased beating, his flesh must still have been quivering. But what I saw was already a loathsome carcass, not a man.

"'I turned away. Gentlemen, there was nothing there for me to help. Nothing but carrion, what an instant before had been my dearest friend, the man I most admired, the most promising youth I ever knew. I bore my part in that charge, did my utmost in the fight. But I was a mere maniac with the riot of my feelings, the turmoil of my thoughts. I was surprised at the clearness of those same thoughts. The rush of the charge, the fury of the fight, the confusion of the retreat were enough to occupy the whole of any man's faculties. The mere physical horror of what I had seen was sufficient to benumb any conceivable intellect. Yet I went through everything like a wound-up automaton, not needing any faculties seemingly, for what I did, thinking independently of what I was doing, and observing my own sensations as one does in the double-consciousness of a dream. I remember what I thought, for I went over it a hundred times, a thousand times in the next year.

"'First of all there was a sort of incredulous amazement at the intensity of the internal, physical sensation of overwhelming grief. It amazed me that it could hurt so atrociously, and I was more amazed that a spiritual smart could feel so entirely corporeal, like a scald or burn. It was as if I had swallowed hell-fire and it blazed in me without consuming me, a suffocating agony.

"'Then there was the bewilderment at my loneliness, the inability to realize that he would never speak to me again, that we should never again exchange confidences. I had gone to college very unformed. There was not much to form a lad on the Eastern Shore in those days. And at Harvard my mind and soul had developed rapidly. But my intellectual growth had been less the effect of Harvard than of Nathan Adams. He had been not so much my guiding star as the sun of my existence from the moment I first saw him. My other interests had been swallowed up in the fascination he exercised over me, and always for good. He was the prophet, preacher, and poet of my college days. My devotion to him was the first passion of my life, its only passion up to his death. To please him, to strive after the ideals he held before himself, to aspire with his aspirations, had been the sum of my aims. Behold, the idol had vanished from my heart's shrine. Life was empty.

"'Also I was dazed with a sense of the loss to the commonwealth. Not only I but all who knew him had regarded Nathan as a natural leader of men, as possessed of transcendent powers, capacities and abilities, as born to a high destiny, as a precious possession of his state, his nation, of the world. I quailed at the irretrievable annihilation of his potentialities for good, of all he was certain to have done had he lived.

"'Likewise I was overwhelmed with the sense of the waste of life the war entailed, of its frightful cost to humanity, and with that sense a crushing weight of my part of the duty to win for the country all his blood had been spilled for, all that was to be bought at the price of such lives as his. I had an access of partisan patriotism.

"'And yet I felt not only that flare of ardor, but the lofty intellectual exaltation of devotion to the cause which had led me to enlist, swamped utterly by a torrent of personal animosity, of revengefulness, throughout that charge. I felt that life's most precious prize would be to have the man who fired that shell helpless before me, to feel my bayonet pierce his breast. That feeling haunted me for months. After I was an officer, after I had my sword and had used my sword, after I knew that gritty, friable, yielding grind of bone under my sabre-point, no other desire so consumed me as to meet in fair fight the man who fired that shell and feel tingle all up my arm the crunching, clinging drag of my sabre-edge cleaving his skull. I was astonished at the elemental fury of my inward savagery. I was as primitive as Agamemnon praying to Jupiter to let him feel his spear-point rend Hector's corselet and pierce his breast-bone. I was as primitive as a Sioux brave at a war-dance.'

"When Melrose stopped, nobody thought of cigars. They sat so still you could hear the breath whistle in Colonel Park's asthmatic wind-pipe. And they were still for some time.

"At last Humphreys asked:—

"'And now?'

"'And now,' Melrose took him up, 'there is not even the ghost of that acrimony left. We meet and you tell of it and I hear of it and know that you are the man. But all that volcano of hatred is burned out in me. I tell of how I felt, but the telling does not revive the feeling it recalls. I have no more animus against you than if those horrors had happened in some past lifetime, or to other men altogether.'"

Wade paused.

"And then?" René queried.

"And then," Wade enlightened him, "they shook hands and we all went out and took a drink."

"Do you know," René remarked, "for a man who calls himself commercial, you tell a story very well?"

"So my wife says," Wade replied shortly.

"Also," René went on, "for a man who disclaims a memory for names you have some rather pat. Agamemnon is not a commercial word."

"Oh," Wade laughed, "I remember names I learned at school. But I get so lost among names of battles, commanders and numbers of regiments, you understand, that I give up altogether. I can repeat a conversation pretty well, though. My wife says it's a wonder that a man who can remember another man's language so exactly can find so few words to express his own ideas. But that's the way I'm built. I remember what impresses itself on me, you understand.

"After we got out on the porch again they were all a little uncomfortable. Melrose's story had been too real. Captain Tupper started in to create a diversion; you could hear that in his tone.

"'Speaking of sighting a shell,' he said, 'the best shot I ever saw was fired from a battery I commanded on the march to the sea. It was just before we reached Columbia. There was really no force in front of us, but they behaved as if they had a substantial body of men, and fooled us for some hours. We got our guns well within range and well-masked. Through my binoculars I could see the enemy's staff as pompous as if they had an army of a hundred thousand men intrenched.

"'There was an officer with a gray goatee seated at a little table, two younger officers, with black goatees, standing on his left, and five or six men on his right, one in front with a long dark beard. They were as cool as if they controlled the situation, orderlies galloping up and galloping off and all that.

"'We had a German named Krebs, a barrel of a man, but a wonderful artillerist: I called him and he sighted our best gun through the scrub pines.

"'He plunked the shell square on that table, I saw the table smash, and the shell exploded as it struck the ground. That was the best cannon-shot I ever saw or heard of.'

"The instant Tupper ceased Colonel Rhett cleared his throat. He spoke in a muffled, choked voice.

"'Strange,' he said, 'a second recognition the same evening. I was one of the half-dozen men on that general's right hand. I was the only one not killed of the nine by the table. The general was my father, and the man with the long black beard my brother-in-law. Two of the others were my cousins.'

"You may be sure we were all uncomfortable after that. And it didn't seem to me another drink was in order, just then, either.

"Colonel Tupper spoke like a man.

"'It was all in the course of duty, Rhett,' he said. 'I wouldn't hold a personal grudge for it against you, if our places were changed, not if the shell had killed all my family and friends.'

"That sort of relieved the tension and we all felt less nervous when Rhett answered,—

"'I hold no grudge, Tupper. We're all friends together, now. And since you mention it, it would have taken an almighty big shell to kill all my kin at one shot.'

"We laughed at that and felt better.

"Captain Bowe cut in. He thought he could change the line of thought.

"'Duty led to some pretty unpalatable acts being forced on a fellow in wartime,' he said. 'Sometimes I think some of the duties that resulted in no bloodshed at all were worse to have to do than any kind of killing. I was in the Shenandoah Valley, and I can tell you turning ladies and children out of doors and burning their homes before their eyes took all a man's resolution and devotion to duty. It took all a man's resolve not to bolt and desert rather than carry out orders. I had some horrible days then.

"'The worst of all was near Red Post, at an estate named Tower Hill, belonging to some people named Archibald. Of course there were women at home, only the women. Mrs. Archibald was not over twenty-six. She had four children, a beautiful little girl of about five years, twin boys, not any too sure on their feet, and a baby not six weeks old. She had two sisters, handsome dark girls, about seventeen and nineteen; Rannie their name was, or something like it. Her mother was an exquisite old lady, all quiet dignity. They were not hard and cold and scornful like some of the women I had had to leave houseless; they acquiesced without protests. Mrs. Archibald said she realized how distasteful my task must be to me. Indeed, I had tears in my eyes when I talked to her, I know. They huddled together just beyond the heat of the fire, and watched the barn and quarters burn and the house catch. They clung to each other, and the girls cried softly. By the Lord, gentlemen, that hurt more than any loss by death, and death took some of my dear ones during the war. That tried my soul more than danger or privations. It was bitter hard to have to do, and it is not agreeable to recall, even now.'

"Janney swore out loud.

"'This seems to be a day of recognitions,' he said. 'Their name was not Rannie, it was Janney. They were my sisters and my mother. I was not two miles away, and I saw the house go. I vowed to kill the man that burned it, if I ever met him, and I meant it too.'

"'Does that vow hold good?' Bowe asked quietly, never stirring in his chair.

"'Time has canceled all the rash vows of those years,' Melrose put in before Janney could speak. 'All the rash vows and all the old hatreds.'

"'Yes,' Janney agreed, 'that is my view too. I consider that vow as completely annulled as if I had never taken it. But if we had captured you, Bowe, among the prisoners we made out of the stragglers then, and if I had known you for the man who burnt Tower Hill, I'd have shot you like a dog, sir; murdered you in cold blood without a qualm, sir!'"

Wade sat silent. The near horse pawed at the turf-grown carriage track and turned his head toward the buggy, wickering softly.

"And what followed?" Des Pertuis queried.

"I don't remember any more that evening," Wade replied. "But next day the nine of them walked down here, arm in arm, Humphreys with Melrose, Rhett with Tupper, Janney with Bowe, and Captain Spence and Parks and Uncle Wade, with seven or eight more veterans. Colonel Melrose stuck that flag on Colonel Spence's grave, himself."

René looked at the flag as if he had never seen it before.

"I perceive the point," he said. "Your experiment is entirely successful. I agree with you. I have seen nothing in America as wonderful as that little faded flag. I understand what it is of which you especially boast. You conceive that here in the United States exists a kind of fraternity more genuine than anything anywhere else in the world. It is this of which you brag."

"Exactly so," Wade affirmed. "That's what I brag of, that's worth bragging of, you understand. What do area and population and wealth and manufactures and trade-balances and prosperity and all that sort of thing amount to, after all? Other nations have had them, and have them, and will have them. But what other nation ever had what that flag stands for? I don't know much history, you understand, but my wife spends her life reading, and I listen when she talks. I'm dead sure no nation ever produced anything to compare with the spirit in which our differences have resulted. I'm sure no nation has it to-day. And if it ever overspreads the world in the future, we made it, we started it, we had it first. That's something worth being proud of."

"I comprehend indeed," René told him. "And I do not wonder at your pride in it."

"Bully for you," Wade cried. "It's some satisfaction talking to somebody who is appreciative, you understand. Now I don't mean to run down the old countries. I acknowledge their culture and manners, their music and poetry and literature, their painting and sculpture and architecture. They've all that and we haven't; we can't compete with them in any of those things. Let them brag of their cathedrals, and art-galleries, and court-balls, and all the rest of it. They are wonderful. But that flag stands for the most wonderful thing in all the world, for the finest thing the world has ever produced yet. Not for talk about brotherhood, but for the real thing. That's my view, you understand."

"I comprehend indeed," René repeated. "And how long will that flag stay there?"

"Till the 30th of next May," his host replied.

"What will they do with it then?"

"Throw it away, I suppose," Wade answered easily. "It will be pretty well used up by then, you see, and they'll stick down a fresh one."

"Shall you be here then?" the Frenchman inquired.

"Sure," said the American. "Why?"

"Could you get it for me?" René queried. "If you could I should like to put it up over the fireplace at Pertuis."

"With what's-his-name's stirrup and thing-em-a-bob's glove?" Wade asked.

"Yes," René answered, "with the gauntlet left by du Guesclin with that hostess who had nursed him back to life; with the stirrup-iron from the saddle which Gaston de Foix gave his boyhood crony, my ancestor; with the other like relics, not a few."

"My wife went wild over that chimney-piece," Wade affirmed. "She said it was the finest she had seen in France and the most wonderful collection of mementos she ever saw in a private house."

"Madame Wade is very kind," René replied. "If you will be so good I should like to place among them this very flag."

Epilogue
THE TWO ARMIES
1863

HENRY TIMROD

Henry Timrod (1828–1867), born and raised in Charleston, was perhaps the leading Southern poet of his day. His first publications date to as early as 1846, and his Poems appeared in 1859. During the Civil War he enlisted as a private in the Confederate army in early 1862, but was given a discharge at the end of the year for health reasons. He moved to Columbia, South Carolina, in 1864, where he wrote editorials for the Daily South Carolinian *until the city was sacked in February 1865. He died of tuberculosis two years later. "The Two Armies," first published in the* Southern Illustrated News *of May 30, 1863, speaks of the army of soldiers in the field and the no less valiant "army" of women who tend to the fallen.*

Two armies stand enrolled beneath
The banner with the starry wreath;
One, facing battle, blight and blast,
Through twice a hundred fields has passed;
Its deeds against a ruffian foe,
Stream, valley, hill, and mountain know,
Till every wind that sweeps the land
Goes, glory laden, from the strand.

The other, with a narrower scope,
Yet led by not less grand a hope,
Hath won, perhaps, as proud a place,
And wears its fame with meeker grace.

Wives march beneath its glittering sign,
Fond mothers swell the lovely line,
And many a sweetheart hides her blush
In the young patriot's generous flush.

No breeze of battle ever fanned
The colors of that tender band;
Its office is beside the bed,
Where throbs some sick or wounded head.
It does not court the soldier's tomb,
But plies the needle and the loom;
And, by a thousand peaceful deeds,
Supplies a struggling nation's needs.

Nor is that army's gentle might
Unfelt amid the deadly fight;
It nerves the son's, the husband's hand,
It points the lover's fearless brand;
It thrills the languid, warms the cold,
Gives even new courage to the bold;
And sometimes lifts the veriest clod
To its own lofty trust in God.

When Heaven shall blow the trump of peace,
And bid this weary warfare cease,
Their several missions nobly done,
The triumph grasped, and freedom won,
Both armies, from their toils at rest,
Alike may claim the victor's crest,
But each shall see its dearest prize
Gleam softly from the other's eyes.

About the Author

S. T. JOSHI is a leading literary critic and editor who has published books about Ambrose Bierce, H. P. Lovecraft, and others, including *The Weird Tale, Lord Dunsany: Master of the Anglo-Irish Imagination,* and *H. P. Lovecraft: A Life.* Joshi lives in New York City.